Paul Burden

May 1997

# SECRETS

# SECRETS

## A Writer in the Cold War

## Paul Brodeur

FABER AND FABER
BOSTON · LONDON

Copyright © 1997 by Paul Brodeur
A small section of *Secrets* first appeared in *The Nation*.

Library of Congress Cataloging-in-Publication Data
Brodeur, Paul.
    Secrets : a writer in the Cold War / Paul Brodeur.
        p.   cm.
    ISBN 0-571-19907-0 (cloth)
    1. Brodeur, Paul. 2. Journalists—United States—Biography.
I. Title.
PN4874.B715A3   1997
070′.92—dc20                                                        96-43622
    [B]                                                                    CIP

Jacket design by Janet M. Clesse
Printed in the United States of America

*To Adrienne and Stephen*

# Contents

# PART ONE

# 1

## Prelude

Now that the Cold War is over and we Americans have proclaimed ourselves and our way of life to be the winner and still heavyweight champion of the civilized world, people are falling all over themselves to give their take on what it all meant—a rush to assessment no doubt encouraged by the fact that just over half a century has gone by since Winston Churchill, on March 6, 1946, signalled the beginning of the Cold War in a speech at Westminster College, in Fulton, Missouri, by declaring that an Iron Curtain had fallen over Europe. As someone whose adult life was more or less encompassed by the Cold War—I was nearly fifteen when Churchill made his famous pronouncement and had just turned sixty when Mikhail Gorbachev was awarded the Nobel Peace Prize in June of 1991—I find myself agreeing with the British journalist Martin Walker, who describes the conflict as "the history of the world since 1945." I take issue, however, with the assertion of the protagonist of John Fowles' novel *Daniel Martin*, who declares that the twentieth century did not begin until that year. It seems to me that the twentieth century began with the 1917 Bolshevik Revolution, which instigated a seventy-year-long struggle between Communism and capitalism—a struggle that was temporarily interrupted by the exigency of having to deal with Adolph Hitler's Nazis, and resumed so quickly during the Cold War that humankind scarcely had time to appreciate the horror of the Russian sacrifice and the Holocaust that had consumed Europe's Jews, before being faced with the prospect of having to live in the shadow of nuclear extinction. When all is said and done, of course, historians down the road, not anyone who actually lived through it, will have the last word about the Cold War. In the meantime, it might behoove those of us who feel obliged to write prefatory chronicles to heed the words of Dr. Bernard Rieux, the narrator of Camus' novel *The Plague*, who informs his readers at the outset that it is not his business to take into account the myriad differences of outlook among the people involved in the story he is about to tell, but merely to say, "This is what happened," and who acknowledges that he would have little claim to competence for the task he has undertaken had not chance put him in the way of gathering information.

My father, who was an orthodontist and a sculptor, invariably referred to the German soldiers who overran Europe in 1939 and 1940 as Boches. That is because he had been a lieutenant in the French Foreign Legion during the prelude that came to be known as the Great War. How he came to join the legion can be told without undue romance. He was born in Webster, Massachusetts, in December of 1894, into a family that had emigrated to the United States from Quebec, where two brothers from Poitiers originally settled in 1675. Two of his uncles were dentists, and upon graduating from high school he went to the Harvard Dental School, where he specialized in orthodontia, graduating in 1916. Since he spoke fluent French, he was selected to go to France to treat refugee children, under the auspices of a charity founded by Anna Morgan, who was a daughter of old J. P. He spent 1917 in Caen, and a year later he did what a number of other young Americans who found themselves in France during the Great War did—he joined up. His friend John Ames had enlisted in the Lafayette Escadrille, a group of American pilots flying for France, and his friend Arthur Dallin, the son of the sculptor Cyrus Dallin, was driving an ambulance for the Red Cross. Since my father was an American citizen, he was required under French law to join the Foreign Legion. He spent the spring of 1918 at the artillery school in Fontainebleau, and that summer he was sent to the front in time to participate in the great bombardment that ended the war.

When I was a child, I used to go up to the attic of our house in Arlington Heights, just outside of Boston, and look at my father's French Army uniform, which consisted of powder blue tunic and breeches, a black kepi with gold braid, a pair of long black leather riding boots, and an ornamental sabre and scabbard. It was a handsome getup, to say the least, and the idea that no one else's father had one made it all the more exciting. There's a mural in the Massachusetts State House, in Boston, which shows a French general decorating the flag of the 104th Infantry

Regiment of the American Expeditionary Force that was sent to France in 1918. Beside the general stands a handsome young adjutant in profile. It is a perfect likeness of my father, who, resplendent in the powder blue uniform, posed for the Gloucester painter Richard Andrew.

Early in the phony war of 1939, Arthur Dallin used to come to our house on Sunday mornings with maps of the Ardennes that he and my father would spread on the living room floor. Arthur was in his early forties, a few years younger than my father, and he had become a stained-glass craftsman whose work can be found in many churches in the Greater Boston area. He was convinced that the Germans would try to outflank the Maginot Line and attack through the Ardennes, but we never got the chance to tell him how right he had been, because he joined the French army later that year and was killed on June 12 of the following year on the banks of the Marne by a German officer, two days before the Germans occupied Paris. He was one of five officers and less than one hundred men—all that were left of an infantry regiment of nearly three thousand men—who had survived a battle at Soissons, on June 8. The day Paris fell was the only time I remember seeing my father cry.

During the war years, we spent summers at a rented cottage on Duxbury Beach, a seven-mile-long sandbar peninsula, some forty miles south of Boston. My father had wanted to join the Free French under de Gaulle, but was persuaded that he was too old and had to content himself with becoming an air raid warden. My younger brother and I were beachcombers. We poached quahogs, collected driftwood, captured minnows trapped in tidal pools, and filled gunny sacks with pop bottles left behind by picnickers. Above all, we considered ourselves patriots. We salvaged tinfoil for the war effort from discarded cigarette packages, helped local residents dry sea moss to collect nitrates for munitions makers, and used the pop bottle refunds to buy Victory stamps at the post office.

The war affected us in many ways during those summers. There was a strict blackout every night, and when we went outside before bedtime the unaccustomed darkness and the profound sea made us feel close and vulnerable to the conflict. Wreckage washed ashore from ships sunk by U-boats, and each day we poked through fresh piles of debris, vaguely aware that we were examining the flotsam of catastrophe. The grown-ups talked incessantly of a submarine that had surfaced off the shore during the First World War and lobbed a few shells into the marshland behind the beach. Had the Germans been aiming at the old cable station? Would they try again? And would they not send a landing party this time? The speculation of our elders filled us with delicious tension. The tin cans my brother and I were forever tossing into the waves became submarines and the rocks we threw at them depth charges, and the constant vigil we maintained for flotsam, pop bottles, and marine life took on a new dimension, for now we were patrolling a stretch of the coast—a strategic flank of the Republic.

The war seemed closer than ever when we noticed that the navy blimps that passed overhead in the mornings, carrying real depth charges that looked like black trash barrels in racks beside the pilots' gondolas, often returned with empty racks at evening. And there was great excitement one night in the summer of 1942, when the old lady who owned the only telephone on the beach heard guttural voices and called the coast guard, which resulted in the temporary apprehension of some Swedish neighbors from Brockton, who were dragging their dory over the sand after returning from a nocturnal expedition for flounder and mackerel. Even more exciting was the day my brother and I found ourselves playing in an abandoned duck-hunting camp halfway out to Gurnet Point, when the beach was mock-strafed by low-flying army airplanes taking part in a training exercise being held by a National Guard regiment that had rumbled out across the wooden planks of Powder Point Bridge, which connected the peninsula to the mainland. The officers whom we encountered as we tried to run home seemed almost as badly frightened as we when they realized that they had failed to clear the beach properly before starting their maneuver, which is how (after being sworn to secrecy) my brother and I came to be adopted for one whole week as regimental mascots and, to the envy of all our friends, were allowed to eat with the soldiers in their mess tent, help them dig foxholes, wave signal flags, stand inspection, and walk guard. The saddest day of my life till then was the day my brother and I stood at attention, after the last tents had been struck and a long line of soldiers had given the beach a final policing, and watched a column of trucks and jeeps rattle back over the old wooden bridge and on to God only knows how many other beaches.

# 2

## Blue Lawns

The autumn after the war ended, I was packed off to Phillips Academy, in Andover, Massachusetts, thanks largely to the intervention of my mother, a former actress and drama teacher, who decided that I was playing too much ice hockey with the neighborhood ruffians and needed to be educated. The motto of the school at the time was "sink or swim," so the attrition rate among the students was high, but those of us who managed to survive its rigors learned how to study and, for the most part, got into the colleges of our choice. Like graduates everywhere, we were full of hopes and high spirits and believed ourselves to be thoroughly grown up. After all, had we not reached our eighteenth birthdays and been required to go to the nearest post office to register for the draft?

I had been a reporter and an editor for the school newspaper at Phillips, and by the time I entered Harvard in the fall of 1949 I knew that I wanted to be a writer. Indeed, I wanted desperately to be a writer. Aside from taking the usual short story writing courses, however, I had no idea how one set about to become a writer, other than to indulge myself in some highly plagiaristic daydreaming, which is how it happened that during a brief but poignant period in the springtime of my sophomore year, when the Korean War had settled down to a hellacious stalemate along the thirty-eighth parallel, I became hell-bent on living a pastiche of what I considered to be the most romantic novel ever written—F. Scott Fitzgerald's *The Great Gatsby*.

How I happened to choose that particular book as my motif is something I have forgotten. "Choose" is not the right word, to begin with. It would be more correct to say that I wandered into *Gatsby* with the same kind of half-wishful involvement that propelled its narrator, Nick Carraway, into the social whirl of West Egg. At any rate, as with most vicarious endeavor, mine had aspects that were superficial, and others that were—by comparison, anyway—profound. As evidence of the former, I submit a sudden addiction to that insouciant salutation "old sport," which I applied with promiscuous delight (as did Jay Gatsby) to friend and foe alike; and as for the deeper side of my posturing, I confess to having derived considerable satisfaction from the fact that, like the early James Gatz, I too had changed my name to conform to a deep, if somewhat imprecisely motivated, need for self-metamorphosis. (In my case, it was not a question of amending my surname and given name, but of quietly dropping the uncommon middle name of Adrian by which I had always been called by family and friends, and which suddenly seemed too bizarre for further service.) As I grew more and more immersed in *Gatsby*—and therefore more determined to see life through the eyes of its characters and in terms of its action—strange things happened; imperceptibly at first, and then with a vividness that comes only with the most extravagant conceits, I began to hear Daisy's thrilling laughter in the Yard, to pass Jordan Baker's wan and haughty face on Beacon Street, and to see all lawns as blue as Carraway saw Gatsby's.

Now, when blue lawns become an integral part of a young man's spectrum, there is no limit to what else he is capable of imagining. I think it was late winter when I first became enmeshed in *Gatsby* as a way of life, but by the time the first shells were skimming over the Charles River I was so submerged in my swamp of conjuration that I even remember nodding to a small, gimlet-eyed man sitting in a Harvard Square hash house just because he corresponded to the image I carried in my head of Meyer Wolfsheim. The most prosaic surroundings were conducive to my new talent for identification. My bedroom bureau, for example, never failed to evoke my favorite passage, in which Gatsby, who is showing Nick and Daisy through his mansion, takes them into his bedroom, where the elaborate pretext upon which he has built his life suddenly confronts the wondrous reality of her presence, and, with the compulsion of a man in crisis, he starts tossing stacks of swank shirts into a sumptuous pile of disarray that soon becomes a lush, colorful handkerchief for Daisy's compulsive tears. In those days, that was for me the most poignant scene in all literature. It affected me profoundly, especially when I gazed into the shallow, paper-lined drawer that contained my own meager supply of shirts that never came back from the local Chinese laundry fluffy with the promise of soft unfolding, but always braced with cardboard, bound with garish blue paper ribbon, and smelling of stale starch. Ah, what would I not have given to have possessed Gatsby's elaborately monogrammed shirts, not have sacrificed if only I could have been so consumed with wonder at a dream come true as to have thrown them in flamboyant offering at the feet of some unattainable girl, who, realizing the agony of my soul, would then have buried her lovely head in them, sobbing out the rebirth of her love for me!

Well, I don't want to create the impression that my efforts to create an alter ego modeled on Gatsby were all that occupied me during this period. On the contrary, they were merely idle moments of speculation in a fairly busy schedule, which is to say that for the most part I functioned normally. I attended classes, studied at the library, and indulged in a suitably relaxing program of athletics. In the evenings, I went over to Radcliffe, or out to Wellesley, or up to the rooms of friends for drink and conversation.

I had two close friends at that time. Louis Kane was my literary friend and Peter Sperling was my roommate and rowing friend. I had planned to spend the spring vacation touring Nova Scotia boatyards with Louis, who also wanted to be a writer, and who was turning out some pretty fair Hemingway imitation as a result of having become involved with *The Sun Also Rises* to the degree that I was with *The Great Gatsby*. At any rate, the summer before, Louis had made a pilgrimmage to Pamplona and run through the streets before the bulls and then taken up with some people and gone down to Madrid with them. He came back to the States in September talking seriously but modestly about good wine, fine bulls, and, of course, women. During the winter, he ran into a bit of trouble trying to live with *The Sun Also Rises*, possibly because the novel was too remote in setting and theme for day-to-day daydreaming, and so he reread *To Have and Have Not,* which he found much more adaptable, and which led directly to his wanting to have a boat built in Nova Scotia. With a good boat, according to Louis, a man could always make ends meet by fishing, and if the engines were fast enough—well, who knows what other business might turn up?

In spite of our friendship, I was not overly enthusiastic about going to Nova Scotia with Louis—perhaps because the fishing towns and boatyards we planned to visit did not promise drama of Fitzgeraldean proportions, so when the opportunity came up to drive down to Miami with Peter Sperling, it was accepted by me as casually as by the people who were forever accepting the chance to tool into old Astoria in Gatsby's yellow roadster. There was one thing to be done before I left— a rather awkward thing, but I wanted to leave my affairs in order. I saw Louis Kane and told him I would not be going to Nova Scotia. As it turned out, I need not have worried. Louis understood perfectly.

"Don't blame you," were his exact words. "Good town, Miami."

"Have you been there yourself?" I asked.

"Just heard about it," said Louis, whose regard for *The Sun Also Rises* had produced in him a marked tendency to omit pronoun subjects. He was a swell fellow, very intense about Hemingway, and those of us who were his friends usually found ourselves playing Bill Gorton to his Jake Barnes, so we continued like that for a while, talking abbreviated dialogue that fills up pages quickly. Then Louis went to his desk, opened a drawer, and pulled out a thick manila envelope.

"Do me a favor when you get to Miami," he said. "Return this to a friend of mine."

"You bet I will," I replied. "What's in it?"

"Long story," Louis said, and he went on to tell me that the envelope contained half a dozen short stories written by a gambler named Sammy Solitaire, who was one of the people he had taken up with in Pamplona the summer before. Solitaire, it turned out, worked for a syndicate that owned a *jai alai frontón* near Miami, and he had gone to Spain to recruit new players. According to Louis, he was a hard-bitten fellow—a regular tough—but with an odd creative streak beneath it all. From Pamplona they had gone down to Madrid together on a spree and done some extensive drinking during which Solitaire had confided in Louis that he wanted very much to get into the "writing game." By the time Louis returned to the States, he had forgotten all about it. Then, out of the blue, Solitaire had mailed the stories to him from Miami.

"How are they?" I asked.

"The stories?" Louis said. "Terrible. Awful stories. Full of sentiment."

"Did you tell this to Solitaire?"

"Couldn't bring myself to do it. Kept remembering the fine time we had in Spain. Leave it to you to say something encouraging."

After a moment's consideration, I decided that there could be little harm in exchanging a few pleasantries with Sammy Solitaire. In fact, the whole idea of meeting him intrigued me. What could fit in better with my own scheme of things than to encounter some mysterious and shady character who, like Jay Gatsby, was obviously bent on following a grand and improbable illusion?

"All right, old sport," I told Louis Kane. "I'll give your regards to Solitaire."

"Have a fine time in Miami," he said.


It was early one morning, several days later, that Peter Sperling and I started nonstop for Florida in another roommate's Oldsmobile convertible. I remember that we crossed the George Washington Bridge at noon, that dusk fell over us in the red clay hills of Virginia, that dawn broke in Georgia, and that during the dark of night we traversed the whole southeast corner of the Republic. Everyone suspects himself of having performed or helped in the performance of at least one notable feat behind the wheel of a car, and this is the result of mine: at eleven o'clock the following morning, just twenty-three hours after crossing the Hudson, Sperling and I were swimming at Daytona Beach. A headline in a local newspaper that someone had discarded on the sand declared that Judge Irving Kaufman had sentenced Julius and Ethel Rosenberg to death for helping the Russians make an atom bomb—a crime the judge described as "worse than murder." The next day we continued to a rooming house in Miami, and late the same afternoon I telephoned Sammy Solitaire.

The quality of Solitaire's voice took me by surprise. It was—and there is almost no other way to describe it—a deadly voice, a voice totally without inflection, a voice that to the scale of human tone was what gunmetal blue is to the spectrum of color. My friend and I should come to the *frontón* for the evening's matches, it said. There would be tickets waiting for us, and if I would come upstairs to the main office at intermission, there would be someone there to meet me.

The *jai alai* proved to be tremendously exciting. Sperling and I sat at midcourt, just behind a net that protects the spectators, spellbound by the speed of the ball and the grace and agility of the players who made incredible leaps to catch it in long, curved baskets called *cestas* that were strapped to their wrists. The *cestas* were swung in great arcs that sent the pellet ricocheting off the concrete walls of the court with the sharp crack of a projectile. After watching two or three matches, we added a new dimension to our interest by joining the murmuring, humming swarm of wagerers before the betting windows; then the intermission came and I had to keep my appointment with Sammy Solitaire.

The noise of the crowd had diminished when I reached the second floor and started down a long concrete corridor toward a door that was flanked by a pair of men wearing sports jackets that bulged noticeably in the region of the heart. It was one of those corridors with the total audibility of a shooting gallery; the echo of my footsteps was ominous. When I drew abreast of the two men I halted, expecting to be challenged, but they merely stared back in silence. Clearly, it was up to me to begin.

"I have an appointment," I said, "with Mr. Solitaire." This produced a flicker of recognition in the eyes of the taller one. "What about, Jack?" he inquired.

"About some short stories he has written," I replied, and then, ever so slowly, as if I were about to take a pledge, I lifted the manila envelope so that it rested across my heart.

The grimace of incredulity that appeared on the face of my interrogator brought home to me with frightening clarity how ludicrous my statement must have seemed to him. I started what I hoped would be a reassuring chuckle, but it turned out to be a kind of nervous whinny. Then I took a deep breath and prepared to launch into a more detailed and convincing explanation. A geyser of unspoken words frothed at my lips, but before I could give them sound, the second guard reached for the door handle behind him and, without taking his eyes from the envelope that was by now stitched to my chest like the bull's-eye of a target, opened it just a crack and spoke to someone stationed on the other side.

"Kid here claims he's brought the boss some . . ." He paused and looked at me with disbelief.

"Short stories," I stammered.

With acute embarrassment, I heard this news relayed at a bellow throughout the room beyond the door. Then the door swung open and, with the jerky step of a mechanical duck, I lurched into an immense office filled with desks, adding machines, and cigar smoke produced by a crew of tough-looking men wearing green-visored eye shades. The general impression was of an accounting firm except that on the desks, in neat stacks bound with thick rubber bands, was more money than I had ever seen. Why, there was enough money in that room for Meyer Wolfsheim to have fixed the 1919 World Series ten times over!

At this point, a squat little fellow with a thoroughly squashed nose bounded off a stool in the far corner of the room and shuffled toward me. "So you're the editor!" he cried.

"Well, not exactly—" I began.

"I am Albert," he continued. "Much as I hate to tell you, Mr. Solitaire has had to go out to the Beach on business of the utmost possible urgence, but not ten minutes previous to your timely arrival has he called me, and this is what he has said. 'Albert,' he has said, 'transmit my apologies to the editor, assure him of my eminent arrival, and spare nothing by the meanwhile to see that he enjoys every hospitable comfort.'"

"Why, thank you," I replied, touched by this elaborate excuse that Albert delivered with his eyes tightly shut, like a schoolboy laboring through a carefully memorized recitation.

"So siddown," Albert said, vacating the nearest chair by tapping its occupant on the nape of the neck with the edge of his palm.

I sat, and Albert sat opposite me, and there followed a rather painful silence during which each of us conducted minute examinations of the room.

Finally, Albert said, "Know Mr. Solitaire pretty good, do you?"

"As a matter of fact, I've never met him."

Albert beamed. "A real genius," he exclaimed. "A man with great powers of brain. Let me tell you, it's an uplift just to be associated with him."

For a moment, Albert stared reflectively at the ceiling; then he went on, "If only the boss could devote himself full-time to the kind of work you represent, there's no telling how high he might perspire."

No sooner had I summoned up the vigorous nod of approval this remark deserved than Albert was on his feet, looking past me toward the door. By the time I gained my own feet and turned around, I found myself confronting a slender and sallowish handsome man of about thirty-five, who proffered me a hand that—with a haste just short of discourtesy—he detached from my grasp and thrust back into the pocket of an elegant blue silk suit. Up close, the face of Sammy Solitaire was more than sallow; it was a parchment mask that threatened to immobilize his lips, the movements of which were almost imperceptible as he returned my greeting. Only his eyes held life—they were large and brown and tragic—but they acknowledged me only briefly before fixing themselves on a distant point in the room, where they appeared to focus upon some scene of sorrow too immense for the heart to bear.

There was a girl with him—a modish, pouting girl who took up a stance some distance away, feverishly twirling a transparent plastic handbag—but Solitaire made no move to introduce us. With an expression of monumental indifference, he seemed bent on absenting himself from our presence. It was a front, of course—detachment of such high order is almost always worn as camouflage—and, wondering vaguely what lay concealed behind it, I engaged him in a hopelessly one-sided conversation that gradually and then suddenly lapsed into total silence.

"You sure got here quick, Mr. Solitaire," Albert said helpfully. "I bet you must've done ninety on the causeway."

"Hunh!" exclaimed the girl with wide-eyed scorn. "Ninety sitting outside in the parking lot?"

With a swift glance—a turning of his head that was as incisive as the short, deft movement of the hand with which Fitzgerald's Tom Buchanan broke Myrtle Wilson's nose—Sammy Solitaire silenced her. A rather strained and awkward moment followed. Then, mercifully, someone announced from the far side of the room that Atlanta was on the telephone, and he disappeared.

The girl giggled nervously. "Hey, don't you love this place?" she asked.

"Very nice," I replied, looking politely in the direction of her gaze as if to find some attractive feature in the concrete walls. Actually, I was trying to decipher a motive for the strange bit of deception that had been exposed, but I could make no sense of it. And just then my vague preoccupations became too much for the girl to bear.

"I mean the money-for-heaven's-sake!" she cried with a mixture of annoyance and ecstasy. Then, in a breathless, confidential whisper: "Hey, don't you just want to scoop it up and run?"

Sammy Solitaire had finished with Atlanta and was standing at a desk close by, smoking a cigarette and nonchalantly flipping through a stack of twenty-dollar bills.

"How long are you and your friend staying in Miami?" he asked.

"About a week," I replied.

"Well, any time you want to come back, give Albert here a ring," he said, glancing at his watch.

Everything in his tone and gesture indicated the termination of our interview. I thanked him and extended the manila envelope. "By the way, here are your stories," I said. "Louis Kane wants me to tell you he liked them very much."

Solitaire took the envelope as if he had never seen it before. Then, with a deprecating wave of his hand, he muttered something about scribbling a few things now and again in his spare time. A second later, he was studying a tally sheet of the night's receipts.

"Well, thanks again," I said, and started away.

Solitaire dropped the tally sheet, thrust his hands into his pockets, and moved quickly between me and the door. "I've never shown my stuff to anyone before," he said, a trifle aggressively. At the same time, he blew a mammoth, unconcerned cloud of smoke toward the ceiling.

There was a silence that begged to be filled. "Well, you should keep working at it," I said heartily.

I don't know why I said that. I suppose I hoped it would provide some reaction on his part. If only he had allowed himself a look of pleasure, however slight, or even the grimace of denial that sometimes passes for modesty, I could have concluded my errand and made my departure. But there was nothing in his face—absolutely nothing—and suddenly I was affronted by his ghostly detachment, and at the same time determined to elicit some human response from him. Or maybe it was that I longed to hear for myself what I ended up telling him.

"Listen, old sport, your stories are better than you think. Why, they're full of promise!"

When I said that, Sammy Solitaire looked at me with such profound reproach that my first instinct was to stammer out an apology. And in that instant I realized that in a curious way I had offended him. It had nothing to do with the lie I had told, it was that I had trampled down his fences and breached the private sanctuary of his hopelessness.

Now his mask began to fall away. With what must have been for him a supreme show of animation, he led us across the room to a large cabinet safe. There, leaning his elbow on the top, he struck a pose that was a burlesque of his old indifference and told Albert to open it.

"Hey, won't there be a wad of money in *there*," said the girl under her breath. She had begun to spin her handbag at a furious clip—faster even than the great revolving rotor blades of the ceiling fans overhead.

Albert was crouching before the safe, his face contorted with concentration as he turned the combination dial. Finally, the last tumbler clocked into place and the door swung open, revealing a pair of handled drawers that, when opened in their turn, proved to be filled with manuscripts—hundreds and hundreds of pages inserted as neatly and evenly as the pages in the binding of a book.

I made a long, exaggerated whistle. "All stories?" I asked.

"All stories," said Solitaire, in a voice that sounded choked and far away.

I looked at him and saw to my amazement that he was trembling on the brink of suppressed delight. He was smiling a strange smile and shielding his eyes with his hand as if to protect them from some dazzling light. Then he was laughing. "It's a crazy thing," he said. "I can't believe—when you told me they were full of promise . . ."

He was consumed with relief, and I realized all at once that everything else—his studied detachment, the reason he had let on to Albert that I was his editor, and the story he had concocted about his late arrival—had merely served to gird him against the possibility of disappointment. Having dreamed his dream so long in private, even the *idea* of exposing it must have filled him with unbearable torment. Now he was laughing almost uncontrollably, and for a moment it appeared that he would not be able to master himself. Then, recovering, he did an incredible thing—something that infinitely stretched the limits of my capacity for awe and against which I have always measured subsequent marvels. He reached into the drawer, took out a whole sheaf of manuscripts, and began tossing them one by one on the floor before us—manuscripts of translucent onionskin, crisp parchment bond, and soft linen, which lost their clips and drifted leaflike as they fell. While we watched, transfixed, he pulled out more, scattering them with abandon, as if consumed with unreasoning joy at the sudden tangibility of a dream, until the white and buff and yellow pages covered the tops of our shoes in a thickening pile that rippled delicately in the currents wafted by the fans above our heads. I looked at the girl, half expecting her, I suppose, to begin weeping like Daisy, but she was staring openmouthed at him, her face rigid with surprise, as if he had just killed a man.

For a moment, I tried to think of something to say, but, of course, there was nothing to say, and Solitaire would not have heard me, anyway. I doubt if he even realized we were there. When I turned at the doorway and looked back, his face was still wreathed with that strange ecstatic expression, and the snow flurry of stories showed no signs of abating.

The last match of the evening was in progress when I rejoined Peter Sperling, but I was scarcely aware of the shouts and applause of the crowd. Suddenly, I found myself afflicted with the kind of dizziness that besets a man who has just walked out of the cinema into the strong light of day. I wanted to tell Sperling what had happened, but he was pounding me on the back and waving six twenty-dollar bills in my face—the proceeds of a winning *quinella* ticket—and all at once the elusive fragment of wonder that I wished to communicate to him became too complicated for the mere precision of speech. So I remained silent, shutting my eyes in an attempt to keep in focus the vision I had so carefully nurtured and which so unaccountably had come true. But it was already becoming blurred and slipping past me. In that room upstairs, I had attained the very apotheosis of the phase I had been living—that phase when we soar on in flights of incredible fancy, straws in the wind, carried back into the illusions of the past. But it was, after all, just a phase. One cannot live forever by seeking to find coincidence between life as it is and as others have seen it; and so, shortly thereafter, I closed out my youthful fascination for *The Great Gatsby*.

Yet our dreams die slowly and nostalgia remains forever.

The following night, armed with the confidence of money easily acquired, Sperling and I met two girls at a Mexican restaurant in Coral Gables. I believe that mine came from Ohio, but I have forgotten her name, and I have only the vaguest recollection of what she looked like. All I remember is that after dinner the four of us drove out across the causeway to Key Biscayne. The convertible top was down, the air was soft, and there was a strange light gleaming on the water of the bay. The car radio announced that earlier in the day President Truman had relieved General Douglas MacArthur of all command in the Far East. Sperling, who was driving, turned the dial to some music that was playing very low but had a familiar lilt.

"Make it louder, old sport," I told him, and suddenly the girl rested her head on my shoulder and tilted her face toward mine.

"'Old sport,'" she said with a funny little laugh. "What a crazy thing to call somebody."

I thought I would choke with joy. How thrilling her laughter was! How careless that face against my shoulder! How wan! When Sperling turned up the volume of the radio, I recognized the George Shearing Quintet picking its way through a nimble rendition of "Moon over Miami."

So I looked up at the night sky and, of course, there was.

# 3

## Family Secret

By the time I got to Harvard, the Soviet blockade of Berlin had been circumvented by a massive American airlift, Alger Hiss had been confronted by Whittaker Chambers before the House Un-American Activities Committee, the Russians had tested their own atomic bomb, and the Cold War was in full swing. With the exception of Yugoslavia, the nations of Eastern Europe had fallen under the Communist yoke, and during the takeover of Czechoslovakia the country's foreign minister and leading patriot Jan Masaryk had gone out the window of his office in Prague under circumstances that were highly suspicious. Here in the United States, people had been alerted to the threat of subversion by the publicity given to the defection of Igor Gouzenko, a young cipher clerk at the Russian Embassy in Ottawa, whose testimony had led to the trial and conviction on charges of spying of the British atom scientist Alan Nunn May. Twentieth Century Fox had capitalized on the situation by releasing *The Iron Curtain,* a film in which Gouzenko was played rather improbably by Dana Andrews, and Gouzenko's wife even more improbably by Gene Tierney. Meanwhile, George Kennan had warned his colleagues in the State Department that the Russians were out to destroy the democracies and dominate the world, and the fiercely anti-Communist Arthur Koestler, author of *Darkness at Noon*, was going about the country giving lectures in which he warned American liberals to stop living on the moon and wake up to the reality of Soviet totalitarianism. Passage of the McCarran Act would soon leave little doubt that the nation's lawmakers regarded Stalin's Russia as a far greater threat to peace and freedom than Hitler's Germany had ever been.

Henry R. Luce's *Life* magazine led the charge from another direction, bemoaning the loss of China and publishing illustrated diagrams that purported to show the standard plan employed by the Reds to enslave unsuspecting peoples. In the winter of 1948, the magazine ran a story warning that within a few years America might not be able to defend itself against an atomic attack. It began with an italicized scenario that read as follows:

> *Ladies and gentlemen, your attention please. We interrupt this program to bring you an important news bulletin. The Associated Press reports that the cities of New York and Los Angeles have just been hit with bombs that appear to be atomic. Because communications to these cities have been cut off, we do not have any further information at this moment. Presumably, the bombs were dropped from high-flying planes. . . .*

I remember this scenario because it was read to me and my classmates by the teacher of our American history course at Phillips Academy, where, during the entire four years of my attendance, I never heard a single word about the Holocaust or any discussion about the ethics of having dropped atomic bombs on cities filled with civilians. Five months later, *Life* ran a story that really caught my attention. It was about a young army sergeant stationed at the American Embassy in Moscow, who had deserted his post for the love of a Russian woman named Galina. She was the wife of a fellow soldier, who had been sent back to the States without her, and she was suspected of being an NKVD agent out to steal military secrets. "Seduction and exploitation!" thundered a State Department spokesman in the best tradition of the guidance counselors at school, whom we suspected of trying to suppress our raging libidos by lacing our breakfast orange juice with saltpeter. A classic example of "how love's sweet mystery can be slyly encouraged by the watchful Soviet authorities," *Life* suggested, ever ready to score a political point. The article went on to describe the boring lives the sergeant and his colleagues had been forced to lead in Moscow, and how easy it had been for them to succumb to the wiles and machinations of women known as "*Mozhno* girls," after the Russian word meaning "if you wish."

It's getting on to fifty years since I read that story. At the time, I had just turned seventeen, and I was sitting in a barbershop in Portsmouth, New Hampshire, waiting to get a crew cut and enjoying a rare day off from the itch-provoking summer haying job I had at a farm in nearby Stratham, and I can still remember the deeper itch that it awoke in me. What would I have given at that age of longing if, instead of the fresh,

freckle-faced girls I wanted but didn't dare ask to the movies, I had encountered a "*Mozhno* girl" to grant my every wish? What betrayal
might I have been capable of? Well, let me tell you, it doesn't do to
think about it.


The fact was that the Cold War into which the nation of my elders had
segued with extraordinary ease did not loom all that large in my life or
in the lives of my friends during our years at school and at college. Like
young people everywhere, we were too full of ourselves and our dreams
to be overly troubled by the catastrophes inflicted upon the world by
the older generation. Besides, we had family baggage to deal with, and
many of us were to some extent or other trying to come to terms with
the troubles our parents had inflicted upon us. In my case, this entailed
an attempt to absorb the meaning of a secret that my mother and father
had kept from me all my life.

The way I found out about the secret was prosaic enough. One
night during my senior year at Harvard, I went to a Christmas dance at
a junior college near Boston, where I met an elderly chaperone, who,
upon watching me sign the guest register, told me that I had my father's eyes and that I resembled my older brother Adrian Paul. Since I
did not know that I had an older brother, let alone that he and I shared
first and middle names (albeit in reverse), this came as a surprise.
There was no reason for me to doubt her, however, because, speaking
slowly enough for me to trace the tenuous trail that linked us together,
she went on to say that she was the mother of the man my father's first
wife had later married.

Naturally, I reviewed what I knew of the chronology of my father's
life, beginning with me and working backward. I had been born in
1931; my father and mother had married in 1928; and ten years before
that he had served as an officer in the French Foreign Legion in France.
The decade between 1918 and 1928 was, however, a blank as far as I
was concerned. As a boy, I had asked my father to tell me about the
Great War, in which he had commanded a battery of 75-millimeter cannon, and as a young man I had questioned him about the crash of 1929
and the subsequent Great Depression, in which he and my mother had
lost our house in Wellesley Hills to a bank. But I had never entertained

any particular curiosity about the intervening years, nor had my father ever volunteered much information about them, except for an occasional reference to his professional life as an orthodontist and sculptor. I remembered him pointing out the building at 240 Commonwealth Avenue in Boston, where he had an office in the early 1920s, but try as I might I couldn't remember anything else that might be pertinent to what I had learned from the elderly chaperone. In the end, all I could do was accept her revelation as a historical possibility.

When I went home for Christmas vacation a few days later, I had a reunion with my brother David and my sister Valjeanne, who had been away at school. My mother and father celebrated by driving us into downtown Boston and taking us out to dinner at a Chinese restaurant on Joy Street, which we had been patronizing as far back as I could remember. Afterward, my father stopped to pay the bill and chat with the proprietor, an old man with hooded eyes, who wore a pair of tiny glasses with thick lenses and sat upon a stool fingering an abacus. Each time I had gone to that restaurant as a child, the old man had written my name for me in Chinese, using a brush and ink and fashioning the graceful, lilting characters with swift sure strokes. I had treasured those scraps of paper for a long time, until, coming upon them in a drawer of my desk one day and placing them side by side, I noticed that each time the old man had written my name he had done it differently. Now I listened as my father reminded him that he had been coming there for nearly thirty years.

"I lemember!" said the old man, laughing and pointing his finger at me. "Little boy all glown up."

"Yes, indeed," my father said. "Good night."

"All glown up!" the old man shouted gleefully as we went out the door. "Good night! Good night!"

It was snowing hard outside. The neon lights of the restaurant were reflected in the swirling flakes, and behind that shifting screen the statuettes and figurines that filled the windows of the shops in Chinatown seemed to shimmer. As I walked along Joy Street with my father, I remembered that when my brother and sister and I had been children, the family dinners in Chinatown had always ended with a visit to one of the shops, where each of us had been allowed to purchase a tiny porcelain animal. Now I recalled a whole parade of fragile horses, elephants, turtles, and dragons, which we had endlessly traded and bickered over, and which had long since broken into fragments and disappeared. For a moment, I thought of reminding my father of the animals, but I was suddenly shy of evoking the past. The thirty years he had recalled for the Chinese proprietor did not seem so much a span of time as a jumble of possibilities that tumbled through my head with the disorder of the falling snow. And as for the myopic old man who had never written my name the same way twice—which little boy did he claim to remember?

On the drive home, I sat up front with my father, who peered intently through the windshield, steering the car over the slippery roads as if he were guiding a ship through dangerous shoals. My mother, sister, and brother were chattering away in the backseat, but I heard only echoes of their conversation. I was thinking that my mother must surely share the secret with my father and that they had decided upon silence together. I was fairly certain that neither David nor Valjeanne were aware of it, but, considering the circumstances of my own discovery, it seemed likely that sooner or later they, too, would chance upon the knowledge of our father's earlier marriage. Did he and our mother believe that it could be kept from us forever? Was he ever tempted, now that we were grown, to take us into his confidence? For a moment, I wondered whether I should assume the responsibility my father was avoiding and take it upon myself to tell my brother and sister about the secret. But suppose there was a reason for my father's silence? Glancing at his grimly intent profile behind the wheel, I wondered if he ever saw his other son.

When we pulled into our driveway, my father turned around, triumphant and beaming. "Well, here we are!" he cried. "Home for Christmas."

While my mother, brother, and sister went into the house, I opened the garage doors so that my father could put the car away. As it moved slowly past me, I saw his face faintly illuminated by the light of the dashboard, which showed the barest outline of his features, leaving all the rest without substance, in transparent shadow, to be imagined. When he switched off the headlights and the engine, the garage became dark and cavernous, and in the silence that followed I found myself wondering whether at this time of year he must not be thinking of his other, oldest son.

On New Year's Day, I went fishing with my father and brother on the Concord River. It was a traditional outing that—weather and ice permitting—we undertook each year. The river was covered with frozen snow, and because of a ridge of ice chunks that had been heaved along either bank by the pressure of the current it looked like a highway winding between the wooded hills. The part we liked to fish was at a bend about half a mile upstream from an old plank-and-girder bridge, and to reach it we walked close to the bank in single file. My father went first, occasionally testing the ice for soft spots with the blade of a long, wood-handled chisel. David followed in his footsteps, and I came last, pulling a box sled that held a dozen tip-up trays, a bucketful of minnows, and our lunch. When we arrived at the bend, we chopped holes in the ice and set out the tip-ups in three clusters that were approximately a hundred yards apart, forming a triangular pattern within the arc of the river bend. Then we separated to tend them.

When I got back to my set of traps, I pulled in each of the lines to see whether the hooks were still baited, and lowered them into the river again. Looking across the ice, I saw that my father and brother were also examining their lines. For a while, I watched their slow progress from one trap to the next, struck by the solitude in which each of them performed his separate tasks. Only the river ice, groaning sporadic protest against contraction, and the planks of the old bridge, which rumbled with the passage of vehicles, made sounds to break the stillness. When my father lit his pipe, a cloud of blue smoke hovered in the chill, wintry air, rose slowly past the bleak wooded hills in the background, and then fled upward into the pale sky—dissolving, disappearing, gone.

Suddenly, filled with a sense of our fantastic visibility against the expanse of ice and snow, I found myself thinking that even if the ice should give way, dropping us into the dark river current, there would still be my older brother. But I could not endure the loneliness that accompanied this vision, and so I forced it from my mind and riveted my gaze upon my father. He's only a hundred yards away, I told myself. I'll cross over and tell him what I've learned. I'll say, "Dad, I know about my older brother." There'll be a look of surprise and relief on his face when I say this. He may even smile. Then he'll tell me all about it, even how I came to be given the same name. He'll probably end by telling me that it doesn't make any difference between us, and I'll say, "I know it doesn't, Dad, but

I'm glad you told me, and I hope you'll tell David and Val someday."
Then we'll shake hands and wish each other a happy New Year.

I started across the ice toward my father, who, when he saw me coming, waved a greeting. But before I'd gone halfway there was a shout
from David, and, turning, I saw him running toward a trap whose un-
sprung red flag was dancing above the snow. Now my father and I hurried toward David, converging upon him just as, hauling in line hand
over hand, he pulled a large fish through the hole. It was a long, sleek
pickerel with brilliant green chain markings on its sides. My father
looked down at the fish flopping on the ice and, grasping each of us by
the shoulder, hugged us to him with elation. "Pickerel for supper!" he
declared. Then, releasing us, he hurried back across the ice to his traps.

I watched him go, wondering if I should follow, but my earlier sense
of isolation had been diminished by my father's embrace, and I decided
against it. Instead, I returned to my own traps. At that point, I found
myself relieved that I had not confronted him with the secret. The secret
had been kept too long and possessed too much history of its own to be
broached except at the right moment. Besides, wouldn't it be better to
wait until he broached it himself? Surely, one day, he would feel bound
to do so.

I had no way of knowing that more than a decade would pass before
this would happen. Nor could I have guessed that in the years to come I
would spend a good part of my professional life exposing secrets and
the harm that secrecy engenders. At the time, looking down at one of
the holes in the ice, I noticed that during my absence a skim incorporat-
ing tiny particles of snow and slush had begun to form and was con-
gealing in faint wrinkles before my eyes. Tonight the temperature
would drop, and by morning the holes would be frozen solid. Thus did
the river keep its winter silence.

What with the discovery of my father's secret, the necessity of writing a
thesis, and one thing and another, I didn't have much time to think
about the Cold War until the following spring, when I was about to
graduate and realized that almost immediately thereafter I would be inducted into the army. No one I knew was anxious to join the fighting in
Korea, but war protests were still far in the future, and none of us would

have dreamed of tearing up his draft card, let alone fleeing to Canada. Some of my classmates sought deferral, others applied to graduate school, a few married in haste, and the rest of us were left to other devices. In my case, this consisted of enlisting for three years in the Army Counterintelligence Corps, with the understanding that if I passed the requisite security check, I would be able to select the theater in which I would serve.

Shortly after graduation, it came home to me that for the first time in my life I was about to embark upon an endeavor from which I would not be able to withdraw. As a result, a certain anxiety set in. My friend Louis Kane, who had been in the Reserve Officer Training Corps, was already in the process of becoming a marine at the boot camp in Quantico, Virginia, and Peter Sperling had been accepted at law school and was out of town, so there was no one I could turn to for reassurance and advice. Finally, I decided to pay a call on Harold L. Humes, with whom Louis and I had shared a short story writing class that winter and spring. "Doc," as people called him, was five or six years older than I was. He had been in the navy at the end of the war and had come to Harvard from Paris, where he had lived for several years and had helped found the *Paris Review*. He was well on his way to completing a long novel about the political situation in France at the outset of the Cold War—it would be titled *The Underground City* and would catapult him into the ranks of the nation's leading young novelists—but, more important to me at the time, he wore experience and political skepticism with an authority that normally only someone older could convey. He had just been married to a lovely young woman he had met at Wellesley, and they were living in an apartment in Cambridge while he was putting the finishing touches on his book.

When I told Humes that I had enlisted in the Counterintelligence Corps, he looked at me askance and shook his head. "Well, just remember to be an apostate," he admonished.

The fact that I was not familiar with the word must have showed because Humes cocked his head to one side and gave a grin—the tolerant grin of an older man who finds himself amused at the foibles of someone younger.

"Bear witness," he told me.

# 4

## "Got You, Sir!"

Not long ago, I read that Fort Dix has been turned into the largest federal prison in the nation. What a laugh and how appropriate! And talk about striking a chord! Historians will tell you that the Cold War began when Churchill made his Iron Curtain speech in 1946, but for me the Cold War began at Dix, in the southern part of New Jersey, where I took sixteen weeks of infantry basic training in the summer and autumn of 1953. The whole time was pretty grim but I remember the last part best.

We had just returned to our barracks from heavy-weapons bivouac in the pine barrens, where we had spent a week firing bazookas and .57 millimeter cannon at papier-mâché tanks, and we were in a rollicking good mood, because we had less than a month to go, and our commanding officer, Captain Miller, had broken his arm and dislocated his shoulder. The captain had won a Silver Star and a battlefield commission with Merrill's Marauders in Burma during the Second World War, and he had been wounded at the Yalu during the subsequent police action that had been conducted by the United Nations in Korea, and he was sure that his proved (and our incipient) valor were still going to be needed there, even though things had cooled down along the thirty-eighth parallel and the two sides that had been arguing with each other at a long table in Panmunjom for most of the year had just signed an armistice. He was a profane and jocular man, the captain—a regular cutup—tough on himself and us, but fair about passes (nobody got them) and guard duty (everybody pulled it) and double-timing in the field (if we did it, so did he), and we had developed a grudging respect for him. Then, on the last day of the bivouac, while we were going through the obstacle course—climbing up walls, crawling under barbed wire, swinging on ropes, that kind of thing—he took it into his head to see how many of us he could make fall off a telephone pole that had been laid across a sand pit by pretending to jiggle the end of it with his boot. I say "pretending" because it's doubtful he could have moved the pole a quarter of an inch one way or the other, but his whooping and hollering made people nervous, and practically everybody in the company lost his balance and had to jump off before reaching the other side. In fact, Bill Collins and I were just about the only exceptions.

Collins was my best friend and tentmate. He was somewhat older than the rest of us—all of twenty-two, perhaps, but reserved and mature—and while we were waiting our turn to get on the telephone pole, he studied the captain's antics and decided that the hazard was psychological. He told me to pay no attention to what Miller was saying, but just run straight along the pole after him, and when we made it all the way across, everyone cheered—even some of the noncoms—which was too much for the captain, who always had to be the main show. He climbed up on the pole and started across, daring anybody to jiggle him off it, and when he was right in the middle a giant black man named Jeremiah picked up one end of it halfway to his knees and dropped it with a thump that sent the captain flying headfirst into the pit and the rest of us dancing gleefully around the edge as if we were serfs baiting a boar in some medieval ceremony.

The captain was in agony, of course, and none too pleased with being made to look the fool, so he had us double-time the whole ten miles back to barracks, carrying full field packs, bazookas, and mortar plates and pipes, while he rode alongside us in a jeep, laughing at our plight and cursing his own and clutching his shoulder. Let me tell you, it was worth it. We felt so good that the noncoms didn't have to sing cadence. We even made up a new chant as we ran along.

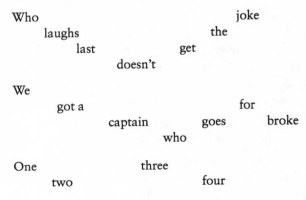

One

       two

            three

                  four                       three-four!

                    One-two

That night, the captain went off to the base hospital to have his arm and shoulder set and placed in a cast, and the next day we got Lieutenant Ramsay as our temporary CO, and crazy time started for Company C.

The lieutenant introduced himself at five o'clock in the morning, after the noncoms' whistles had screeched and we had fallen out of our bunks and then out of the barracks and into formation on the parade ground next to the battalion motor pool. He was a red-faced fellow about our age, and he stood on a wooden reviewing stand in front of us with his arms akimbo and his feet spread apart. Right away you knew there was something strange about him because his fatigues were at least a size too small and so new they hadn't yet been laundered and faded in regular army style, and the bottoms of his pants weren't bloused and folded down over the tops of his combat boots, like those of our noncoms and other officers, but tucked straight inside, which made him look like a civilian deer hunter.

"The name's Ramsay!" he shouted. "Lieutenant Ramsay! My orders are to maintain this company's combat readiness until Captain Miller is able to resume his duties, and I intend to carry out those orders. You got me?"

There was stony silence from the ranks.

The lieutenant's face grew redder. "You got me?" he said again.

Not a sound came from anyone.

"The correct answer to my question, gentlemen, is 'Yessir!'"

This time a couple of people murmured the correct answer, but almost inaudibly, as if they were reluctant to swim against the general tide of silence.

The lieutenant's face grew even redder. "Give me fifty!" he shouted. "Everybody!"

While we were grinding out the push-ups, the noncoms paced up and down through the ranks, looking for malingerers, and the lieutenant pumped his folded arms and spread his legs farther apart, as if to plant himself more firmly on the reviewing stand. When we were on our feet again, he told us that unless our attitude changed there would be no Thanksgiving passes. Since Captain Miller had already informed us that this would be the case, the announcement was greeted by a ripple of faint but unmistakably derisive laughter.

"Down and give me fifty more!" the lieutenant yelled. His face was lobster red.

When we struggled to our feet again, the lieutenant told us that if we so chose, we could be doing push-ups all morning. "It's your option, gentlemen!" he shouted. "You got me?"

"Yessir!" we shouted back.

"That's more like it," he said. "Now, I want the barracks cleaned. I want them cleaner than your mother's wash. Got me?"

"Yessir!"

"Otherwise, I intend to volunteer this company to battalion for guard duty every day from now on until and including Thanksgiving. You got me?"

"Got you, Sir!" we roared back.

"Get you, motherfuck," whispered someone from behind me.

"Now fall out!" the lieutenant commanded.

"Aaarrgghh!" we roared, and raced for the barracks whose walls, floors, and rafters had not yet dried from previous applications of soap and water.


The line on Lieutenant Ramsay came down while we were on our knees, scrubbing the barracks floors. One of the corporals said he was Reserve Officer Training Corps from the University of Rhode Island and hadn't been in the army any longer than the rest of us. The idea that he was an ROTC college boy set everybody's teeth on edge. As it happened, Bill Collins and I and at least a dozen other members of Company C had gone to college, but it wasn't the kind of thing you got any mileage out of in basic, so we acceded silently to the general imprecations about the adverse role of higher education upon Lieutenant Ramsay's character and conduct, except for Collins, who, perched on a stepladder as he wiped off the rafters, quietly pointed out that Ramsay was probably insecure in his first command, because of his lack of experience, and was simply trying to act tough in order to compensate.

That was Collins for you—fair, analytical, and unassuming. He was engaged to a girl back in Boston, and his plans were to marry her as soon as he got out and became an accountant. We had met on a sultry morning in early August at the cavernous South Boston army base, where we had reported to a sergeant at the recruitment office of the Counterintelligence Corps, in which we had enlisted for three years with the option of selecting our overseas theater, rather than be drafted for two years with the attendant likelihood of being shipped to Korea. The sergeant informed us that CIC recruits had to go through sixteen-week basic, like other regular army enlistees, but that if we passed a background investigation by the Federal Bureau of Investigation, to be conducted during the same period, we would end up at the Army Counterintelligence School at Fort Holabird, in Dundalk, Maryland, just outside Baltimore. He then advised us not to discuss our CIC connection with anyone else, thus creating a shared secret that bound Collins and me together. That same morning, we boarded an olive-drab bus that took us to a reception center at Fort Devens, where, after the usual shearing, we spent a week swabbing barracks floors and policing up parade fields; then we were shipped in another bus to Dix, where we were still swabbing and policing away three months later.

When Lieutenant Ramsay arrived to inspect our most recent efforts, he marched down the middle of a center aisle between rows of bunks and those of us who had been frozen in place by the corporal's shrieked "Tennn-shut!" until he came to Collins' footlocker, which he hopped up on and used as a launching pad to leap high, grab hold of a rafter with one hand, and, while swinging like a monkey, wipe the forefinger of his other hand across the rafter's upper surface. When he jumped down, his face was redder than usual from exertion, and he held his forefinger in front of Collins' nose.

"See that, soldier?"

"No, sir," Collins said.

"That's *dirt,* soldier!"

"Sir," Collins said, "I cleaned that rafter myself and I don't see any dirt, sir."

"Soldier, when I say there's dirt, there's *dirt.* You got me?"

"No, sir," Collins said quietly. "I don't get you."

"Corporal!" the lieutenant bellowed. "Get this man into full field pack and have him do a hundred laps around battalion perimeter!"

It was the worst sort of chickenshit—straight out of *From Here to Eternity*, which had just been released and was showing at the post theater—and some of the guys who had seen it kidded Collins as he was pulling on his field pack by calling him "Pruitt." It also evoked Camus' "Myth of Sisyphus," which I had been reading as an antidote to the inherent despair of army life, for it established the irrevocable fact that no matter how clean we might scrub the barracks, "Got Me" Ramsay, as he was now called, would always see to it that we failed inspection, just as the gods kept seeing to it that the stone would always escape Sisyphus' weary grasp and roll once again to the bottom of the hill. The merging of flick and philosophy produced in me a sense of futility so profound that it seemed to give meaning to the very meaninglessness of scrubbing the barracks floor. In this mood, I not only kept an eye out for the plodding figure of Collins, whose gallant progress around the battalion perimeter gradually grew slower and slower with the onset of exhaustion, but also found it possible—indeed, necessary—to imagine Collins happy.

Of more immediate consequence than literary allusion, however, was the quiet rage that Ramsay's unreasonableness and Collins' plight engendered among the other members of Company C. There were one hundred and twenty of us in all, including some eighty blacks and Hispanics from Harlem and the Bronx, and since the lieutenant had confined the entire company to barracks, many of us were at the windows that evening to watch him leave his quarters for a night out in Trenton with (according to the duty sergeant) a nurse from the very hospital where our captain lay in pain. The lieutenant wore loafers, gray flannels, and a gaudy plaid sport jacket—the kind that gets worn at country clubs with lime or lemon yellow slacks—and at least two troopers swore they could whiff his after-shave from across the parade field. But it was his car parked out in front of company headquarters that drew everyone's attention, for the lieutenant drove a reconditioned cerulean blue 1937 Nash convertible, with white sidewall tires, leather mud guards, and a raccoon tail hanging from the radio antenna, and with bumpers, trim, and radiator screen of such sparkling and reflective chrome that some people claimed they saw the drivers of oncoming vehicles flicker their headlights before he had even climbed into it and driven away, leaving poor Collins with thirty laps to go and bitterness in every onlooker's heart.

The plot was hatched that very night—I forget by whom, but I seem to remember that among the ringleaders were Jeremiah and some friends who had worked together in an auto body shop in the Bronx. In any event, practically everybody in the company had a hand in the affair before it was over. Things got rolling when the lieutenant returned, shortly before midnight, checked in with Corporal Hernandez, who had relieved the duty sergeant, and took himself off to bed. Luis Diaz, a cheerful and diminutive Puerto Rican, who was posted outside the lieutenant's window, and who claimed to have three wives and children by each of them—something none of us believed until three ladies carrying infants appeared together at the orderly room one Sunday afternoon in late October—said that Ramsay had begun to snore as soon as he turned the light out. At that point, while Diaz and some friends regaled Hernandez with pornographic photographs of one of the friend's cousins making love to herself with a banana, Jeremiah and his cohorts surrounded the lieutenant's car, and like soldier ants tugging at a scarab beetle, wheeled it off to a storage shed next to the battalion motor pool, where, during the next several hours, it was completely dismantled.

When I came on the scene at about 3 A.M., the floor of the shed was piled high with fenders, doors, bumpers, seats, dashboard, axles, tires, and other assorted auto body parts. It was surprising how small the various components of the Nash turned out to be, and disconcerting how many of them there were. The largest pieces were from the skeletal chassis, which had already been cut up with an acetylene torch "borrowed" from the motor pool; the heaviest was the engine block, which became the first thing to be interred by the dozen or so of us who had volunteered to bury the remnants of the dismembered Nash in the company parade ground. Few graves have ever been dug more briskly than those into which we lowered to their final resting places the mutilated remains of the lieutenant's beloved vehicle. It was a cloudy, moonless night, and the parade field soon became a tableau reminiscent of an illustration from my childhood edition of Robert Louis Stevenson's *Treasure Island*, except that no lanterns were held high to illuminate the scene. The worst part came shortly before daybreak, while we were planting the fenders in separate holes and had to jump in on top of them when the lookouts signalled that someone was coming. Hugging the graceful curve of metal that until recently had flared over a front wheel of the Nash, and shivering in the dankness emanating from the wet sand, I waited for the beam of a flashlight to shine into my pathetic hiding place, and for subsequent retribution. I imagined being convicted at court-martial for the unpardonable crime of destroying property belonging to an officer. I saw myself being remanded to the post stockade for a term of hard labor. I thought of the FBI agents, who were even then interviewing friends, classmates, teachers, and former employers, in order to determine my loyalty to country and my fitness for a position of trust and confidence in one of its secret services, and how the final pages of their background investigation—a judgment that would follow me all the days of my life— would reveal the ignominy of my having been discovered embracing the corpse of a vandalized car. All these things passed through my mind until the all-clear was given, a few minutes later, after the occupants of an MP jeep, who had sneaked a smoke by the motor pool, had driven off. Then the last pieces of the Nash were safely buried and covered over, and a crew of twenty men raked every inch of the parade field to obscure all traces of our nocturnal excavations. By now it was almost daybreak and the only man not awake was Collins, who was dreaming in the sleep of exhaustion with his mouth open and an arm hanging limply over the side of his bunk.

Reveille sounded over the company loudspeaker soon thereafter, and when the noncoms entered the barracks, whistles shrieking to reinforce the shrill awakening bugle, we nearly trampled them down in our haste to rush out into the gray light and line up before the reviewing stand to await the appearance of our tormentor. The very fact of our presence on top of his car made us incredibly buoyant. We literally danced upon the sand—a dance of joy and triumph upon consecrated ground containing holy relics—as we extended our arms smartly and looked left to align ourselves in proper formation. The puzzled lieutenant barely had time to add the familiar interrogative to the announcement that we would be double-timing out to the firing range and back that day, when we bellowed, "Got you, sir!"

After that, things were anticlimactic, though not uneventful. Captain Miller returned at the end of the week with his shoulder in a cast and his arm in a sling, and Lieutenant Ramsay was assigned elsewhere on the base. The captain seemed subdued and withdrawn, and we heard a rumor that word about the telephone-pole caper had got back to the battalion commander, who had called him on the carpet. Not surprisingly, there was a minor hullabaloo over the disappearance of the lieutenant's car, which became the subject of an investigation conducted by a pair of military policemen, who appeared in the orderly room, a day or two after the great interment, but left after asking some routine questions.

Bill Collins had begun to feel listless around that time—a symptom he attributed to the aftermath of overexertion caused by the hundred laps he had been required to run around the battalion perimeter. Then his eyes grew puffy and his upper lip swelled up, and on the day before we were slated to go out into the field for our final firing tests, he could scarcely get out of bed. I urged him to go on sick call, but we were nearly at the end of our sixteen-week ordeal and the firing test was mandatory—you could be held back and sent through basic all over again if you missed it or didn't pass it—and Collins wanted to avoid that at any cost.

On the march out to the firing range, he staggered and nearly fell a couple of times, so I carried his field pack the last few miles. By the time we pitched our tents at the end of the day, he was ashen, except for his upper lip which had become an angry red and so swollen that it misshaped his whole face. With typical army luck, he got tabbed for perimeter guard duty that evening, but I was able to talk the field sergeant into letting me pull it in his place. I was relieved around midnight, and when I got back to the tent, I could hear him groaning. When I crawled inside, I found him delirious and thrashing about in his sleeping bag, and when I put my hand on his forehead it felt like an overheated radiator. I took a long look at him in the beam of my flashlight and then went off to find the captain, who, after the duty sergeant had awakened him, scrambled out of his tent, looking dishevelled and none too happy to see me.

"Sir," I said, saluting and standing at attention. "My tentmate, Private Collins, is very ill."

"What's the matter with him?"

"He's got what looks like a large boil, sir. On his upper lip. And he's got a high fever."

"Nobody bugs out of the sixteenth-week bivouac," the captain told me.

"Sir, I think he needs medical attention."

"Ask the medic for some aspirin. I'll look at him tomorrow."

"Sir, I think he should go to the hospital."

The captain gave me a baleful look. "Get the hell out of here, soldier," he said.

"Yes, sir," I replied. Then I saluted and went back to the tent, where Collins was moaning in his sleep. Ten minutes later, I had bundled him into the captain's jeep and was barreling down a dirt road between stands of pitch pine, toward the base hospital. When we arrived at the emergency room, a sleepy medic took one look at Collins, who could barely stand, and went off to wake the duty physician, a captain, who took Collins' pulse and temperature, and then got on the telephone. Within twenty minutes, the lieutenant colonel who was in charge of the hospital had arrived, and Collins was undressed, put into a white gown, and taken off to an examining room. I was worried about him, of course, but I was also worried about having taken Captain Miller's jeep, so after half an hour or so, I asked a sergeant sitting behind the admissions desk if I could speak to one of the doctors. The sergeant, who was reading a copy of *Police Gazette,* looked at me askance and asked what outfit I was from and if I shouldn't be getting back to it. I told him I was from Company C, Sixteenth Infantry Battalion, and had brought Collins in from the field, and that there was a problem about my return transportation.

"How'd you get here?"

"By jeep," I said.

"Where's it at?"

"Outside."

"No reason to bother the doctor then. Go back the way you came."

"It's about the jeep I have to talk to the doctor," I told him.

"Why you need to see a doctor about a jeep?" the sergeant inquired, tossing the magazine on his desk to reveal a picture of a tall brunette who was kneeling on a bed, wearing spike heels, black mesh stockings, a garter belt, matching lace panties and bra, and an expression of shocked surprise.

"Because I stole it."

The sergeant gave his eyes a weary roll, got to his feet, and went off down a corridor. When he returned, a few minutes later, the light colonel was with him.

"What's this about a stolen jeep?" the colonel said.

"Sir, it was the only way I could bring Private Collins in here from the field."

"Don't you have a commanding officer?"

"Yes, sir, but he—" I paused here, not wanting to get Captain Miller in any more hot water than he was already—"didn't seem to appreciate how sick Collins really was."

"He's sick, all right," the colonel said. "He's got a major infection close to the brain stem. Could be encephalitis."

"Will he be okay?" I asked.

The colonel shrugged, sat down at the admissions desk, and wrote a note. "Give this to your CO," he said. "Tell him I said if he has any questions to contact me."

The captain had no questions, but as he read the note in the first light of day, all the gray seemed to drain out of his face. As for me, I passed my firing tests, and even made expert in the Browning automatic rifle by squeezing off rounds in short bursts. At the end of the week, we returned to the company compound to await orders, and when they came through, a few days later, there was anguish in the barracks. Except for Collins and me, and two guys who were being sent to language school at Fort Ord, everybody else in Company C was scheduled to ship out to Korea from Hoboken in January.

Meanwhile, Collins was in the hospital on the danger list. In fact, his condition was so serious they wouldn't even let me visit him. I left him a long note at the front desk, telling him the news, giving him my address at Fort Holabird (the FBI hadn't dug up anything inimical) and promising to write. I saw him only once after that—about ten years later—but we passed a few letters during the winter. It was never wholly clear what had been wrong with him, but whatever it was he had very nearly died of it, and he wasn't released from the hospital until after Christmas. Then he was sent home for a couple of weeks before starting basic all over again the middle of January. He said that Company C had run into some bad luck soon after I left. Two men had come down with spinal meningitis, and one of them had died. As a result, the company was quarantined, Christmas leaves were cancelled, a bunch of people went AWOL, and Luis Diaz, who had become despondent because he couldn't see his wives and children, hung himself from a rafter in the furnace room of his barrack. Somebody cut him down but not in time, and, according to Collins, he was permanently brain damaged. Captain Miller was relieved of his command and later court-martialed and busted to sergeant—rumor had it because of the telephone-pole incident, but there had to be more to it than that—and Lieutenant Ramsay was brought back as temporary CO. That was the last straw as far as the troops of Company C were concerned. They refused to pull KP on Christmas Day, and when Ramsay volunteered them for guard duty on New Year's Eve, they deliberately failed inspection by turning out with sand in their rifle bolts. Collins said he'd heard they'd been escorted to Hoboken by the MPs and marched on board a troopship there at gun point. He also said he owed me, because I'd saved his life.

# 5

## Insubordination

Fort Holabird was a picnic. All of us who attended its CIC school had graduated from college, and you could almost imagine you were back in academia, except for having to make your bed and march to classes in formation. The curriculum was somewhat unusual, of course, consisting of courses in interrogation, evidence gathering, report writing, subversion, surveillance, and techniques of counterespionage and countersabotage. Surveillance was everybody's favorite because we were allowed to go out into the streets of Baltimore in civilian clothes and practice following instructors, who pretended to be subversives and tried to "make" us by picking up our reflections in store windows. It was a tactic we attempted to counter by using three men—two across the street, who constantly switched off positions with a third, who, keeping close behind the subject, was called the "tail."

The course in subversion was taught by a large florid-faced Irishman named Walker, who was either on loan or retired from the FBI—it was never quite clear—and who had the disconcerting habit of referring to our Soviet adversaries as "Commies" in much the same inflection then being used by Joseph McCarthy, the junior senator from Wisconsin, who had recently switched his search for left-wing sympathizers from the State Department to the army. Like McCarthy, Walker was convinced that a *Fifth Column*—one of his favorite phrases—was at work to undermine democratic values in the United States. To prove this thesis to those of us in the captive audience that made up his class, he dwelt at length on the case of Ethel and Julius Rosenberg, who had been executed as spies, six months earlier, and regaled us with tales of conspiracy and subterfuge whose provenance he invariably cited as residing in the FBI's voluminous files. According to Walsh, *Grapes of Wrath*, *Cannery Row*, and other works of John Steinbeck clearly fell into the category of left-leaning literature whose aim it was to foment discontent among the working class, as did Hemingway's *For Whom the Bell Tolls*, which, he solemnly assured us, was a "Commie" political tract from beginning to end, if you knew where to look and what to look for.

Next to Fitzgerald, Hemingway had been my chief literary hero, and to experience some aspect of the expatriate life he and his friends had led in Paris and Spain in the twenties had become one of my deepest aspirations. Indeed, it was a dream that, almost as much as the apprehension attending the prospect of being sent to Korea, had encouraged me to enlist in the CIC whose recruiters had practically guaranteed assignment in Europe as a reward for signing on for the three-year hitch. Thus, Walker's characterization of Hemingway as a political tool of the Reds was especially painful to me, but when he launched into a half-hour-long dissection of *For Whom the Bell Tolls*, in which he described those who fought for the Loyalists as "creatures of the Kremlin," and Pilar and Pablo's ragtag guerrilla band as a group of dedicated Gypsy-Jewish Marxist terrorists, I began to suspect that he was talking through his hat. So did Aaron Wascowitz, our group leader whom I sat beside at lunch that day. Wascowitz was not only disturbed, as I was, by the inaccuracy of Walker's literary interpretations, but, being Jewish, he was also distressed by what he perceived to be the anti-Semitic undertones of our instructor's remarks.

"This guy's an ignoramus," he told me. "What d'you say we show him up?"

The prospect was appealing to someone who had recently helped bury the fenders of an obnoxious officer's car, and so, that same evening, Wascowitz and I put our heads together and cooked up a scheme. Under the guise of seeking clarification and engendering further discussion, we decided to ask a series of questions about *For Whom the Bell Tolls* that would demonstrate to our classmates that Walker had little knowledge of the Spanish Civil War and had probably not even read the book.

When the subversion class convened the next day, Wascowitz raised his hand, and, after professing puzzlement about Walker's thesis that the novel was an out-and-out Communist tract, asked him to elucidate on some specific points.

"What's giving you trouble?" Walker inquired.

"Well, for example, sir, how does Anselmo fit into the picture?"

"Anselmo . . ." Walker said.

"The sentimental old guide who hates killing. He reminds me of my grandfather."

"Oldest trick in the book," Walker declared. "Straight out of 'Little Red Riding Hood.'"

"Sir, how about Comrade General Golz and the other Russians who hang out at Gaylord's in Madrid?" I asked.

Walker looked at me and frowned. "What about them?" he said.

"Well, Hemingway doesn't exactly keep it a secret that they've been trained and sent to Spain by the Comintern." By this time, some of our classmates were smiling.

"Sir, the person I really can't figure out is Maria," Wascowitz said. "The Ingrid Bergman character in the movie, who gets raped by the Fascists and has all her hair cut off. D'you figure she's some kind of dupe?"

"A classic example," Walker said.

"What about the Gary Cooper character?" I said. "Robert Jordan."

"What about him?" Walker replied, looking hard at me.

"Well, isn't he more than your typical academic pinko?"

A ripple of laughter ran through the class.

"Suppose you tell me," Walker said.

"Maybe he's Jewish," Wascowitz said helpfully. "Maybe he changed his name."

It continued like that until Walker caught on to what was happening and dismissed the class. Wascowitz and I became instant folk heroes, and remained so for the rest of that day and night, but the next morning, we were called out of formation and told to report to the commandant's office.

We never got to see the commandant, who was a brigadier-general, but were ushered into the office of his adjutant, a major, who had the thinnest lips of any man I have ever seen. The major was seated at a large desk before a pair of crossed flags, and for what seemed an interminable period, he perused some papers; then he looked slowly up at Wascowitz and me, who were standing at rigid attention before him.

"Do you know what insubordination is?" he asked, locking his gaze upon me like radar on a target.

"Failure to obey orders, sir," I ventured.

"What d'you think it is?" the major asked Wascowitz.

"Same thing, sir," Wascowitz replied.

"Insubordination can take many forms, gentlemen. It can be deliberate disobedience, or it can be the willful creation of an atmosphere of disrespect. Do I make myself clear?"

"Yessir," Wascowitz and I said in unison.

"Upon reviewing the report of your instructor, Mr. Walker, it is my opinion that you are guilty of the second form of insubordination, which, in any form, will not be tolerated at the Counterintelligence School. Therefore, you are hereby placed on notice that any further transgression of any kind on the part of either of you will result in immediate expulsion and reassignment to the combat infantry branch. Have you understood me?"

"Yessir," Wascowitz and I chanted, once again in unison.

"Dismissed," the major said.

Needless to say, no further discussions were initiated by anyone taking Walker's subversion course, and for the next three months we sat in silence as our instructor led us through thickets of deception and duplicity from which the FBI had ferreted out the poetry of William Carlos Williams and the politics of Owen Lattimore and John Service. During that time, Roy Cohn and G. David Schine discovered books inimical to the best interests of the United States in several army libraries in Europe; Dien Bien Phu fell to General Giap and the Vietminh; and midway through the Army-McCarthy hearings, Joseph Welch began the senator's slide into oblivion by asking a simple question with an earnest inflection that defied response: "Have you no sense of decency, sir, at long last? Have you left no sense of decency?"

The senator, you will remember, had unfairly called into question not only the loyalty of some young clerks in the Army Signal Corps, but also that of several senior officers—among them one General Zwicker, commander of a military base where a dentist named Peress had been promoted even though he had refused to fill out loyalty forms. Some of McCarthy's allegations in the matter appeared to have been derived through the use of wiretaps, which so alarmed Secretary of the Army Robert Stevens that he ordered two dozen counterintelligence agents who were deskbound at the Pentagon into the field to determine how the senator and his aides could be conducting the kind of surveillance that was generally considered to be the prerogative of the FBI and other agencies entrusted with the right to invade privacy in the name of national security. The vacuum thus created in the world's largest office building was filled by members of a clerk-typist class, who were scheduled to graduate from Holabird at the same time as were we—May of 1954—and among whom I had several acquaintances, including a fellow from New Hampshire whose name I have forgotten. He and his classmates were assigned to temporary duty at the Pentagon in order to record the results of the army's investigation of McCarthy's latest gambit, but I would not find that out until a year and a half later, when I bumped into him at the Jeu de Paume in Paris. At that time, he told me that he and his coworkers had spent the late spring and early summer of 1954 typing up reports of the army investigators' findings in ten carbon copies, and that a number of these documents identified their primary source of information as Robert F. Kennedy, who had served on McCarthy's staff for nearly two years, before resigning the previous winter. According to my former colleague from Holabird, Kennedy informed his military interlocutors in some detail about how, when, where, and by whom the wiretaps had been installed—mostly, it appeared, by retired or moonlighting FBI agents who were sympathetic to Senator McCarthy's views—which makes one wonder whether this was when Kennedy developed the penchant for eavesdropping that, once he became attorney general, would not cause him to hesitate before ordering FBI agents on active duty to install wiretaps and microphones to record the conversations of congressmen, journalists, academicians, generals, and whoever else's private discourse was considered to be of interest to the White House. One day, Attorney General Robert Kennedy would authorize J. Edgar Hoover to tap the telephones and bug the hotel rooms of Martin Luther King, whom he and President Kennedy had come to consider a major political liability (thus recording King's sexual activities), and following the Bay of Pigs disaster he and his brother would approve President Eisenhower's earlier endorsement of a CIA plan to eliminate Castro, whom they had come to consider their mortal enemy. The idea to kill Castro had been proposed early on by an Agency employee named E. Howard Hunt, and it subsequently became the chief aim of a presidential-sounding project called "Executive Action," which provided alternatively for the *Comandante* to be supplied with his favorite cigars in lethally explosive form, or given a poisoned wet suit for scuba diving, or injected with poison secreted in a fountain pen designed to serve as a syringe, or handed a drink laced with botulin toxin by Cubans recruited by members of the Miami Mafia, whose gambling casinos in Havana had been confiscated in the Socialist Revolution. The support of these Cubans as go-betweens in the assassination plot had been enlisted by a former FBI agent named Robert Maheu, who had formerly worked for the CIA but was now employed by Howard Hughes for whom he later served as confidential emissary and financial conduit to President Richard Nixon. Leaving messy footprints in this supposedly faint trail, and thus threatening to make a shambles of the doctrine of plausible denial that had been designed to protect chief executives who take out contracts on other world leaders, was a mafioso named Sammy Giancana whose girlfriend, Judith Exner, had been calling President Kennedy at the White House on Giancana's home telephone, which, as it happened, was being tapped by the FBI as part of an ongoing criminal investigation.

But all this would come out only years later in the wake of Watergate.

Upon graduating from Holabird, I was given a two-week leave, and then I was shipped from the army's Staten Island Terminal to Bremerhaven on the USS *General Darby,* a troopship carrying nearly two thousand airmen and soldiers, a hundred or so officers, twice that number of dependent wives who were bound for Germany to join their husbands, and six of us who were members of the Counterintelligence Corps. The airmen and soldiers were packed in the bowels of the ship, while the officers, the dependent wives, and we six in the CIC were given cabins. During the trip across the Atlantic, which took ten days, we were informed of world events over a loudspeaker by the ship's captain, which is how we learned that the Socialist (the captain said Communist) government of President Jacobo Arbenz, of Guatemala, had been overthrown by an army officer named Colonel Carlos Castillo-Armas.

Among other things, Arbenz had had the effrontery to expropriate several hundred thousand acres of unused farmland owned by the banana-growing United Fruit Company, of Boston, for distribution to the landless peasants who had helped elect him to office. Nobody including the ship's captain had any idea, of course, that the CIA was behind the whole affair—even to the point of flying the B-26s that had bombed and strafed targets in Guatemala City—nor would any of us find out for many years to come that the ubiquitous E. Howard Hunt had served as Political Action Officer for the operation, which was directed by one Richard Bissell, who would subsequently manage the Bay of Pigs debacle, and mastermind plots to assassinate Castro and the Congolese leader, Patrice Lumumba. At the time, we were smack in the middle of the Atlantic, so when the ship's captain—our only link to the world—announced triumphantly over the loudspeaker that a Red-led threat to peace and freedom in the hemisphere we were leaving behind had been thwarted, we gave a faint cheer, before resuming our various shipboard pursuits. Mine happened to be playing piano in a makeshift dance band that held forth nightly in the ship's lounge, where I could be seen gazing dreamily at the freckle-faced wife of a tank battalion commander, who perched like a nightclub thrush on the edge of the piano lid, warbling slightly off-key lyrics to ballads such as "I Cover the Waterfront," while I pounded away at the ivories in a vain attempt to keep pace with the wildly erratic beat provided by an artillery-lieutenant drummer and a bass-playing infantry warrant officer, both of whom had fallen as deeply in shipboard love with her as I. Who cared if the sky cared to fall into the sea, or that the CIA had made Guatemala safe for democracy—an accomplishment that over the next four decades would turn out to cost the lives of tens of thousands of that impoverished nation's Mayan peasants, and allow the Guatemalan army to arrange for the "disappearance" of forty thousand others? We had been at sea a full week, and on the following day the *General Darby* was scheduled to dock for thirty-six hours in Southampton to disgorge eleven hundred airmen bound for bases in England. Better still, it had been announced that the cabin-class passengers would be given twenty-four-hour passes and allowed to go ashore. Best of all, the tank battalion commander's wife had agreed to go sightseeing with me in London.

Anticipation kept me awake half that night, so imagine the letdown the next afternoon when, as the *Darby* was being warped to her berth, my counterintelligence colleagues and I learned from a self-important major who had been designated as our group leader that twenty-four-hour passes would be issued to all cabin-class passengers with the exception of the six of us. The major tried his pompous best to put the best face on this omission, theorizing that the decision not to issue us passes had no doubt originated at the highest level of command, and probably had to do with the fact that our top intelligence people considered England and its government to be riddled with Communist spies. (He was undoubtedly alluding to the defections of Guy Burgess, of the British Secret Intelligence Service, and Donald Maclean, of the British Foreign Office, which had been hidden from the public up to then, but would shortly be revealed.) He went on to surmise that our potential contribution to the struggle against Communism had been deemed far too valuable for our identities to be compromised by premature exposure in England where Soviet espionage agents . . . He never got around to finishing his tortuous rationale, probably because the collective look on our faces told him he was lucky we weren't still at sea.

The losses we suffer in our lives have a way of lingering, and I can still recall the profound sense of deprivation I experienced as I stood by the rail of the *Darby,* an hour or so later, and watched the tank battalion commander's wife skip merrily down the gangplank and onto the waiting arms of my two colleagues in the ragged rhythm section. But the bitter disappointment of that moment may well have been a blessing in disguise, because the ship's captain had apparently been told by his officers that illicit liaisons were being formed among the cabin passengers—a suspicion that could have been reinforced as he gazed down from his bridge and observed the happy pairing that was taking place at the bottom of the gangplank in Southampton. In any event, appalled by the prospect of sexual license aboard his vessel, the captain initiated a close watch on the nocturnal comings and goings of his charges during the three days it took the *General Darby* to pass through the North Sea to its final destination. As a result, when the ship docked in Bremerhaven, it was not met, let alone serenaded, by the customary military band, but by a company of white-helmeted and white-spatted military police, who proceeded to detain a dozen or so army wives, including the tank battalion commander's wife, and a similar number of army officers for questioning, which ultimately led to disciplinary action being taken against several of the officers, and charges of adultery brought against a number of women, whose husbands were informed of this in telegrams that asked whether they wished their allegedly delinquent spouses to be sent on to them, or returned to the United States.

I never did find out if the tank battalion commander's wife was among those whose arrival in the Old World had been so inauspiciously announced, but a few months later, when I was back in Bremerhaven on assignment, a chaplain's assistant whom I met in a PX told me that virtually all of the aggrieved husbands had selected the first option. I was about to conjecture in jocular fashion about the ensuing scenes of tender reunion, when the chaplain's assistant informed me that because the evidence was largely circumstantial, the charges against most of the women had been dismissed, and that most of the officers had been let off with mild letters of reprimand. He went on to observe that it was fortunate no enlisted personnel had been involved, because—shades once again of *From Here to Eternity*—any enlisted man suspected of consorting with an officer's wife would have been sentenced to hard labor and packed off to the disciplinary barracks at Fort Leavenworth.

# 6

## The Music of Our Time

The ominous welcome at Bremerhaven notwithstanding, I was thrilled to have arrived in Europe. The day after I landed I reported for duty to the Seventh Army's CIC Detachment in Ludwigsburg, just outside of Stuttgart, where I was charmed to find Duke Ludwig's palatial copy of Versailles surrounded by a web of cobblestone streets that were lined by cottages with red-tile roofs and filled with chickens, cattle, and children in lederhosen. By the middle of summer, I had managed to visit the Hohenstaufen Castle in the Black Forest, an old church with famous altar carvings at Breisach, the brick cathedral at Speyer, the *Schloss* at Heidelberg, and the university at Tübingen. I also spent a weekend in Munich, where I enjoyed drinking beer and carousing in various *Gastuben* until I met a solemn Jewish artillery lieutenant named Garber, who insisted on taking me on a pilgrimage to the remnants of a place called Dachau, which was on the Amper River, a few miles north of the city. There were, to be sure, certain military duties that had to be performed—anal chores for the most part, such as inspecting offices where classified documents were logged and stored, and surveying perimeter fences, guard postings, and security procedures at various posts and encampments throughout the region.

My first counterespionage assignment came in late August, when the captain who commanded our detachment selected several of us—I was included because I could speak a smattering of German—to accompany him to the town of Hof, near the conjunction of the borders between West Germany, East Germany, and Czechoslovakia, in order to debrief a captain and two enlisted men from a medical detachment in Worms, who had just been returned to the West after having been snatched by Czech border guards while on a sight-seeing trip to the Iron Curtain border. The captain and his men had been held for nearly ten days in a military dungeon in Prague, but since the medical detachment was singularly lacking any classified mission or information, it was not immediately clear what all the fuss was about. Our captain, however, was ecstatic about the mission, and as we sped in a tiny Taunus over the Autobahn through Bavaria, he regaled us with its possibilities. Through painstaking interrogation of the medical captain and his men, we could hope to glean valuable insight into the "essential elements of information" (EEI, our captain called them), which the enemy had been seeking to learn through his interrogation of them, thus indicating what the enemy did not know about us and what we, in turn, must henceforth redouble our efforts to keep him from knowing about us, unless, of course, he already knew and was merely pretending not to know, in order to lead us astray and keep us guessing. It was all rather dizzying, like the glorious scenery streaking past the windows of the Taunus, but our captain was persuasive and, in addition, in possession of a voluminous FBI report on the medical captain's background (he came from Orlando and had recently graduated from the University of Florida's medical school in Gainesville), which advised us to make sure that he had not been "doubled" (persuaded) by his captors to become an agent for them.

Hof turned out to be a somewhat dreary town, and we found the medical captain and his men quartered in a smelly *Kaserne* that housed a detachment of horse-mounted constabulary used to patrol the nearby border. They had already been questioned by agents of the Central Intelligence Agency who were chiefly interested in the interior layout of the prison in Prague, and they had also been examined by physicians from the military hospital at Regensberg, who had pronounced them physically and mentally fit, except for the medical captain whom they found to be suffering from anxiety.

The first interrogation we conducted took place in an office borrowed from the constabulary's S-2 officer, and contained little more than a desk behind which our captain sat, a chair for the medical captain, and a chair near the door for me and whomever else our captain might designate to take notes, fetch coffee, and run errands. There was no question that the medical captain was a shaken man, because when he entered the room and saluted our captain, the fingers he held to his brow were palpably quivering. Our captain invited him to be seated and tried to put him at ease by telling him how glad everyone was to have him and his men back safe and sound, and asking him if he had yet had a chance to telephone his family in Florida. Then he led the medical captain through the story of how he and his men had taken three-day passes, driven out to the Czech border, and were photographing each other near some big stones that marked the demarcation, when they were surrounded by soldiers carrying automatic weapons, blindfolded, and hustled off to the prison in Prague, where they were placed in separate cells. Up to this point, the medical captain recounted the experience calmly enough, but when he told how the prison guards had kept him awake for the next twenty-four hours by periodically sliding open a small window in the door of his cell, his voice quavered, and when he tried to describe his first interrogation at the hands of his captors, he started to unravel and began to cry.

"Keep in mind you're safe now," our captain told him. "You're back with friends."

The medical captain nodded and took a deep breath. "They had me believing I never would be," he said.

"How'd they manage to do that?" our captain inquired.

"They knew everything about me."

"Everything," our captain said.

"They knew where my mother lives, and the name of my fiancée, and the names of my sister's two kids and where they go to school, and how much my stepfather's trying to get for the land he's selling over in Ocala."

"How d'you suppose they got to know those things?"

The medical captain swallowed hard and shook his head. "It was uncanny," he said.

"Unnerving, perhaps, but not uncanny," our captain said. "So how did they bring all this stuff up? Your fiancée, for example."

"They told me I'd never see Jennifer again."

"And you believed them?"

The medical captain was weeping softly. "They said I could forget about the cypress house in St. Augustine—the one her grandmother wants to give us when we get married."

Our captain's voice was soothing. "So what did you tell them besides your name, rank, and serial number?"

"That's all."

"You trying to kid me?"

"No," the medical captain said.

Our captain's voice grew harsh. "They had you scared shitless about never seeing your mother, sister, nephews, nieces, and the house you and your girlfriend were going to live in, and you want me to believe you didn't tell them anything besides your name, rank, and serial number?"

"What else could I tell them?"

"That's exactly what the army wants to know," our captain said. "The army wants to know what the enemy wanted to know and how much of it you told him."

It went on like that for another hour, with the medical captain remembering that his interrogators had shown considerable interest in where his detachment had been sent during the previous autumn's maneuvers; how and where the theoretically wounded had been evacuated; and what specific treatment had been given the personnel who had been burned and contaminated during the several theoretical atomic strikes that had theoretically neutralized a number of divisions. The medical captain remembered that he had been able to answer all of these questions, except the last, for which there was no real answer.

"What d'you mean no real answer?" our captain said.

"Well, there isn't much you can do for nuclear burns and radioactive contamination in the field," the medical captain replied. "I mean except for Unguentine and rudimentary showering."

"Which is what you told them."

"I figured they probably knew that to begin with," the medical captain said.

"Like they knew about Jennifer and the cypress house and the land your stepfather's selling in Ocala."

"Am I in trouble?" the medical captain asked.

"Get some sleep," our captain said. "We'll talk some more tomorrow."

When the medical captain left the room, our captain sat for a long time, smoking a cigarette and drumming his fingers on the S-2's desk. "What d'you think?" he said finally. "Was he telling the truth?"

"He seemed pretty believable to me," I replied.

"But that's what he'd like us to think, wouldn't he?"

"Yes, sir."

"So let's review what we know. We know that after they softened him up with all that family stuff, they got some valuable information out of him, didn't they?"

"They did?" I said.

"Sure they did. They found out that a tactical atomic strike made against our forces in the field will be severely damaging from a medical as well as military standpoint. The question the army and the FBI want answered is, was he scared enough to be recruited? In other words, did he agree to keep in contact with them if they sent him back?"

That seemed highly unlikely to me, and I said so. I also wondered aloud how we would be able to tell one way or the other.

"By breaking him down," the captain replied.

"The poor devil seems close to that already."

"Wait'll I get through with him," the captain said grimly. "Wait'll I start him thinking about being court-martialed for giving aid, comfort, and information to the enemy."

I had begun to feel sorry for the medical captain. "Does he really pose all that much of a threat?" I asked. "I mean, to the military?"

"The army's the least of it," our captain replied. "He'll never see a classified document for the rest of his tour. It's afterward you have to worry about, when he's back in Orlando. Will he be an agent in place? Someone they can activate a few years down the road?"

The phrase *agent in place* intrigued me, smacking as it did of Graham Greene. "I hadn't thought of that," I said.

"Well, you want to," our captain told me. "How d'you suppose they found out all that stuff about his family to begin with?"

"D'you mean they already have agents in place in places like Orlando?"

The captain gave me a pitying glance. "Not in Orlando," he said. "Right here! Why, probably half the janitors and trash collectors at all the military posts in Germany are low-level agents in place! A whole army with no other mission than to sift through garbage, collect envelopes and letters—especially those addressed to people with serial numbers that begin with O for *Officer*—and then send them back across the border where they get read, analyzed, alphabetized, and stashed away in huge files that end up containing just about everything anybody'd ever want to know about any officer who's ever served here. That way, when one of them strays too close to the border . . ."

At this point, our captain lifted his hands and held them apart, as if to indicate a breadth of possibility beyond imagination, and I found myself conjuring up the file that the FBI would now open on the medical captain in anticipation of his return; a file that would swell with the record of the debriefing just begun, and grow fat to bulging as it became bloated with interviews of former professors, classmates, and acquaintances; with lists of patients, colleagues, and correspondents; and with all manner of information about the beliefs of family, friends, and fiancée—the whole of which, when coupled with the contents of similar files being compiled on thousands of other people in hundreds of other cities and towns across America, together with the dossiers being collated in Prague and the ancient capitals of Eastern Europe from a mass of minutiae plucked out of wastebaskets on military posts throughout West Germany, France, Italy, and other NATO lands, set the mind to reeling.

For some moments longer, the captain and I remained silent—each of us lost in contemplation of the intricacies of the music of our time— and then we went out to dinner. Two days later, after the medical captain had been reduced by further interrogation and sent off to recuperate in the psycho ward at Regensberg, we tooled back across Bavaria to Ludwigsburg. Just south of Stuttgart, while I was taking my turn at the wheel, a four-engine transport attempting to land in dense fog at the airport adjacent to the Autobahn mistook the highway for a runway, touched down on the road just ahead of us, and roared back up into the night sky, inducing reverberations in my brain, which, when transmitted to the steering wheel, sent us veering off on a shoulder—a swerve our captain attributed to timely evasive action on my part. "You just saved our lives," he said matter-of-factly, after I had driven us back onto the macadam and we had continued on our way.

A week or so later, our captain selected me and Eddie Calabro—a tough, handsome Italian kid from Detroit—to ride shotgun for Charles D. (Engine Charlie) Wilson, the former chief executive officer of General Motors, who had become secretary of defense in the Eisenhower administration. Wilson, who had acquired his nickname because he liked to wear a railroad engineer's cap, had achieved notoriety by declaring that what was good for GM was good for America, thus equating corporate profits with the national well-being, and by expressing a metaphorical preference for bird dogs over kennel dogs while giving a discourse on why he thought laid-off workers should be required to forage for new jobs instead of being allowed to become dependent on unemployment benefits. This tendency toward outspokenness undoubtedly lay behind the decision to show our colors to the Soviets by having him ride part of the way from Bremerhaven to Frankfurt in the cab of one of several .280 millimeter atomic cannons that had just been shipped over from an arsenal in Watertown (outside of Boston) to bolster the firepower of the Seventh Army in Europe. By way of preparation, our captain sent Eddie and me off to the firing range at Bad Canstatt to become proficient in shooting the submachine "grease" guns with which we were supposed to ensure the secretary's safety. Neither of us, it turned out, was able to hit the broad side of a barn door with a grease gun—for that matter, few people could, because the weapon kept jumping up on you as soon as you pulled the trigger—but the sergeant in charge of the range had been instructed to train us for an important mission, and, rather than fail in this assignment, he presented us with marksmen's badges for stitching cardboard silhouettes full of holes at ten paces. At that point, cocky as gangsters, we returned to detachment headquarters, where our captain pronounced himself pleased with our readiness for the job that lay ahead, and proceeded to send us on our way by jeep to Bremerhaven.

The .280 millimeter cannon were massive ordnance, nearly two stories high and so long they had to be hinged and driven from the rear as well as the front, like hook-and-ladder fire trucks, which didn't prevent them from knocking off the corners of several fourteenth-century churches when they were subsequently sent out on maneuvers in Bavaria. There were three of them in all, and, according to *Stars & Stripes,* they were fearsome weapons, capable of lobbing a shell carrying an atomic warhead at least fifty miles, which would give our side a tactical advantage if and when the Soviets sent their tanks pouring through the Fulda Gap. When Eddie and I first saw them, however, they were sitting on a dock by the River Weser, shrouded with huge tarpaulins that made them look like lumpy dinosaurs, which was kind of prophetic considering that they would not only prove to be incapable of negotiating the narrow streets of most German towns but also of being supported by most German roads, and so ended up by getting hopelessly mired in soft ground and swamps from one end of Bavaria to the other.

There were about twenty of us in the group that had been assembled to protect the secretary of defense, and our briefing for this task, which was conducted by two colonels, took up a large part of the afternoon of the day we arrived in Bremerhaven. It began with a description of the route the convoy would follow and the positions we would take in relation to the cannon carrying Secretary Wilson, and it concluded with a lecture on the nature of the threat we were supposed to guard against, which was based upon a detailed report compiled by agents of the CIA, who warned that subversive elements of the outlawed KPD (*Kommunistische Partei Deutschland*) might try to embarrass the army and Chancellor Konrad Adenauer by disrupting the cavalcade and inflicting harm upon its illustrious passenger.

That night, Eddie and I were so nerved up we could hardly sleep, and the next morning we were still excited when Eddie drove our jeep into Lilliputian position beside the behemoth bearing Engine Charlie Wilson. In fact, I was trembling so I scarcely dared keep my finger on the trigger of my grease gun, as I had been told to do. At precisely 0900 hours the procession got underway, and ten minutes later we were rumbling over the highway that led from Bremerhaven to Bremen.

The Adenauer government had declared a holiday, and when we reached the outskirts of the city, thousands of people lined the avenue on either side, waving flags, shouting greetings, and straining against rows of black-booted German cops, who linked arms to hold them back. Among the multitude were hundreds of schoolchildren, dressed for the occasion in starched shirts, pleated skirts, and gray lederhosen, who threw flowers under the massive wheels of the cannon, as well as *Hausfrauen* who hung over second-story windowsills padded with airing bedclothes and blew kisses down upon us. Following our instructions, Eddie kept pace with the cannon that carried the secretary of defense, and while I anxiously scanned the crowd and the windows of houses and buildings for the glint of a gun barrel or the arc of a lobbed grenade, the secretary—gray haired and red faced—stuck his head out of the truck cab of the cannon that towered above us, waving his arms and doffing the famous cap that made him look like a popover rising out of a baking pan. It took a while—probably half the length of the street—for us to realize that our mission was futile, but it was Eddie who knew it first. Pointing toward a phalanx of cheering children, he asked me what I would do if I saw someone raise a rifle among them, and when I said I didn't know, he inquired whether I would fire into them to protect the secretary, and when I said, "Hell, no," he said, "Me either," so I took my finger off the trigger of the grease gun and kept it off for the rest of the ride, while Engine Charlie, who had no idea he was on his own up there, kept waving his goofy cap and giving everybody the thumbs-up sign.

# 7

## North Point

Eddie Calabro and I received special commendations for our part in helping protect the secretary of defense, and upon returning to our detachment in Ludwigsburg, we became our captain's fair-haired boys. As a result, when several outpostings became available during the autumn, we were given first pick. Eddie, who liked to ski, took Bad Tölz on the Austrian border, which was the headquarters for a tank division, and I selected Weierhof, a tiny village in the Rheinpfalz, which was in the middle of the French Zone, only a six-hour drive from Paris. No one, not even our captain, seemed to know what was up there, and I did not find out until I arrived at a former Wehrmacht *Kaserne* on the outskirts of the village, and reported to the man I was replacing, a first lieutenant, who was being returned to the United States for special training. From him I learned that the *Kaserne* housed an ordnance battalion that had been formed as a special weapons unit at Sandia Base, New Mexico, and that its personnel, who for the most part were electricians and electrical engineers, spent their working hours sealed beneath the earth's surface in subterranean storage vaults, called igloos, at an underground site in a nearby forest. Buried in the igloos were nuclear warheads for the recently arrived .280 millimeter cannon, as well as for the Honest John rockets that were then being deployed to counteract any Soviet attack.

During a two-year stay in New Mexico, the members of the ordnance battalion had been under a strict surveillance conducted by agents of the CIC and FBI, and I soon realized that the memory of this scrutiny had lingered, with the result that my presence inevitably imposed a certain constraint on any gathering I might happen to attend. To avoid such awkwardness, I stopped living at the bachelor officer quarters and taking my meals at the officers' mess, and moved off post to a requisitioned house on the edge of Kircheimbolanden, a town on the way to the storage site where I maintained an office that, once I learned the significance of some red and green light bulbs, I visited as infrequently as possible.

The storage site, called North Point, was surrounded by double chain-link fences topped with barbed wire. The area between the fences was patrolled by armed guards accompanied by police dogs, and the forest beyond the fences was patrolled by the members of an infantry company. Access to the installation was gained by passing through a gate manned by an officer and several enlisted men, who examined credentials and waved visitors to a parking lot beside an operations building that was only partly visible. Once inside the fences, all perspectives shrank into the earth. Built as an underground arsenal for the Wehrmacht, the site had been renovated by American ordnance engineers and camouflaged with subtlety and nonchalance by nature. Beneath a vault of trees, the subterranean igloos wrinkled the forest floor into elongated mounds of turf and needles, sprouting ventilators that looked like giant fungi. The whole place seemed eerie and unreal, because it was the citadel of a future too close at hand to be comfortably imagined. Would it survive, I sometimes wondered, as had the Celtic rubble of the surrounding countryside, with sufficient evidence of its secrets for distant historians to explain? Or would the excavators be forced, as with Stonehenge, to speculate on unknown treasures, obscure gods?

On the day of my first visit, I introduced myself to the battalion S-2, a chain-smoking captain, who gave me a tour of the premises that excluded the igloos to which, because I did not possess a "Q" clearance (one reserved for people working with nuclear weapons), I had neither permission nor need to go, and then he invited me to his office for a cup of coffee. When I remarked upon the stringent measures that had been taken to provide security, he gave a harsh laugh and pointed out a window toward a group of German civilians who, under the watchful eye of a guard, were raking up leaves from the grounds.

"Place is a goddam sieve," he said. "They probably know more about what goes on here than I do."

Remembering what I had been told about the role of janitors and trash collectors, I maintained a judicious silence.

The captain nodded toward the doorway, above which were mounted twin light sockets—one holding a green bulb that was illuminated, the other a red bulb that was off. "Green means everything's okay down in the igloos," he told me. "When the red comes on, there's a problem."

"What kind of problem?"

The captain shrugged. "Some kind of short circuit, usually. Happens when they're arming or de-arming the warheads. I never know for sure because I don't have a need to know, but our German friends know, which is how I find out."

"I don't follow you," I said.

"Wait'll you hear Bertha."

"Who's she?"

"I don't want to spoil the fun for you. Some night, when the red light's on and you're sick of listening to hillbilly on the Armed Forces Network, tune in to East Berlin. Bertha comes on around midnight. She plays great jazz and classical."

I glanced at the doorway and saw that the green bulb was still illuminated. "How often does the red light come on?" I asked.

"Often enough," the captain said. "There was one week I hardly ever made it back to the *Kaserne*. My poor wife was worried sick."

"Couldn't you phone her?"

"Red light comes on, the telephones shut down. Automatically."

"Why's that?" I asked.

"To prevent the spread of panic," the captain said dryly. "Red light means nobody—not even the colonel who commands this bunch of electronic hot shots—is allowed outside the building. Anyone who tries to leave gets cut down. The guards even have orders to shoot each other." The captain grinned—no doubt at the expression he saw on my face—and bared his teeth. "How we avoid traffic congestion on the road to Kircheimbolanden."


I was lonely and restless in the Pfalz for the first few months. Then, in early March, I was marooned for ten days by a series of heavy snows. The roads became impassable, and only by throwing my jeep into four-wheel drive could I get about. Suddenly, I was truly alone—a vassal lord in a remote province, a latter-day palatine enchanted with the brilliance of my solitude and already disaffected with the Empire. I went skiing on the Donnerberg, a nearby mountain, breaking out a slalom course through trees that covered its steep eastern face, and pausing from time to time to gaze out over the motionless landscape that only I could traverse in freedom.

During the spring, I leased a stretch of trout stream that entered the valley at the base of the mountain, flowed past the *Kaserne* housing the ordnance battalion, and fed into a larger stream in the flatland near the Rhine. By then, I was taking dinner almost every night at the *Gasthof Post*, in Kircheimbolanden, where they served the usual Weiner Schnitzel, potatoes, and oxtail soup. The villagers went to bed early, and in order not to disturb the quiet I would sometimes switch off the engine of my jeep at the top of the hill above the town and allow the vehicle to coast, silent as an owl on nocturnal wing, over a cobblestoned street that descended to the market square past darkened, tightly shuttered houses that huddled together like blocks of pumice soaking up the moisture and color of the red-clay earth. Like other hamlets that nestled in the hollows of the Pfalz, this one slept soundly, as if night were a blanket it had pulled up over its head. There was always a stale, heavy odor of sleep in the air, and the cobblestones of the market square glistened with a slippery film, as if the breath of some slumbering animal were condensing into rime and falling back upon its nocturnal lair. Before me, slivers of light showed through the shutters of the dining room on the first floor of the *Gasthof*, where a red-haired waitress who longed to leave for the city told me that we were living *hinter Mond*—behind the moon—the German way of saying "in the sticks."

By that time, I had begun to sever relations with headquarters in Ludwigsburg. My method was simple: I stopped writing the kind of reports that aroused curiosity and query and brought about a desire for further clarification and, finally, more reports. I did not, of course, cut off all correspondence. At regular intervals, I sent down routine surveys of perimeter security and inspections of document-logging procedures—seasonal plantings to reassure the gardeners who tended the master files at headquarters that the district of their tenant was still fertile. In this way, I ensured my freedom, assuring my superiors and telling myself, as if to satisfy a flagging sense of duty, that I was "keeping an eye on things," while I took care never to alarm the analysts at headquarters, who were forever sticking colored pins into huge wall maps and nodding solemnly at one another in recognition of vast patterns of conspiracy that were unfolding before them. So jealous did I become of my domain and solitude that by the time summer rolled around even the thought of someone poring over a map of my district would have been enough to fill me with anguish.

Of course, the world I wished to leave behind—the one sporadically lit in red above my office door—soon managed to intrude. On a fine spring morning, when the wet hills of the Pfalz were being plowed and laced with human manure that had been collecting all winter in the "honey wagons" of the sugar-beet farmers, I got a call from *Polizeiwachtmeister* Brausch, in Weierhof, whose voice crackled with excitement as he told me that an airplane had crashed into the Donnerberg. When I arrived on the scene a short while later, I found the police sergeant sitting on his mud-splattered motorcycle, waving off a small group of peasants who had gathered along the roadside. The plane had gone into a stand of trees at the edge of a grassy meadow on the lower part of the mountain, not far from the stretch of trout stream I had rented, and as Brausch and I hurried toward it I could see long pieces of crumpled wing dangling in the branches of the trees and a thin tube of fuselage and tail section sticking out of the ground. The airplane had spun into the woods at a fairly shallow angle, because its wings had been sheared off by the trees, and only the front part—the nose, the cockpit, and what looked like the air-intake casings of a jet engine—had been mangled by contact with the earth. It was light gray in color and it bore no visible markings, except for a number painted in blue on the tail, and there was no smoke, no smell of fuel, and no sign of the pilot. After examining the wreckage for a few minutes, I left the *Wachtmeister* to guard it, drove back to my office, and called the duty officer of a Canadian Night-Fighter Squadron that was stationed near Langmeil, a few miles to the south. When I got through, I told him what had happened, and he said he would look into it. Ten minutes later, he called me back to say his outfit had nothing down, and he had checked with the Americans at Ramstein, who told him they didn't either.

"That can't be right," I said.

"All I know is what they tell me," the duty officer replied. "Ramstein says not only don't they have anything down, but there's no report of anything missing or down in all of Europe."

No sooner had I hung up the telephone than it rang again. This time it was the police sergeant in Alzey—a fairly large town about fifteen miles to the north—who told me that one of his men had found the body of an American pilot in the middle of the main road leading to Mainz.

"How do you know it's an American pilot?" I asked.

"Because I haff seen it," he replied. "And I haff seen what is an American flag painted on the back."

It took me nearly half an hour to drive to Alzey. As I approached over the treeless plateau above the town, I had no trouble finding the police sergeant, because he and two other policemen were directing traffic through an intersection formed by the main road leading north to Mainz and the east-west road from Worms to Bad Kreuznach, and they were surrounded by a dozen or so bystanders who, dressed in the customary black garb of the local peasantry, stuck out of the bare landscape like a flock of crows. The body of the pilot, who appeared to be wearing some kind of laced pressure suit over long underwear, and whose parachute had obviously failed to open, lay facedown in the very center of the crossroads. It had been horribly compressed and misshaped upon impact with the macadam. A huge stain of blood had soaked the pressure suit and seeped outward over the roadway, obscuring everything except the outline of a decal of the Stars and Stripes, which had been stitched to the back of the suit.

I didn't stay long, because there was nothing for me to do, but when I tried to return to my office at North Point, a sentry turned me back, telling me that a red-light alert was in progress. At that point, I drove over to the *Kaserne* in Weierhof, put through a call to air force headquarters in Weisbaden, and left a message for the duty officer there, suggesting that he ought to check his radars for a missing plane. Then I drove back out to the Donnerberg, where I found *Wachtmeister* Brausch standing in the roadway with some onlookers, gazing at a crew of twenty or so air force enlisted men, who were dragging pieces of the downed plane out of the woods and loading them into a pair of ten-wheeled canopied trucks that had been driven up into the meadow. I was about to ask Brausch what was going on, when I noticed a black Mercedes parked at the lower end of the meadow, near the roadway.

I knew the car and its occupants, because I had seen them several times as they cruised through my district looking for a Zis driven by members of a Soviet military liaison team, who, although the entire area for miles around North Point had been declared a forbidden zone, came through periodically to test the perimeter security. They were agents from the CIA station in Kaiserslautern, and when I walked up to the Mercedes, the one in the driver's seat to whom I showed my credentials told me that everything was under control and that my services were not needed. That aroused my territorial instincts, so I let him know that I'd already been there, a couple of hours earlier, and suggested that instead of hanging around and doing nothing, he and his colleague might want to drive up to Alzey, where they would find a dead American pilot smack in the middle of the intersection of Route 40 and the road to Bad Kreuznach. Then I walked back down to the road to chat with *Wachtmeister* Brausch, and after the Mercedes took off, tires squealing, in the direction of Alzey, I drove back to the *Kaserne* and wrote up a report of the whole incident, which I stuck in my filing cabinet and promptly forgot until five years later, when I was back in civilian life and living in New York City, and saw the photographs released by the Soviets of the long-winged plane flown by Francis Gary Powers.

About twenty years after that, while sitting in a dentist's office, I came across a lengthy article about the U-2s in one of those high-tech military magazines that became popular during the 1970s and 1980s. It contained interviews with former U-2 pilots who said that the prototype planes flown during the fifties were difficult to control, unforgiving of the slightest mistake, and prone to flame out, and that more than a dozen of them and their pilots were lost during the early years of the overflights. The same article said that the photographs of Powers' plane suggested that it had been belly-landed, instead of falling out of the sky, which sent me to the library to read Powers' book, *Overflight*. In it, he claimed that he had been knocked out of the sky by an exploding SAM missile, and that he had ridden his plane all the way down to fourteen thousand feet before bailing out. What I found interesting was that the plane he flew had been equipped with an automatic ejection seat, but that he had chosen not to use it, apparently because of suspected defects in some switches that operated the seat catapult system and a destruct system—a three-pound charge of cyclonite—which was supposed to blow the airplane into little pieces once the pilot had got clear of it.

This tended to make me skeptical about why Powers would choose to trust his parachute, especially in light of the fact that the early U-2 pilots had been supplied with (and encouraged to use in case of capture) needles tipped with curare, but that was just the beginning of my doubts. What I found downright suspicious was Powers' account of a U-2 flight that had "crashed near Kaiserslautern" during the middle 1950s, after supposedly being buzzed by two curious Canadian Air Force interceptors, whose wake turbulence as they passed close by had caused the spy plane to disintegrate in midair. Believe that if you will, as well as the story that Powers, who, like all U-2 pilots, had been trained to keep an eagle eye on fuel consumption, died a few years later when the traffic-watch helicopter he was flying for a Los Angeles TV station crashed after running out of gas.

Whatever the case, on the night of the day the plane crashed into the Donnerberg, I remember climbing into bed and tuning into Radio East Berlin, just in time to catch the tail end of Sibelius' Seventh and to hear a refined and faintly accented woman's voice wonder in perfect English what had gone wrong that morning in Igloo Number Seven at North Point, and whether it could be remedied, as the manual claimed, by the replacement of a diode in the arming console, or, like some metastasizing electronic tumor, it would allow a fatal current to spread to the brain of the warhead the next time the arming procedure was initiated. Then I drifted off to sleep, listening to Benny Carter soloing on "Doubletalk" and wondering about the pilot who had plummeted to earth at Alzey—the old Altaia of the Romans, where Julius Caesar had camped on his way to the Rhine more than half a century before the birth of Christ—and why his parachute hadn't opened.

# 8

## The Jewish Question

By this time, I had already begun to take dinner once or twice a week at a restaurant in Alzey that specialized in venison, wild boar, and other game, a welcome respite from the veal cutlet and potatoes of the *Gasthof Post*. Since I liked to eat late, the place was usually empty when I arrived, except for three men dressed in black suits who always sat at a table in the far corner of the room near the kitchen, drinking coffee and after-dinner schnapps. From the way the proprietor and his wife and their waitress bustled about them, I gathered that they were prominent citizens and, indeed, soon learned that they were none other than the *Burgermeister,* the *Doktor* who ran the local hospital, and the *Schuldirecktor* of the high school.

The three of them could have been plucked straight out of central casting. The *Burgermeister* was a hearty, blunt-spoken, white-haired man of commanding presence and substantial girth; the physician was a slender, pinch-faced fellow who wore tiny rimless spectacles; and the school principal was a sad-eyed chap with a drooping mustache, who seemed to defer to the other two. For the first week or two, they paid no attention to the young American in civilian clothes, who was always seated on the other side of the room. Then one evening, after they rose from their table in unison and bade farewell to the proprietor and his wife, the principal nodded in my direction. The next time I ate there, he made a point of saying *"Guten Abend"* to me, and soon all three of them were bidding me "good evening" (and I them) not only when they left, but also when I arrived. Before long, I was invited to join them in their after-dinner brandy, and all at once as if we had been friends forever we were discussing everything from international politics to local cultural events—West Germany had just become a sovereign nation again, and a month-long music festival was being held in Weisbaden, an elegant spa town a few miles to the north. I had recently heard the

Weisbaden Symphony Orchestra play Beethoven's Ninth in the *Grand Saal* of the city's *Kurhaus*—a wonderfully ornate structure that had been built by the Emperor Franz Josef I around the time the town became a haven for sufferers of rheumatism—and this impressed my new friends so much that they began to vie with one another in recommending other cultural forays (visits to museums, castles, cathedrals, and the like) for my consideration. As for me, I welcomed the willingness of these older men to take me into their company, as any young stranger might have, particularly one stuck away in a region so remote, and I proceeded to do my best to engage their interest and satisfy their curiosity about life in the United States.

I forget exactly how the subject of what had happened to the Jews came up. All I remember is that it came out of the blue one night, not long after I had begun to meet with them on a regular basis, and that it came up inadvertently. It may have been triggered by some mention of the tension that was developing between Israel and Egypt over control of the Suez Canal, or by something as remote as a passing reference on my part to my having heard the violinist Yehudi Menuhin. Whatever triggered it, I remember that a long silence fell upon the table, which was not broken until the *Burgermeister* removed his after-dinner cigar from his mouth, set it in an ashtray, and informed me in a voice that brooked no contradiction that "we here knew nothing of the Jewish business," before adding another "Nothing!" as a mark of final punctuation.

"Nothing," the physician seconded with a shake of his head.

"*Nicht*," the school principal echoed softly.

Clearly, the burden was on me to say something, but what was I to say? I was less than half the age of any of them, a stranger in their town, a guest in their newly sovereign nation. In the end, I did the most politic thing I could think of. I changed the subject. I talked about a tennis tournament I had recently attended in which a young Italian named Pietrangelli had beaten Vic Seixas, which allowed the physician to observe that he had once seen Von Cramm play Tilden. And so the awkward moment passed.

Not long afterward, the subject of what had happened to the Jews was touched upon again—this time by the *Doktor*, who said that he had spent most of the war with a medical unit stationed in France, and had thus escaped the horrors of the eastern front. As for the concentration camps whose existence had been discovered at the war's end, all of them, he told me, had been located far to the east as well. "Nothing of that sort ever happened in the Pfalz, I can assure you," he declared.

"Nothing," the *Burgermeister* agreed.

"Surely not," the *Schuldirecktor* murmured.

At that point, I felt constrained to say that I had visited Dachau the summer before, during a visit to Munich. I was about to ask whether any Pfalzers had been required to visit death camps under the program that was enforced during the immediate postwar occupation, but before I got the chance the *Burgermeister* inquired if I had yet visited the new casino that had opened in Bad Durkheim.

During the next few weeks, the subject of what had happened to the Jews kept popping up, as if it were a nervous tic that had a life of its own. On one occasion, the *Burgermeister* hinted at it when he assured me that, except for Swabia, the Palatinate was Hitler's least favorite part of Germany and that many of the excesses practiced by the Nazis had not found favor in the Pfalz. On another occasion, it came up when I told my dinner companions of meeting an old shepherd out by the trout stream I had leased, who boasted that he could count in English, Polish, and Yiddish.

"*Ein Judisch Schäfer!*" the doctor exclaimed. "How unusual! There were no Jews here during the war."

"None," the *Burgermeister* agreed.

I was tempted to ask how there could have been, but once again I kept still, and another silence ensued that begged to be broken.

It finally got so that I could expect—indeed, count upon—one or another of my new friends to bring up the subject of the Jews at least once during each of our twice-weekly meetings. Such mention invariably engendered some form of denial on the part of the *Burgermeister* and the *Doktor,* and uncomfortable agreement, or, as often, silence on the part of the *Schuldirecktor.* It aroused in me a nagging suspicion that there must be some reason behind their compulsion to return again and again, no matter how indirectly, to a subject from which one might expect any decent German to cringe.

Late in May, I was summoned to Seventh Army headquarters in Stuttgart to attend a briefing to be given by the chief of army counter-intelligence, General Boniface Campbell. Like most of the agents who had been brought in from the field, I went to the meeting in civilian clothes and listened attentively as the general described how important it was for us to be vigilant against the growing threat of Communist penetration of the military establishment and of the democratic institutions of our newly sovereign German allies. He went on to say that since the end of the Second World War the Counterintelligence Corps had provided a bulwark against Soviet infiltration of free Europe, and that we should consider ourselves the proud inheritors of a protective role that was now a decade old. He did not mention (nor did I or any of the rest of my colleagues in the audience know at the time) that army counterintelligence agents had been aware of what Klaus Barbie had done to the Jews of Lyons during the war and had protected and paid him for five years afterward, in return for his cooperation in informing them about Communist activities in France and Eastern Europe. They later looked the other way when he escaped to Bolivia by way of Italy in 1951.

I had driven down to Stuttgart from the Pfalz on the Autobahn in order to make certain that I would be on time for General Campbell's pep talk, but on the way back I decided to take a more scenic route, driving north from Stuttgart to Heilbronn, and from there along the Neckar River to Heidelberg, which was the headquarters of the United States Army in Europe (USAREUR). Never have I seen such a beautiful valley as the valley of the Neckar between Heilbronn and Heidelberg—fifty miles of lush rolling hills that were covered as if by snow with flowering dogwood, crowned by ruined castles, and striated with stands of dark fir trees that plunged to the narrow river, where barges plied tortuous passage between villages that sat beneath terraced vineyards.

Heidelberg, an old university town, had been almost untouched by the war, which no doubt accounted for why it had been selected to be USAREUR headquarters. As such, it contained a huge complex of offices, liaison missions, and procurement divisions, and it was home to dozens of generals and admirals and their wives and children, who lived in elegant requisitioned villas and luxurious hotels, in an atmosphere that had been rendered as exclusive as the most restricted stateside suburb, which is to say that all military personnel assigned there were carefully screened, and that Negro troops had only recently been allowed to visit the town on pass. More important from my perspective, however, Heidelberg was the repository for a vast store of military occupation records and captured German archives.

When I arrived in town and looked up an old Andover classmate, a navy attaché and admiral's aide, who had been described in a recent issue of the school alumni bulletin as living in a gay social whirl, I found him inhabiting a posh villa next to a magnificent *Schloss*. He was kind enough to put me up for a couple of days, and that evening he took me on a round of cocktail parties. The next day, he arranged for me to gain access to the military records division, which is how I came to find myself thumbing through index cards listing prewar activities in the various towns of the Rhineland-Palatinate until I came to the heading *"Krystallnacht"*—Night of the Broken Glass—and found what I had been looking for.

A week or so later, I was having dinner with my three friends in Alzey, when the *Doktor* remarked that Soviet authorities were engaging in harsh reprisals against Jews who were petitioning to be allowed to emigrate to Israel. The *Burgermeister* seized this opportunity to observe that although severe measures had undoubtedly been undertaken by the Nazis against certain Jews in Germany before and during the war, Communists and left-wingers were trying to inflame resentment against the German people by dwelling on such deeds and by exaggerating their extent. He went on to say that now that our two nations had finally joined together in the struggle against the Soviets, we must be careful to recognize the sinister tactics that lay behind such distortions.

At that point, I told my dinner companions that I had been to Heidelberg, made a search of the military records there, and discovered that on *Krystallnacht*—November 9, 1938—Jewish families throughout Germany, including some in Alzey and nearby towns, had been taken forcibly from their homes. I observed their neighbors must have had good reason to believe that these Jews would not be returning anytime soon, because by the following morning many of their homes had been thoroughly looted. I tried to say this as unemotionally and as matter-of-factly as I could, and when I had finished the *Burgermeister's* face flushed with anger, the *Doktor's* wizened features contracted further within themselves until they seemed to shrink behind his tiny spectacles, and the *Schuldirecktor's* eyes filled with tears. Then we all stood up in unison and said *"Guten Abend"* to each other and to the proprietor and his wife, before walking out into the cool spring night—they to their nearby homes, and I to the car in which I had driven from Kircheimbolanden to that restaurant for the very last time.

# 9

## Spycatching

During the summer, I caught a spy. I was sitting at the typewriter in my office at North Point, laboriously pecking out the report of a monthly security survey in seven onionskin carbons, when I happened to look out the window and saw a man in civilian clothes crouching behind a surveyor's tripod that was aimed in the direction of another man, who was driving a chaining pin into the sod covering the roof of Igloo Number Two. I could hardly believe my eyes, so I called down to the inner security gate and asked the second lieutenant, who was manning it that day, who he'd let inside.

"They're from the *Kreis Landvermessensamt*," he replied.

"What's that?" I said.

"The county surveyor's office. They're measuring all the boundaries in the district."

"How do you know?" I inquired.

"Because their papers say so, and they have a permission signed by the French commander in Mainz."

After calling for a guard, I went outside, walked up behind the man behind the tripod, and tapped him on the shoulder. He jumped a mile. Then, while the guard kept him and his colleague to one side, I examined the surveyor's compass on the tripod and found a miniature camera mounted on it. So I had both of them brought inside, and after examining their papers and other belongings, I questioned the man with the tripod, who refused to say anything except that he was a surveyor for the county on official business.

"*Warum Eine Kamera haben Sie?*" I asked, which produced a shrug.

At that point, I told him and his colleague that I would have to detain them for a while. Then I called down to headquarters in Ludwigsburg to let them know what had happened and asked what I should do. A short while later, I received a call from an intelligence colonel at

United States Army Headquarters, in Heidelberg, who told me that he was sending a major over to pick up the prisoners, and that I was to release them into his custody. So I typed up a release form—by that time, I had learned to cover my ass—but when the major arrived, an hour or so later, he refused to sign it.

"I wasn't told I'd have to sign anything," he said.

"Well, what's the harm?" I asked.

The major regarded me with suspicion. "You know something about these birds I don't?"

"All I know is they had a miniature camera on their surveying tripod," I replied.

"So you figure they're from the other side."

"Where else?" I said.

The major laughed out loud. "Listen, you've gone and nabbed a couple of Reinhard Gehlen's boys, and I'm here to let them go."

Reinhard Gehlen had been a big wheel in the German counter-intelligence service during World War II, and rumor had it he had been put in charge of setting up another such *Abwehrdienst* by our new allies, the recently emancipated Federal Republic, in Bonn. As for the major, he had suddenly become another unwelcome intruder in my territory. To wipe the smirk off his face, I told him that if he wanted the prisoners he would damn well have to sign for them, and after making a telephone call to USAREUR, he agreed to do so. The incident threatened to get me into trouble, because the colonel in Heidelberg complained to my superiors in Ludwigsburg that I had been rude to the major, but after cautioning me to henceforth treat USAREUR people with kid gloves, my people let it all blow over.

What didn't blow over was the Warshawsky affair. Adam Warshawsky was a Polish kid, from a town in the coal fields south of Pittsburgh, who had enlisted in the army right out of high school and had become an electronic specialist with the ordnance battalion. The whole thing started with a memo from headquarters, informing me that Warshawsky's "Q" and Top Secret clearances were being lifted as a result of newly developed information that cast doubt upon his loyalty, and instructing me to conduct a discreet inquiry into his conduct and activities since his arrival in Germany a year earlier. The lieutenant in charge of the igloo to which he was assigned told me that he had performed his duties at North Point (whatever they were) in such an exemplary manner that he had been made a squad leader. From his barracks sergeant, I learned that he had not earned a single demerit. From the post chaplain, I found out that he attended mass every Sunday at the Catholic church in Weierhof, had studied German in order to understand what the priest was saying, and had joined the local German-American Friendship Club. From the post librarian, I discovered that he had taken out books about the history of the Pfalz. A check of his company file showed that he had received weekend passes to visit Cologne, Mainz, Worms, and Speyer—cathedral cities all—and had recently taken a two-week leave in Rome, where, according to one of his friends, he had spent several days at the Vatican. I wrote all this up as simply as possible, letting the facts speak for themselves, and sent it off to Ludwigsburg. Several days later, I received another memo, telling me to call Warshawsky in for interrogation. At that point, I reached for the telephone and called Joe Moran, who was my immediate superior down there.

"Joe," I said, "what's the story on this Warshawsky fellow? What's he done?"

"Beats me," Moran replied. "What's the file number?"

After I read off a series of digits from the top right-hand corner of the memo, there was a clatter as Moran dropped the receiver on his desk, followed by a squeaking noise as he wheeled his chair to his filing cabinet, and a pause during which I could hear the clacking of typewriters in the office. When he picked up his telephone again, he said, "This one's got a high priority. It's straight from the FBI."

"But what's he done?"

"They don't exactly say."

"If I don't know what he's supposed to have done, how do I know what to ask him?"

Moran chuckled. "Apparently, they think he's been involved with one of the organizations on the attorney general's list."

This was a list that had been drawn up during the late 1940s by President Truman's first attorney general, Tom C. Clark, and updated by his second attorney general, a man named J. Howard McGrath, and updated again by Eisenhower's appointee to the post, Herbert Brownell. "Which organization?" I inquired.

"They don't tell us," Moran replied.

"Back to square one," I said. "Maybe they think we don't have a need to know."

"I'll send out a request for clarification," Moran told me. "Meanwhile, why don't you call him in and have a chat?"

"About what, for God's sake?"

"Just call him in and feel him out," Moran said wearily. "About his politics and stuff."

"Look, Moran, the kid's a model soldier, a squad leader, and a regular churchgoer."

"Stop giving me a hard time," Moran said. His voice was friendly but cool. "You've been around long enough to know that once the FBI puts something like this down on paper, we have to go by the book. We get the machinery in motion and we check it out."

After I hung up the telephone, I told myself there was no point antagonizing Moran, who not only had no choice in the matter, but also had left me alone to handle things in the district on my own. Then I took an elevator in the corridor outside my office and descended several levels into the bowels of the operations building to the office of Colonel Mallory, the battalion commander, whose adjutant had called earlier to say that he wanted to see me. When I went in, I didn't come to attention or salute, because, even though I held the rank of an enlisted man, I was in civilian clothes and considered to have civilian status—at least for the purpose of my visit—and to be in no way a subordinate of the military commander. I was careful to be correct, however, for the colonel ruled his command with all the patriarchal jurisdiction and prerogatives of his rank, and was accustomed to treat me with the reserve a patriarch accords an outsider who holds a position of autonomy within the tribe. As I advanced across the room, he applied the flame of a match to the end of a cigar and blew a billow of blue smoke in my direction. The colonel always seemed full of composure and sure of himself beneath ground level.

"Good morning, sir," I said. "You wanted to see me?"

"It's this business about Warshawsky. I've been told I have to yank his clearance. What the hell's going on?"

"I'm not sure, sir. The FBI has apparently dug something up on him back in the States."

"Fucking pheobes," the colonel said. "They made our life miserable at Sandia."

I had never heard anyone refer to the FBI that way before, and it was all I could do not to burst out laughing. Perhaps the colonel wasn't such a bad egg after all. "I'll do my best to straighten things out," I said. "Will that be all?"

"That'll be all," the colonel said. "Thanks for coming down, and by the way"—he had plucked the cigar from his mouth and was aiming it at me like a dart—"this Warshawsky's a fine lad. Be sure you treat him well."

I ended up treating Warshawsky like a younger brother. How could I not? He was an intelligent, clean-cut kid, who loved being an electronic specialist, and he was understandably puzzled and unhappy about having been transferred to the battalion motor pool.

"Sir, I'm considering reenlisting," he told me at the start of our interview in the S-2's office at the *Kaserne*. "Can you give me any idea what's going on?"

I had already decided to be as forthright with him as possible. "Something's turned up in an ongoing background check in the States," I said. "It may prove to be nothing important, but they want me to ask you some questions."

"Sir, you can ask me anything. I haven't got anything to hide."

"You don't have to call me 'sir,'" I told him. "Let's start with your family."

And so, for the next hour or so, I heard all about Warshawsky's family. One of the first things he described was an all-night vigil that had taken place while he and his mother waited to hear about his father, who had been trapped with half a dozen other men in a gas explosion in one of the mines. Then he told me about having nightmares when his uncle, an organizer for the United Mine Workers who had evidently tried to fill the gap left by the father's death, went off to fight in the war, and about a big party up in McKeesport when the uncle came home and married his mother. During his second year in high school, he remembered that the cops had caught him and a couple of friends drinking beer under a bridge over the Monongahela, and it went on like that until I brought the subject around to the union activities of the uncle who had become his stepfather. I did it because I figured that something like that must have triggered the FBI's suspicions. "Your uncle ever take you to any union meetings?" I asked.

Warshawsky shook his head. "Not that I recall. They were usually held at night when I had to study."

"D'you remember any strikes?"

"Sure," he said. "The miners were always striking. Mostly because they wanted safer conditions. Better ventilation and stuff like that."

"Did you ever go on a picket line?"

"No," Warshawsky said.

"And you never went to any meetings?"

"I could call home," Warshawsky said helpfully. "My uncle would probably remember."

I thought about that a moment, and then advised against it. My reasoning was that since the FBI was already suspicious of him, they might have tapped into the family telephones, in which case a call home would only exacerbate the situation. "It would be better if you could remember on your own," I told him.

"I'm trying to," Warshawsky said. "But my uncle worked the night shift during the last couple of years I was in school, and I didn't see much of him except on weekends."

"What'd you do then?"

"Sometimes we went fishing."

At that point, I stood up and ended the interview by shaking hands. "If you think of anything else, be sure to get in touch," I said.

When he left, I sat down at the S-2's desk and started typing up the notes I had taken. I had barely gotten past the part about the mine disaster when there was a knock on the door, and Warshawsky came back in, all out of breath, as if he had been running. "Sir, I just remembered something," he told me. "My uncle took me to a dance once. It was on a Saturday night. Up at a Ukrainian place near McKeesport."

"Can you describe the place?"

Warshawsky shrugged. "It was maybe a roadhouse. The women were dressed in costumes—embroidered blouses like they sometimes wear over here—and everybody was flying around, doing the polka."

"What year?" I asked.

"It would've been my next to last year in high school—1950 probably."

"Do you know why your uncle took you there?"

"No," Warshawsky said, "but the men were miners so it may have been what you thought—something to do with the union."

When I asked Warshawsky if he remembered the name of the place, he said he didn't, and when I asked him if he'd ever gone back, he said he hadn't. Then I asked him if he could think of any way someone might know he'd gone there, and he thought a moment before telling me that he might have signed his name in a register book at the doorway. "I seem to remember that," he said. "The reason is it was unusual for me to do it."

After Warshawsky left a second time, I picked up the S-2's telephone, called Moran, and told him I'd conducted the interview he'd requested and come up with nothing.

"Not so fast," Moran said. "We just got another FBI twix. This one says they've definitely connected the suspect to one of the organizations on the attorney general's list. In fact, they want us to put him on the lie detector and see how he reacts when he hears the name."

"What name?" I said, looking out the window at the solitary figure of Warshawsky, who was trudging across the compound toward the Motor Pool.

"I think it's called the Ukrainian-American Club," Moran replied.

Suddenly, I had one of those tremendous renewals of faith—like the one Nick Carraway experienced when he learned that Gatsby had told the truth about having gone to Oxford. I wanted to reach all the way across the compound and hug Warshawsky, who was just about to pass from sight behind a barracks building. Instead, I spoke into the telephone. "I bet it was near McKeesport," I told Moran.

"How'd you know?"

"Because Warshawsky told me. For Christ's sake, Moran, he went there only once. To a dance. With his uncle. On a Saturday night. When he was seventeen. Five years ago. *Back in nineteen-fifty!*"

There was a long silence at the other end of the line, and when Moran came on again, his voice was kind of fatherly and sad. "What're you trying to tell me?" he asked.

"I'm telling you that it's probably nothing, and certainly not something that should ruin this kid's whole military career."

"That's not for you or me to decide," Moran replied.

"No, it's for the fucking phoebes to decide," I said.

There was another long pause, during which I could hear Moran draw a deep breath. "You know, I think you've been up in the boondocks too long," he told me.

"You may be right," I said. "What d'you want me to do about this interview?"

"Write it up and send it down with the next dispatch," Moran replied. "The latest FBI twix went to USAREUR, as well as Seventh Army, so we want to stay on top of things."

When I tried to explain the situation to the colonel the next day, he just stared at me and shook his head, and two weeks later, Warshawsky was transferred to a tank outfit in Baumholder to finish out his time. On the day he left, I went over to his barracks to tell him I was sorry and to wish him well, and found him packing the contents of his footlocker into a duffel bag. He shook my hand and tried to smile, but his face was drawn and there was a look of terrible deprivation in it.

It was the middle of October by then, and when I looked out over the barren hills of the Pfalz on my way to supper, the earth seemed to be twinkling and whispering into the night through soft coils of vapor. The rich smells of autumn filled me with an exhilarating melancholy, but what had happened to Warshawsky had left its tarnish, and I no longer relished the heavy, muffling fog that lay upon the land like a wet compress in the mornings, nor looked forward to being snowbound again in the coming winter. The following week, I applied for an advance discharge, under a program that let you out of your enlistment three months early if you enrolled in school. Then I started counting the days until spring.

It was a long wait, because the winter—one of the coldest in recorded history—dragged on. It got so frigid that to get a jeep engine going you had to squeeze half a can of lighter fluid into the carburetor, then jump inside and crank the starter fast before the lighter fluid could evaporate. Trees that had lined the roads for decades froze to the core and died in the first big thaw of spring, while carp locked in the ice of a pool in the garden of the requisitioned house I lived in came flopping back to life. Nothing could revive my spirits, however, not even what happened out at North Point on a bitter cold night at the beginning of February, when I was preparing to brief the duty officer of an infantry company that had just arrived from Worms to conduct the twenty-four-hour patrols beyond the perimeter fence. I looked up from my desk to find "Got Me" Ramsay standing at attention. He didn't remember me, of course, but I could not have mistaken that flushed and beefy face, notwithstanding the name stencilled on the breast of his parka. He was still a second lieutenant, and he still hadn't learned to blouse his pants, and for a second I was tempted to ask him what kind of car he was driving these days. But the Warshawsky business had taken the fun (whatever there had been) out of things, so I just gave Ramsay his instructions and watched him pull on a helmet and ear flaps, go out into the brutal cold, and trudge off with his men over the umbilical ribbon of macadam that, gleaming in the light of a desolate moon, ran through the trees beyond the control gates.

# PART TWO

# 10

## Paris

Three months later, I got an early discharge in Ludwigsburg and went off to Paris to study French, start a novel, and spend my spare time day-dreaming Hemingway pastiche in various sidewalk cafes. The scene in Ludwigsburg was not a happy one, because the army was undertaking one of its periodic purges of the reserve officer ranks, and senior people in the counterintelligence detachment were being demoted. Among them was my former commanding officer—the same captain with whom I had traveled to Hof almost two years earlier to interrogate the unfortunate medical doctor, who had been tricked by the Czechs into believing that he would never see his fiancée again. The captain had recently received word that he was going to be reduced to the rank of sergeant, and had gone to the States on a two-week leave to assess his nonmilitary options. In his absence, the usual procedures that should have accompanied an overseas discharge from one of the intelligence services—a thorough debriefing, an admonition to avoid association with left-wing foreign nationals, and a sworn statement promising not to reveal classified information—were omitted entirely, and I was let go after turning in my credentials and revolver and passing a medical examination whose findings were summed up in a sentence of stunning understatement: "Subject is physically and mentally fit for discharge."

It was the middle of May and I was in a desperate hurry to be gone. That same day, lugging a duffel bag that contained a small Remington portable and all my belongings, I took the train from Stuttgart to Basel, where I converted five hundred dollars in savings and discharge pay into French francs, and the next afternoon I took a train to Paris, arriving at the Gare de l'Est at the hour of dusk. It was the day before my twenty-fifth birthday, and I was elated, to say the least. My military service was behind me, my life and what I would make of it lay ahead like a narrative in progress, and I could now devote myself to the glorious task of becoming a writer.

What better place to start than the Left Bank of Jean Paul Sartre and Simone de Beauvoir—the district that Hemingway, Stein, and other expatriates had made famous for several generations of Americans—where the living was still relatively cheap and the sensitive antennae of an incipient novelist could easily be tuned to the intellectual ferment that emanated nightly from the Flore and the Deux Magots? I was already familiar with the Latin Quarter as a result of having spent several weekends there with an American girl I had met while on leave in Spain, the summer before, who was studying painting at the École des Beaux Arts. She lived on the top floor of the Hotel Lenox, on the rue Jacob, in a tiny garret whose porthole-sized window looked out over the rooftops of the Quartier Saint-Germain-des-Prés, and we had some lovely times together.

On Thanksgiving Day of the previous year, we had spent the better part of a cold, gray afternoon at the Jeu de Paume, looking at the dancers of Degas, the portraits of Renoir, scenes of the Midi by Cezanne, Picasso's little boy with the dove, and the absinthe-loving denizens of Toulouse-Lautrec's dance halls. That's when I bumped into my colleague from the counterintelligence school at Fort Holabird, who was stationed with a CIC detachment at La Rochelle, in the Charente-Maritime. He was accompanied by an attractive young woman who worked at the American Embassy at 2 avenue Gabriel, and the four of us had drinks together at a cafe on the rue de Rivoli, which is where I heard about Robert Kennedy's early involvement with wiretapping. Afterward, my girl friend and I walked across the Pont Neuf to the Left Bank and wandered through some murky side streets that gave off the rue de Seine, until we came upon one of those enchanting markets that spring to life at dusk in Paris—a cluster of lighted stalls manned by men in stained white aprons and patronized by women wearing kerchiefs and carrying *filets*. One of the stalls was hung with fat hares, partridge, pheasant, and quail from the Auvergne; another was stacked high with cylinders of cheese from Normandy; several were filled with crates of cabbages, cauliflowers, and Brussels sprouts from Brittany; others displayed piles of oranges, lemons, and fragrant Algerian melons; and still others held boxes of iced halibut, sardines, tuna, and herring from the

Pays Basque, which infused the night air with a sweet smell like that of freshly cut cucumbers. When darkness fell, we followed several of the aproned vendors into a steaming bistro, where we ordered a botttle of Cote de Rhone and ate piping hot onion soup and *choux fleur aux gratin*. Then, emboldened by the wine, we sneaked past the sharp-eyed concierge of the Lenox, whom we called "Madame de la Vigilance," and climbed soundlessly on carpeted stairs to the garret, where we spent the rest of the night floating on a sea of rooftops in each other's arms.

That was the vision of Paris that had sustained me through the numbing cold and isolation of my final winter in the Pfalz, and carried me from Stuttgart to Basel to the Gare de l'Est from which I now took a taxi to the Lenox—the only hotel I knew in the city. There I submitted myself to an inquisition conducted by Madame, who described the departure of my American friend to New York several months earlier, and inquired sternly whether or not we intended to marry. The next morning, I got up early and began scouring the neighborhood for cheaper and more private digs, until I found a room for two hundred francs a day. It was a room with a large window, running water that was supposed to be (but wasn't) hot on weekends, and a bricked-up fireplace, and it was on the top floor of the Hotel de la Havane on the rue Saint-André-des-Arts—an address that seemed altogether appropriate.

I moved in that afternoon, and on the following day I started classes at the Alliance Française, where I met and had coffee with a tall, willowy Italian girl from Bologna named Natalia Maltoni, who was working as an au pair for a French family in Neuilly, and hoping to enroll at the Sorbonne in the fall. I also started work on a short story that would one day be published in *The New Yorker* and lead to my becoming a staff writer there. Like most stories, this one had some autobiographical underpinnings. It was about a counterintelligence agent in Germany, who, by reporting a possibly rabid fox to the local authorities, triggers a chain reaction of events that brings trouble upon an elderly shepherd, who is falsely suspected of being a subversive. The story, which I called "The Sick Fox," was meant to be a comment on the paranoia that informs intelligence work, as well as on the inclination of Germans to mistrust and harass strangers, and although it was set in the Pfalzer hill country, I was still sufficiently mindful of security considerations to avoid any mention of the underground nuclear storage site at North Point, or the special-weapons ordnance battalion that manned it.

By the end of the week, I had managed to crank out a rough first draft, and when I finished it I decided to reward myself with a lunch of *steak pommes frites* at one of the local student restaurants. The Hotel de la Havane had a winding iron-rung central staircase that descended through five floors and as many half-landings, where the common toilets were located, and as I drew opposite the w.c. between the *premier étage* and the *rez-de-chaussée,* I heard someone ask for me by name. Since the stairwell was deserted, I knew that it was not I who was being addressed, so I paused at the landing and peered down through the iron-grill railing to the ground floor, where two men stood before the desk clerk, who sat perched on a stool behind a counter with a cigarette hanging from a corner of his mouth.

The man who had inquired for me was a thickset, balding man in his middle forties, who spoke fluent French and supported himself on the palms of his hands as he leaned over the counter toward the clerk. His companion, who was slender and blond to the point of being semi-albinic, was at least ten years younger and wore a sport jacket whose cut was American. He took no part in the conversation with the clerk, but leaned his elbows on the counter and faced in the opposite direction, as if he was expecting someone to enter from the street or descend the staircase. At one point, he glanced up with a pair of cold blue eyes whose gaze swept past me like that of a scanning radar.

Meanwhile, the thickset man had asked to see my passport, which I had surrendered to the desk clerk upon my arrival. After thumbing through it, he asked what room I was in.

The clerk's eyes following the smoke of his cigarette toward the ceiling. "*Numero quarante-et-un.* Top floor."

"How often does he go out?"

The clerk shrugged. "He's only been here a few days."

"Tell me something I don't already know," the thickset man growled as he pocketed my passport.

"Yesterday, I saw him in the morning and at noon, and once again in the late afternoon. Today, I haven't seen him at all."

"What about at night?"

"You'll have to ask the night porter."

"Any visitors?"

"None that I've noticed."

"Telephone calls?"

The clerk glanced at the phone on the counter. "Not yet."

"Letters?"

"Nothing so far."

"We'll want to know of any calls or letters."

"*D'accord,*" the clerk replied.

"*N'oubliez pas de demander le clef,*" the blond man said in an accent that was unmistakably American.

The thickset man turned the palm of his hand upward on the counter in a silent request that was immediately rewarded by the clerk, who reached behind him and plucked a key to my room from a large board.

"We'll be back," he said as he and his blond companion left the lobby for the street.

"*Je vous attendrai,*" the clerk called after them, wearily.

I climbed back up the stairs and returned to my room in an agitated state of mind. The thickset man was apparently a French cop, and the albinic blond was clearly an American, but what was I to make of it? I had broken no laws, done nothing wrong, yet I had somehow come under suspicion. For the first time in my life, I realized how unpleasant that could be. It was the American who worried me the most, of course, because it seemed likely that he was connected with the profession I had so recently relinquished. Perhaps someone in Stuttgart had come to the belated realization that I had been discharged without a proper debriefing and was now roaming the streets of Paris with the secrets of one of the nation's most sensitive military installations rattling unfettered in my head and ripe for the picking by the ubiquitous agents of the Kremlin. Yes, that was the most logical explanation—the Cold War giving one last tug at my coattails. No matter, I would act as if nothing had happened. And why not? Nothing *had* happened. In this mood, I descended the staircase again—all the way to the ground floor—and walked past the desk clerk whose head was wreathed in smoke.

"Anybody ask for me?" I inquired in a jaunty voice.

"*Personne,*" he replied without looking up.

Out in the narrow street, I glanced both ways, saw nothing out of the ordinary, and sauntered off toward the student restaurant, which was near the Saint-Germain. But the idea that they had obtained a key to my room weighed on me like a sea anchor, and for some moments I wondered if I should check out of the Havane on the sly and find a room in some obscure *quartier* where they would have trouble locating me. Then I realized that I would still have to surrender my passport no matter where I registered, which is probably how they had found me in the first place. Besides, why should I try to shake them when I had done nothing wrong?

The quandary I found myself in did not help me to enjoy the lunch I had anticipated with such relish only an hour earlier. To make matters more puzzling, when I returned to the hotel, the desk clerk handed me my passport, which, of course, meant that they had come back. As I climbed the stairs to my room, I cursed myself for not having stuck a hair from my shaving brush across the door jam, or a speck of lint on the top page of my story manuscript, but once inside I found everything as I had left it, so I decided to get back to work.

The second draft of the story went well. Except for my morning French class and coffee with Natalia, I kept pretty much to my room and worked steadily for almost a week until I put the finishing touches on it late one night. The next morning, I was in a mood to celebrate, so when I met Natalia at school, I asked her if she would like to go to the Roland Garros Stadium that afternoon and watch the tennis matches at the French Open, which I had read about on the sports page of the Paris *Herald Tribune*. Luckily, it was her day off, and after our class we took a bus out to the Bois de Boulogne, where we ate a picnic of wine, cheese, and bread and talked about ourselves to each other. I told her about some of my military adventures in Germany and how I hoped to become a writer, and she told me about wartime life in Bologna, where her parents had been in the underground, and how she planned to get a degree in education so that she could teach.

The first tennis match we saw was a marathon five-set affair in which a second-seeded Budge Patty lost to a young Belgian named Brichant. Afterward, an Australian named Cooper beat the Czech player Jaraslov Drobny, and after that a tall black woman named Althea Gibson crushed her British opponent with a flat, almost untouchable serve that skimmed the net and skidded low off the red clay surface of the court. Late in the match, the tiring British player lunged for one of Gibson's offerings, barely getting the wood of her racket on the ball, which sent it spinning in a high, lazy arc over the crowd on our side of the stadium. Along with almost everyone else, we looked up to follow its trajectory, and when it came down, half a dozen rows behind us, several spectators ducked as others jumped to their feet in an effort to catch it, and—*voila!*—sitting unmoved in all the commotion was the blond American who had reminded the French cop to ask for the key to my room.

The match was about to end, so I grabbed Natalia by the hand and on the pretext of avoiding the crush bolted for the nearest exit in an effort to get lost in the crowd. I knew I had succeeded, because when we emerged from the stadium I caught sight of the blond American standing by an adjacent exit, his head swivelling slowly from side to side as he scanned the throng of spectators who came pouring out into the Bois. If I had wanted to be clever, I could have waited until he realized that he had lost me and then proceeded to follow *him*, but I had Natalia in tow and, in any case, I found the whole business so disconcerting that turning the tables was the last thing that entered my mind. During the next few days, however, I remembered enough of the countersurveillance techniques they had taught us at Fort Holabird to be able to spot him and at least one of his colleagues accompanying me at a discreet distance along the rue Saint-André-des-Arts whenever I emerged from the hotel to attend my morning class, went for a late afternoon aperitif at one of the local cafes, or met Natalia on the evenings she didn't have to tend the children of her employers.

A week or so after the tennis matches, Natalia's eighty-four-year-old grandmother died, so she went home to Bologna for the funeral. She was crying when she called the hotel to tell me what had happened, and I gathered that she had been extremely close to the old lady, who had taken care of her when her mother and father had been forced to go into hiding during the war. A day or two later, I was standing in line for my mail at the American Express Office near the Opera, when I was hailed by the woman I had met six months earlier with my colleague from intelligence school at the Jeu de Paume. I seem to remember that her name was Miriam. In any case, she had auburn hair and stunning green eyes and a self-assured way about her, and when I told her that I had wangled an army discharge in Europe and had recently arrived in

Paris, she invited me to come by the embassy that evening and join her at a reception for some Indonesian diplomats. I wore a shirt and tie and my best (and only) Harris tweed jacket for the occasion, and Miriam put me at ease by introducing me to a number of her colleagues in the trade mission she worked for, as well as a number of other comrades who worked for the State Department. We then spent a pleasant hour drinking champagne, nibbling the usual canapes, and listening to shop talk that centered on the importance to the Free World of Indonesia—the third largest democracy in the world—and of its dynamic leader, Sukarno, who, following the Afro-Asian conference he had hosted at Bandung a year earlier, had been espousing the cause of nonalignment in the Cold War.

Anyone overhearing the conversation that evening would have concluded, as I did, that the State Department genuinely respected Sukarno's neutralism, and that President Eisenhower's praise of the Indonesian prime minister's pronouncements about the freedom of the individual had been motivated by the highest regard. In fact, however, Eisenhower and John Foster Dulles feared and despised Sukarno and his Third World colleagues—Nasser, Nehru, and Nkrumah—and had already decided to make an example of the Indonesian and Egyptian leaders, in order to demonstrate to the Third World that the American colossus was not to be trifled with. Indeed, even as Miriam and I and her coworkers were sipping champagne with the Indonesian diplomats, the CIA was installing a new station chief in Djakarta with orders to "hold Sukarno's feet to the fire," and Dulles was preparing to cancel an American loan designed to help Egypt build a dam on the Nile River at Aswan.

The latter decision caused Nasser to nationalize the Suez Canal in July and led to the ill-fated attempt by the British, French, and Israelis to take over the waterway by force that fall, while the former decision led the CIA to support a doomed rebellion on Sumatra mounted by army officers opposed to Sukarno. This action resulted in the capture and imprisonment of a CIA pilot named Allen Lawrence Pope, who was shot down in his B-26, in 1958, while carrying out a mission for the rebels in which he mistakenly bombed a church and killed most of its congregation. A similar debacle would take place almost three decades later when a CIA pilot named Eugene Hasenfus was shot down by Sandanista troops in Nicaragua, while ferrying weapons to the contra rebels in a Fairchild C-123K cargo plane in defiance of a congressional ban. But Hasenfus, who was quickly released after being found guilty of conspiracy to commit illicit acts, was luckier than Pope, who spent four years in an Indonesian jail.

At the time Pope was shot down, Dulles lied to the Congress by denying that there had been any intervention whatsoever by the United States in the internal affairs of Indonesia, and Eisenhower lied to the American people by solemnly declaring that the nation was not involved in any way in the revolt against Sukarno. Both men were believed and vigorously defended by the *New York Times,* which denounced the Indonesian government for claiming the contrary, which happened to be the truth. Meanwhile, in order to discredit Sukarno with his Muslim followers, the CIA commissioned Robert Matheu to make a pornographic film showing an actor who resembled the Indonesian leader engaging in a series of explicit sexual acts with a blonde who was supposed to be a Russian woman whom Sukarno had encountered while on a state visit to Moscow and had subsequently invited to Djakarta.

The idea for the X-rated movie had probably not even been thought up at the time I attended the reception for the Indonesians at the American Embassy, but I was about to learn for myself about the CIA's inclination toward sexual intrigue in a series of revelations that began as Miriam and I were saying good-bye to her colleagues before going out to dinner. The first of them occurred when I happened to look across the room and saw the blond American talking with one of Miriam's colleagues in the trade mission.

"That guy over there," I said to her. "The one with the white thatch of hair."

"What about him?"

"D'you know him?"

"Sure."

"What does he do?"

"He works here."

"Well, he's been following me all over Paris."

"Really? I can't imagine why."

"Me either," I said grimly. "Let's go ask him."

Miriam frowned and placed a hand on my arm. "If you promise not to make a scene, I'll see what I can find out."

She was gone at least twenty minutes—long enough for me to have another glass of champagne and listen to more shop talk about the Third World from the State Department types—and when she returned, she was all smiles. "Guess what?" she said. "We've been checking up on you." Then she laughed and took my arm, and promised to explain everything over supper.

# 11

## Cover

What Miriam explained at a swank bistro on the rue des Capucins was a typical Cold War scheme that I'll relate pretty much as she did, except for a couple of interrogatory interpolations of my own. To begin with, I had come under French suspicion because I had been seen meeting with a young Italian woman named Natalia Maltoni, who was under surveillance because she worked for the family of a French Air Force general, who was being investigated by the DST (the French Counterespionage Service) for reasons unknown but of sufficient importance for the boys in the DST to ask their counterparts at the American Embassy for assistance in finding out who I was and how I might fit into the picture. Second, I had come under American suspicion, because when my military records showed that I had been a counterintelligence agent at a top secret nuclear weapons storage depot in the French Zone of Germany, it was decided that my relationship with Signorina Maltoni should be scrutinized to make certain that our encounter had occurred by happenstance (like, for example, my encounter with Miriam at American Express?) and was not in any way connected with why a French Air Force general and his Italian au pair were under surveillance. And, finally, since the suspicions about me had in the meantime been checked out to everyone's general satisfaction, those in charge of running the case had decided that I would be the ideal person to gain Natalia Maltoni's trust and confidence and thus learn about the true nature of her association with the French general and his family, which, as Miriam concluded by raising her glass of St. Emilion to mine, "is why this dinner's on Uncle Sam."

"Hold on a minute," I said. "Are you telling me that Natalia Maltoni's being investigated because she's taking care of some French general's kids?"

"It's more complicated than that," Miriam replied. "She comes from a notoriously left-wing city and has a family background that raises eyebrows."

"She comes from Bologna and her mother and father were in the underground during the war."

"The Communist underground."

"Was there any other kind in Bologna?"

"The French are our allies. When they ask us for help, we try to oblige."

"Is that official trade commission policy?" I inquired.

"Don't be a smart aleck," Miriam replied. "You know we have to work undercover."

"My cover these days is that I'm a civilian."

Miriam appraised me coolly as the waiter poured the last of our wine. Then she ordered another bottle. "Think about duty, honor, country."

"Natalia Maltoni's a friend of mine. Someone I'm fond of."

"We want you to keep on being fond of her. And she of you. In fact, if it'll help things along, we'll lend you an apartment."

By this time, Miriam and I had drunk a fair amount, but there was no mistaking the suggestion she was making. No mission of that kind had ever been assigned to me in the Counterintelligence Corps, and for a moment I found myself tongue-tied by the very idea. Then I saw that Miriam's green eyes were gleaming with mischief, and realized that she was getting a kick out of my discomfiture.

"You don't have to decide now," she said, and with that she dropped the subject and began to talk about Albert Camus' adaptation of William Faulkner's *Requiem for a Nun*, which would be coming to the Paris theater at the end of summer.

We finished the second bottle of wine with some roquefort, and ordered fresh pears for dessert. Then we went to a nearby cafe for espresso, and some time later we wound up at Miriam's apartment on the rue de Varenne, where we sat side by side on a sofa as she showed me a scrapbook filled with elegantly mounted photographs of black-gartered women initiating and submitting to flagrant acts of sex. By now, of course, I realized that I had encountered an adventuress.

As I might have anticipated, the steamy affair I embarked upon with Miriam that night turned out to have a decided downside. For one thing, it complicated the decision I made as soon as Natalia returned from Italy not to betray my friendship with her by becoming an informant for the people Miriam worked for—I assumed, of course, that she was an employee of the CIA—and for another it placed a considerable strain upon my relationship with Natalia, whom one half of me felt I should warn that she was under surveillance, even as the other half realized that to do so might compromise an investigation into matters of serious consequence. For a couple of weeks, the ambiguity of the situation provoked an indecision that left me in suspense, which is to say that I found myself swinging back and forth between opposite poles like a man trapped on a trapeze with no way to get off and no safety net below. On the one hand, when I was having coffee or lunch with Natalia, whom I had no reason to suspect of being a spy any more than I had Warshawsky, I experienced an overwhelming desire to let her know what was going on; while on the other hand, I wondered how I could possibly tell her about the secret activity that was swirling about her without revealing the essentials of what Miriam had told me, which would surely constitute a breach of faith if not of national security. Further complicating matters, of course, were the evenings I was spending with Miriam.

In the end, I could see no way out of the predicament I had gotten myself into with these two women other than to withdraw from both, which I did to the distress of one and the fury of the other. In some ways, it could have been taken as a good lesson in how not to conduct one's personal life, but how was I to know that by inviting a tall, willowy Italian girl to have coffee, I would be engaging the gears of suspicion that had driven the Cold War for a decade and would keep on driving it for at least three more?

During the last week of June, I told Natalia that I had decided to leave school and spend the rest of the summer traveling in the south of France. As things turned out, this was reasonably close to the truth, because I had already planned to take a ten-day trip through Normandy and Brittany with an old army friend, and soon thereafter I would be invited to spend the month of August in the Pays Basque and the Pyrenees with a French acquaintance named Pierre Girrou, who I had met at a dinner party given by one of Miriam's embassy colleagues. In any event, Natalia accepted my decision with a touching and wistful resignation and insisted upon taking me out to a farewell dinner that must have cost her a week's wages.

As for Miriam, she greeted my announcement in considerably less accommodating fashion. In fact, when I told her that I was withdrawing from school and would no longer be seeing Natalia, she accused me of leaving her in the lurch. (Perhaps she had assured her superiors that I was a sure thing for the mission they had in mind for me, and felt that my defection from the project might embarrass her standing with them.) Once she calmed down, she tried to get me to change my mind by insisting that my participation in the case could be an important factor in strengthening a fragile relationship that existed between her people and their French counterparts, and when that failed to move me she threatened to expose my impending truancy at the Alliance Française to the military authorities who had discharged me early on condition that I attend classes there. It was a hollow threat and we both knew it, and when we stopped laughing we went out to dinner, but things were never quite the same between us, which is to say that I was never again invited to spend the night at her apartment on the rue de Varenne.

The rest of my stay in France was relatively uneventful. During the swing through Normandy, I visited the vast American cemetery at Saint-Laurent-sur-Mer, near Omaha Beach—it was the day the *Andrea Doria* sank—and early the following month Pierre Girrou and I drove his aging Panhard to the Pays Basque and spent two weeks at a pension in Ascain, a tiny village in the foothills of the Pyrenees behind Saint-Jean-de-Luz, where we were awakened each morning at daybreak by the sound of booted and bereted paratroopers from a nearby military post, who were training for the coming bloodshed in Algeria by running in full field pack down the mountain to the sea and back. Like many French children, Pierre had been sent to unoccupied France during the early part of the war, and when we left Ascain we drove east through the Hautes-Pyrenees and the Haute-Garonne, stopping at Tarbes and Toulouse, where he had been taken in by Catholic priests, who, I was surprised to learn, often voted as Communists out of solidarity with their parishioners. Then we visited the brick cathedral at Albi, where there was a small museum housing some of the early work of Toulouse-Lautrec, and returned to Paris through the central part of France by way of the caves of Figeac and the Dordogne.

In September, my sister came to town en route to the University at Aix-en-Provence, where she had arranged to spend her junior year at college, and while she was there I borrowed Pierre's car and we drove out to the Cathedral of Chartres one evening to hear the Boston Symphony under the direction of Charles Munch. On the way, we chatted about the family and what everyone was doing—in particular our brother David, who had gone to Denver to seek relief from his asthma—and, caught up in the intimacy of catching up, I decided on the spur of the moment to tell her what I knew of our father's secret. "You know, there's something I've been meaning to share with you," I said. "Something Dad should probably have told us years ago."

"You mean that he was married before and has another son?"

"Then he did tell you!" I exclaimed.

"No, but I've known about it a long time," my sister said. "Ever since I was a little girl. I woke up one summer night during the war and heard him and Mother talking. He was terribly upset, which is why I remembered even though I didn't really comprehend all of what they were saying until much later, when I'd spoken to Aunt Bella. Evidently Daddy had heard from his other son for the first time in many years. His son was at Fort Devens and was about to go overseas. He called Daddy up and they made a dinner date for that night, but the boy never came."

"Maybe he couldn't get a pass," I said. "Maybe he got shipped out."

"I don't know," my sister replied. "Aunt Bella didn't either. She was guarded, of course, because she knew I'd found out accidentally, but she told me that Daddy hadn't seen his other son for nearly ten years. She said he'd seen him fairly regularly up until the time he was eight years old or so, but that just after you were born, his first wife remarried and went to live out West."

"Did Aunt Bella tell you they'd given me his name?"

My sister looked at me, uncomprehendingly.

"His name is Adrian Paul."

My sister shook her head. "Aunt Bella said the divorce had been bitter—not an amicable settlement as the saying goes—so there hadn't been much correspondence. Also, it was the middle of the Depression. The bank had foreclosed on our house in Wellesley, and when Dad couldn't keep up payments on the car, we lost that, too. Meanwhile, David and I had been born and—well, according to Aunt Bella . . ."

For some moments, I found myself trying to assess what my sister was telling me in the context of how the secret had unfolded for each of us, but the incongruity between the various places of disclosure—a rented summer cottage in Duxbury, a junior college on the North Shore, a restaurant in Chinatown, and this borrowed car in which we were speeding toward Chartres—blurred my ability to take it in. "Did it bother you very much?" I asked finally. "Knowing?"

"No, I don't think so. I just accepted it."

"Perhaps we ought to tell David."

"David!" my sister exclaimed. "Why, he's known about it almost as long as I have. One of our cousins told him."

"But that's impossible," I protested. "David would have told me."

"Would he?"

I glanced across the seat at my sister's face and saw laughter lurking in her eyes. "That's right," I said. "You didn't."

"Why bring up something that might have disturbed us? Father and Mother must have decided there was no point in telling us when we were young. Then, with one thing and another, but mostly time, it no longer became a question of not telling us but rather of simply going on the way we always had. Do you know what I mean?"

"Maybe Dad finds it too painful to talk about."

"That's something we may never know," my sister said. "That's a subsidiary secret. One begets another."

The exterior of the cathedral had been illuminated with searchlights so that it could be seen for miles around, but its vast interior was only dimly lit, thus diminishing the presence of thousands of people sitting in shadows cast by the enormous columns that supported its vaulted ceiling. Then the orchestra opened with the crash of Beethoven's Ninth, and scores of startled bats came swooping out of dark recesses to the sudden fluster of the crowd. They disappeared an instant later, and I remember sitting as if alone in all that gloom and grandeur, thinking of the secret I was afraid to discuss with my father.

When we returned to Paris, we went to a late-night party that was being given by Miriam and some of her embassy friends for the members of the orchestra, who had recently returned from a concert tour in

Russia. I had not seen Miriam since July, and when I inquired what had happened with the investigation involving Natalia, she took me aside and said she'd heard that the whole affair had turned out to be much ado about nothing, but would have to make further inquiries because she'd spent most of August and the first part of September with the symphony.

When I reacted to that disclosure with a look of surprise, she laughed, placed a forefinger to her lips, and said, "Great cover."

# 12

## Home Again

My money had all but run out when I boarded the French liner *Flandre* at Le Havre in early October and sailed back to the United States. I arrived in New York shortly before the temperature of the Cold War took a precipitous drop with the Suez invasion, the bloody suppression of the Poznan strikers by the Polish Army, and the even bloodier suppression of the Hungarian Revolt by two hundred thousand Soviet troops supported by more than two thousand tanks. My father came down from Boston to meet the ship, and as it docked I caught sight of him in a crowd of people standing on the pier. At first, he seemed to be wearing an overcoat that was far too large for him, but as the tugboats warped us closer to our berth I saw that it was a coat he'd had for years, and that he'd aged and shrunk. I found it hard to believe that the frail-looking, gray-faced man I gazed down upon was the same man who, only four years earlier, pipe dangling from a corner of his mouth, beret pulled rakishly down over one ear, had smiled jauntily at the camera as he accepted the trophy for winning the Massachusetts field archery championship. But when he saw me, he waved wildly and smiled a broad smile, and by the time we embraced on the pier, he was flushed and happy and looking better.

On the drive home, he confided that things hadn't been going all that well with his orthodontia practice, and that he was thinking of closing up the office he'd maintained in Fitchburg for more than twenty years. When I asked how mother was, he said that she was fine, and told me how he had tried to overcome her disapproval of his going to the racetrack by getting up early one morning and papering the stairs in the house with ten one-hundred-dollar bills—part of the proceeds of a winning *quinella* ticket—before calling her down to breakfast.

That night, after dinner at our home in Arlington, I heard the rest of the story from my mother, who seemed tired and anxious. "Your father's practice has dropped off badly, and the bills have been piling up for more than a year," she told me. "The money he won at the racetrack went to catch-up payments on the house mortgage, which the bank was threatening to declare in default, and on the loan for the car, which they've been threatening to repossess. There are still outstanding bills for water, gas, telephone, electricity, real estate taxes, and Lord knows what else. Your father stuffs them into his pockets and tries to pretend they don't exist, but the truth is he's worrying himself sick and I'm worried about him."

My mother was right to worry. Four months later, my father suffered a coronary heart attack one morning after breakfast and was rushed by ambulance to the Peter Bent Brigham Hospital, in Boston. Fortunately for him, he was cared for there by an old friend, Samuel Levine, who, along with Paul Dudley White, Eisenhower's physician, was considered to be one of the foremost heart specialists in the world. While he was in the hospital, the fiction editors at *The New Yorker* accepted "The Sick Fox" for publication, and the magazine sent me a check for thirteen hundred and something dollars plus some change. It was a gift from heaven because it paid off all the outstanding bills, which meant that my father wouldn't have to worry about them during the several months he would have to recuperate.

That summer, my mother took a badly needed vacation and went to Europe to visit my sister, while I stayed home with my father and set out to recoup my fortunes by writing another story for *The New Yorker*. This one was titled "The Only Casualty," and like "The Sick Fox" it was based on an experience I'd had in Germany. It was about the adventures of a young second lieutenant with a penchant for abstract thought who, while assigned as an artillery umpire to a NATO maneuver designed to simulate nuclear war in a Hessen valley close to the Iron Curtain, realizes that he is involved in a dress rehearsal for mass suicide, and, in impulsive defiance to the maneuver scenario he is supposed to follow, declares everything around him to have been destroyed. That night, as he is driving through the valley in dense fog, he comes across a gruesome accident in which a woman lies dead in the wreckage of a small car that she has driven headlong into a parked and disabled tank. A Kafkaesque investigation and jurisdictional nightmare ensue, during which the German police discover that the woman is traveling without identification papers in a stolen vehicle, and they assume that she must have been fleeing toward the border. The contrast between the abstract and the real—the idea that the valley has merely been destroyed in theory, while the woman lies dead for real—unnerves the second lieutenant, who, after being chastized by his superiors for not following the maneuver scenario, leaves the valley a greatly disturbed young man.

It seemed like a good enough story at the time—indeed, an allegory for the Cold War. But that was the trouble with it. I was thinking in abstract literary terms—the valley of death, an unknown victim, an Everyman second lieutenant, that sort of thing—and simply couldn't bring my characters to life. The editors at the magazine did everything they could to help by offering suggestions for revision and by patiently reading at least a half dozen different versions I mailed down to them, but try as I might I couldn't pull it off. In retrospect, I realized that I'd made two mistakes. One, of course, was to set out on the murky sea of literary import; the other was to try to write fiction with the idea of making money right up front.

While my mother was in Europe, my father and I got along pretty well, except when I nagged him about sticking to his fat-free diet, or tried to become too much of a nursemaid. In any event, he recuperated strongly and by the middle of the summer he was back at work and acting like his old self. I realized that for sure, one incredibly hot July afternoon, when I returned home from a trip into Boston to find the garage empty and his car gone. I knew exactly where he'd gone, because his favorite hunting bow and arrow were missing from their rack in the cellar, but I hated to think of him out in the woods alone in such appalling heat—the temperature had soared into the nineties—so I took off after him in my mother's car. By the time I arrived at the field archery range—it was in a forest out in Weston, about fifteen miles away—I was beginning to worry, and when I saw his car sitting in an otherwise empty field beneath the broiling sun, I found myself imagining the worst. For the next ten minutes, I ran through the woods from one target to another in a twenty-four-target course, shouting my father's name in the stifling heat and wiping the sweat from my eyes, until, all of a sudden, I came into a sun-drenched clearing and saw him sitting in the shade of a tree on the other side. At that point, I stopped running and began walking very slowly toward my father, who was sitting with his shoulders resting against the trunk of the tree, with his head slumped to one side. I couldn't tell if he was breathing, and he looked awfully pale.

"Dad?" I asked, fearfully. "Are you okay, Dad?"

My father opened one eye and then the other, and looked up at me askance. For some time, he looked at me without saying anything. Then he gave a sigh and told me that he was feeling fine, that I had been fussing over him too much and getting to be a royal pain in the ass, that he loved being in the woods alone, and that if anything were going to happen to him he would just as soon it happened in a peaceful place like this. He said all this without rancor, and then he held up his hand so that I could pull him to his feet, and when I had done that we walked slowly and in silence back to the cars.

In October, the Soviets launched Sputnik—the first man-made space satellite—which unravelled the nation's psyche and shook its confidence by lending credence to reports that the USSR had surpassed the United States in missile technology. The top-secret Gaither Report warned that America was entering a period of extraordinary peril, and Edward Teller, father of the hydrogen bomb—"It's a boy!" he had telegraphed triumphantly when the first one had been detonated at Eniwetok—contributed to the national disquiet by describing the Soviet achievement as a defeat far worse than that inflicted by the Japanese at Pearl Harbor. Teller, who founded the Lawrence Livermore nuclear weapons laboratory, proved to be a pitchman of grandiose schemes. The following summer, he and some fellow physicists from Livermore went to Alaska, where they proposed to excavate an instant harbor near Point Hope, on the Chukchi Sea, by burying and detonating four thermonuclear bombs in the shallow earth. In order to sell Alaskans on the idea, Teller boasted that he could dig them a harbor in the shape of a polar bear, and told them that "if your mountain is not in the right place, just drop us a postcard." As things turned out, his nuclear public works project, which would have contaminated the Arctic tundra for generations, was vetoed by the Eskimos of Point Hope, at which point, deflected but undaunted, he directed his energies and much of the nation's treasure into a scheme called Star Wars, in which the firing of X-ray lasers triggered by exploding nuclear bombs would set the heavens alight and save Western civilization.

For his part, my father looked upon Sputnik as a grand accomplishment and the harbinger of great adventure. A day or two after it had been sent aloft, he awakened me at 4 A.M., handed me a cup of coffee, and insisted that I accompany him out to a schoolyard at the end of the street, where we watched an orgiastic green light, bright as any star, trace a slow path through the night sky as Sputnik traversed the heavens. My father put his hand on my shoulder as we stood there and marveled at what we were seeing. "It reminds me of Lindbergh," he said. Then he thanked me for staying home with him while he'd gotten back on his feet, and told me that I should now feel free to leave and resume my life.

I came close to telling him then and there that I knew about his other son. "Dad, I know about my older brother," I could hear myself saying. Once again, I was sure that if I said this there would be a look of surprise and relief upon my father's face. I imagined him smiling as he told me the whole story, which he would conclude by saying, "This doesn't make any difference between us, you know," and with me replying, "I know it doesn't, Dad, but I'm glad you told me."

But Sputnik and the moment passed, and there was nothing above us except a sky of fading stars that would soon seep into daybreak—a disappearing void from which as both child and man I had invariably flinched, yet found mysterious, inscrutable, profoundly calm.

A few months later, I went to New York and, on the strength of the story I'd published, got myself hired by *The New Yorker* to be its newsbreak editor. This was an entry-level job that entailed the culling of hundreds of newspaper gaffes and non sequiturs sent in by readers each week, and selecting the best and funniest for E. B. White to append his inimitably deadpan taglines. I had very little money with me, and during the month I spent looking for work and trying out for the newsbreak job I slept on an equally impoverished friend's floor. He was renting a room in a transient hotel on the Upper West Side while attending the Columbia Graduate School of Education. One evening, after a particularly discouraging day, I walked up Fifth Avenue in the enchanted metropolitan twilight Fitzgerald talks about in *Gatsby,* feeling the loneliness of one of those young clerks of his who loiter in front of windows at the hour of dusk, "wasting the most poignant moments of night and life." When I got to the corner of Fifth and Fifty-ninth, I sat down for a few moments on a bench just inside the park, looked up at the windows of the Plaza, which were coming alive as golden lights winked on, and wondered whether or not I had a future in the city.

It was a chilly evening in early April, and an elderly couple wearing threadbare overcoats were sitting on the next bench, feeding the pigeons. The old lady was holding a burlap sack on her lap, and the old man was holding a bag of grain from which he was broadcasting whole handfuls far and wide to an ever-increasing flock of birds. As I watched, his grand sweeping gestures became more and more constricted, until he was casting just a few pieces of grain at a time to fewer and fewer pigeons, and then perhaps only one or two kernels to a solitary bird that, as if sleepwalking, came peck, peck, pecking its way closer and closer until, with a quick movement, the hand that had been feeding the pigeon snatched it and wrung its neck and plopped it into the gunnysack that the old lady opened and closed in the blink of an eye. It all happened so fast I could scarcely believe what I was seeing, until I saw him do it several times again, without ever once missing, and realized that he and she were harvesting a supper of street squab.

I came close to packing it in right then and there and going back to Boston, but *The New Yorker* came through the following week and I started work instead. It was a dreary business selecting the newsbreaks, but I soon found myself able to winnow the stack of mail that arrived each morning in an hour or two, which left me time for my own writing. Needless to say, the thousands upon thousands of gaffes that crossed my desk each week have long since merged into a forgettable blur. In fact, the only one I can remember wasn't fit for use in the magazine—at least not in those days. Someone sent in a brochure put out by a company in Queens that pronounced itself capable of storing wedding dresses for future generations. A photograph of a lovely young bride wearing an elegant gown was accompanied by a flowery text that urged its readers, "let us take your wedding dress and preserve it for perpetuity in one of our special temperature-controlled facilities, where it will retain all of its pristine glory for some future occasion. Who knows but that one day your own daughter, or even your granddaughter, may wish to consummate her marriage in it."

Scrawled beneath this exhortation was the query, "Can she take her shoes off?"

# 13

## Talk of the Town

During the next few years, I worked hard to expand "The Sick Fox" into a novel about Cold War Germany, married a girl named Malabar whom I had met at Radcliffe during my college days, fathered a son, and became a Talk of the Town reporter. My first major assignment was to interview Werner Heisenberg, the German physicist and Nobel Prize winner, who was in this country to discuss a theory he had devised to explain and predict the characteristics of the elementary particles that are believed to hold the solution to the matrix riddle of the universe. He was a stocky man in his late fifties with a pink, cherubic face, a mischievous smile, and a halo of gray hair splaying out from the sides of his head and giving him the look of a kindly impresario. Only years later would it come to light that during the war he had been suspected—wrongly it turned out—of leading a German effort to build an atomic bomb, and that in 1943 a former major league baseball catcher named Moe Greenberg, who was then serving with the Office of Strategic Services, had been sent to Switzerland to assassinate him while he was delivering a lecture at the Federal Technical University in Zurich. Greenberg had aborted the assignment at the last moment, when Allen Dulles decided that the Germans weren't building a bomb after all and that killing Heisenberg might result in blowing the cover of other American agents who were operating in Switzerland under his direction. When I asked Heisenberg about his new theory, he started out by telling me that he had become convinced that the symmetry principles that must govern particle interactions hold the secret of the nucleus. He went on in that vein for a while; then, no doubt realizing from the expression on my face that I had little ability to understand his abstruse world, he undertook to talk about it in ways I might comprehend, telling me that music and physics had properties and characteristics in common, that his chief interest outside of physics was music, and that he and his wife and their seven children played chamber music together. "You see, it is really a harmonic world," he said. "The trouble is that we have split it into too many complex details. People are confused today. They have lost the sense of harmony that underlies everything. They do not see the big connections."

As a result of the piece about Heisenberg, William Shawn, the editor of *The New Yorker*, decided that I should report on scientific matters, and he proceeded to assign me a series of articles about the latest developments in cybernetics, which meant that I soon found myself writing about prodigy machines that could play chess, teach humans to solve technical problems, and put through hundreds of telephone calls in a matter of milliseconds. It would never do, of course, for the sovereign-voiced narrator of the Talk of the Town of that era to act nonplussed about any mere technological innovation, so it was necessary to introduce each of these devices in a manner that was appropriately tongue in cheek. "We intend to keep on informing our readers of all the latest developments in the field of automation until the creepy technological point is reached at which a machine is devised to inform our readers of all the latest developments in the field of automation and our poor old brains and beat-up Remington are put on the shelf," one of my stories began.

Not surprisingly, the Cold War was rarely out of sight or mind in those early days of mutually assured destruction. When the Soviet cosmonaut Gherman Titov spent twenty-five hours in orbit, I was sent to the New York Public Library to research a fact piece on weightlessness— a condition that man was experiencing for the first time in his history. Among other things, I learned that a satellite and the man inside it are weightless, because a perfect equilibrium has been achieved between the earth's gravitational pull and the satellite's orbital velocity of nearly eighteen thousand miles an hour, and that it is this same nice sort of balance that keeps the earth and its fellow planets circling the sun, and the moon circling the earth, and the whole universe spinning splendidly along. I also learned that in addition to the sense of touch the human body obtains information about its external support from the pressure sense of the skin, which records changes in acceleration, thus accounting for the expression "flying by the seat of the pants." Best of all, I found out that the sensation of weightlessness had been simulated as early as

1928 by a German scientist-aviator named Hubertus Strughold, who took a biplane up from an airport near Cologne after anesthetizing his buttocks with Novocain. It was the first time that the word *buttocks* found its way into the pages of the magazine, and Shawn—an intensely modest man—deliberated for some time before deciding that the anecdote would be lost without it. What didn't find its way into the magazine for reasons of extraneousness was that Strughold, like Wernher Von Braun and other German scientists, had been brought to the United States after the war to work on the development of missile weapons.

Another thing that didn't find its way into the magazine was a story I wrote around the same time about a demonstration that I and several other journalists had been invited to witness at the Bell Telephone Laboratories, in New Jersey. The security at that place made North Point look like an open house. After being led by a company official through a series of chain-link fences, guarded gates, and laby-rinthine corridors connected by electrically controlled doors that were opened and closed by operators who observed us through closed-circuit television, we found ourselves in a room divided by a thick glass shield. There, we watched an invisible beam projected by a tubelike contraption called a "maser"— an acronym standing for "microwave amplification by stimulated emission of radiation"—burn a hole through a stack of several hundred stainless steel Gillette razor blades in the blink of a microsecond. As the puff of blue smoke that accompanied this phenomenon evaporated into thin air, our host informed us that we had seen the progenitor of wondrous devices (lasers, of course) that would one day be used to benefit humankind. When I got back to the magazine, I wrote a piece that described what I had seen as the progenitor of the next generation of modern weaponry, which Shawn found too troubling (or, perhaps, too extraneous) for publication at a time when the nation seemed to be heading into a period of terrible peril.

The previous three years had seen a steady escalation of the Cold War. Eisenhower had dispatched the marines to Lebanon as a reminder to the Arab world that Middle Eastern oil should stay in Western hands; Gary Powers' U-2 had been downed over Russia; Khrushchev had cancelled

the Geneva summit; Fidel Castro's introduction of Socialism into Cuba
had gone undeterred by the Bay of Pigs adventure; and the Berlin Wall
was about to go up amid threats of thermonuclear retaliation. The Vienna conference with Khrushchev had gone badly for Kennedy, who
saw no other way to reassert himself and the nation he led except to increase the defense budget, call up the reserves, and threaten to go to war
if the Soviet leader carried out his threat to cut off western access to
Berlin. Everyone was anxious and afraid during that summer of 1961—
scared witless, in fact—including me and the slightly supercilious first-
person plural narrator of the Notes and Comment piece I wrote for the
issue that came out in the first week of September, just after the Soviets
broke a three-year moratorium on nuclear tests by detonating some hydrogen bombs that were hundreds of times more powerful than the
weapons that had devastated Hiroshima and Nagasaki. After deploring
the age of surveillance, with its secret satellites, metal detectors, radiation badges, and whatnot, the "we" of the piece turned our attention in
the customarily oblique fashion of Talk of the Town to a proposal made
by the National Geographic Society and the National Science Foundation that the grizzly bears of Yellowstone National Park, which were
feared to be heading for extinction, be fitted with plastic collars carrying
miniature radio transmitters that would enable conservationists to keep
track of them during warm-weather wandering and in hibernation. "We
are a conservationist ourself, but we were disheartened to read of the
poor grizzly's new bondage, because it suddenly brought to our mind a
vision of all that is absurd, futile, and grotesque in our time," the article
concluded. "For one brief moment, we saw the earth in ash and ruin,
and the last grizzly blissfully asleep in his cave, signalling his position to
a world of men who could no longer scrutinize the puny devices with
which they had managed merely to preside over their own extinction."

From the beginning, Shawn had not only been profoundly troubled
by the threat posed to the existence of humankind by the weaponry of
the nuclear age, but also had been determined to do something about
it. As the managing editor of *The New Yorker*, he had been instrumen-
tal in persuading its editor, Harold Ross, to send John Hersey to Hiroshima to write about what had happened there on August 6, 1945,
and about the consequences of that event for humanity. Hersey wrote

his piece in a white heat—taking only a few weeks to do so—and it ran in *The New Yorker* on August 6, 1946. It was titled "Hiroshima" and it was accompanied by an unprecedented announcement that marked a turning point in the history of the magazine and that read as follows:

> The New Yorker this week devotes its entire editorial space to an article on the almost complete obliteration of a city by one atomic bomb, and what happened to the people in that city. It does so in the conviction that few of us have yet comprehended the all but incredible power of this weapon, and that everyone might well take time to consider the terrible implications of its use.

Following Ross' death in 1951, Shawn became the editor of *The New Yorker*, and in the years that followed he saw to it that the insidious drift toward nuclear proliferation and its potential consequences remained before the eyes of the magazine's readers—a not altogether popular undertaking as the climate of the Cold War grew even chillier and it became a tenet of national faith that the doctrine of massive retaliation provided the only possible deterrent to disaster. Not surprisingly, Shawn also seized every opportunity to explore various ways in which a nuclear catastrophe might be avoided, and it was for this reason that I found myself assigned to write about a compelling (if somewhat unorthodox) scheme for preventing war and preserving the peace that had been dreamed up in late 1961 by a brash and indefatigable advertising copywriter named Stephen D. James. Under James' plan, the threat of war could be dramatically reduced if the United States and the Soviet Union would agree to exchange peace hostages on a massive scale. James proposed to start things off at the top. "Let one of President Kennedy's brothers or sisters go with his or her family to Russia in exchange for the family of one of Khrushchev's children," he told me. "Let other high-ranking officials follow this example. Then broaden the base until it includes exchanges at all levels of society for periods ranging from six months to two years. Eventually, the peace-hostage program will develop into population rotation—millions of Americans, Englishmen, and Frenchmen living and working in the Soviet Union, and millions of Russians living and working here, in England, and in France. Talk about cultural exchange! Talk about peaceful coexistence!"

During the next two years, James traveled to Russia and Africa to pitch his peace plan and in the process got the signatures of nearly a thousand volunteers on a peace-hostage pledge, including those of the Reverend and Mrs. Robert L. Pierson, the son-in-law and daughter of Governor Nelson Rockefeller, who was then pushing for the construction of bomb shelters. Meanwhile, in early October of 1962, the peace-hostage exchange program was extolled before the Senate by Republican Senator Jacob K. Javits of New York and by Democratic Senator Hubert H. Humphrey of Minnesota. In fact, Humphrey read the Talk of the Town story I had written about it into the *Congressional Record*, after declaring that, like the narrator of the piece, "I, too, have a 'perennial admiration for people who think up fresh approaches to knotty problems.' "

What neither of the senators nor any of the rest of us could possibly have known was that the boys at Langley, who kept busy by thinking up their own fresh approaches to the knotty problem of how to survive the Cold War, had apparently devised a plan under which every living soul in Moscow (including the Americans living and working in the Embassy there) would become an unsuspecting hostage to the very technological terror that the peace-hostage plan proposed to avoid. I say "apparently," because, like many other supersecret operations concocted by the Agency in that era, it was and is still carefully concealed under the rubric of national security, and will no doubt remain there for many years to come. Under this plan, the components of a nuclear weapon were to be brought into Moscow in State Department shipments and assembled within the walls of the Embassy in order to override the possibility that an anti-ballistic-missile system the Soviets were then installing around Moscow might be able to counter the American deterrent by destroying our incoming missiles in the event of nuclear war. One of the ways I came to suspect its possible existence was because of something my sister told me almost fifteen years later. Back then—October of 1962—she was more than halfway through a three-year hitch she had signed on for with the State Department, and was working as a researcher for the department's political section at the American Embassy in Paris. Only she wasn't, as I would one day find out, working for the State Department; she was working for the assistant chief of the CIA station.

My little sister.

But as Miriam would have said, "Great cover."

Crises could arise with bewildering speed during the Cold War. In the middle of that October, U-2 flights over western Cuba produced photographs showing that launch sites for medium-range ballistic missiles were being constructed near San Cristobel, and during the following fateful week the world came uncomfortably close to Armageddon. The sense of anxiety with which we live through momentous events fades with time, but I can still remember the fear I felt in the pit of my stomach as I got into my car after President Kennedy spoke to the nation on Monday night, October 22—it was the speech in which he threatened thermonuclear war if the Soviets did not remove their missiles from Cuba—and drove to Manhattan from a small weekend cottage my wife and I had rented in the woods of Connecticut, in order to be with her and our infant son if the worst came to the worst.

No doubt Kennedy was frightened, too—in fact, his biographers say as much—just as Eisenhower had been made nervous six years earlier by the prospect of Soviet miscalculation at the time of the Hungarian uprising and the Suez invasion. Once undertaken, however, the use of nuclear brinkmanship in times of crisis could not easily be abandoned, and for this reason the two presidents (together with their bellicose adversary Khrushchev) had little choice but to keep venturing out along the tightrope of international tension. Fear breeds anger, of course, and the anxiety accompanying the knowledge that any false step might result in catastrophe for humanity may account in part for the fact that during the late 1950s and early 1960s both Eisenhower and Kennedy took to using the Central Intelligence Agency as an instrument for dealing with troublesome foreign leaders on the more individual basis known as "executive action."

Late in Eisenhower's first term, the CIA was not only encouraged to hold Sukarno's feet to the fire by supporting his foes on Sumatra but also encouraged to formulate preliminary plans for assassinating him. In addition, the Agency was involved in several unsuccessful plots to kill Colonel Gamal Abdel Nasser, the leader of Egypt, including one dreamed up by the British Secret Intelligence Service (MI6) at the behest of Prime Minister Anthony Eden, in which Nasser was to have been done in by a Remington Rand electric shaver that had been stuffed with plastique and rigged to explode when turned on.

Thanks to the concept of "plausible denial"—a process by which covert actions were proposed and approved with language so circumlocutory and euphemistic that a president and his most senior officials could deny knowledge of an operation should it be disclosed—these early flirtations with the use of murder as national policy have remained in the murky realm of allegation. Not so, however, in the case of Patrice Lumumba, who had become premier of the newly independent Congo in the summer of 1960 and had threatened to invite Soviet troops to hasten the withdrawal of Belgian armed forces that still occupied large areas of the country. That August, Eisenhower expressed strong feelings to the members of his National Security Council "on the necessity for very straightforward action" regarding Lumumba. A week later, the president's feelings were translated by members of the Special Group—a subcommittee of the NSC made up of his assistant for National Security Affairs, the director of the Central Intelligence Agency, the deputy director of defense, and the undersecretary of state for political affairs—into a decision not to rule out consideration of "any particular kind of activity which might contribute to getting rid of Lumumba." The language became more precise with distance from the White House. On the next day, Allen Dulles sent a cable from CIA headquarters at Langley to the station chief in Leopoldville, telling him that Lumumba's "removal" was a "high priority of our covert action."

A few weeks after that, Richard Bissell sent Dr. Sidney Gottlieb, his special assistant for scientific matters, to Leopoldville with syringes containing a deadly virus (possibly anthrax) provided by the Army Chemical Corps at Fort Dietrich, Maryland. (Gottlieb had been in charge of the CIA's experiments with the hallucinogen lysergic acid diethylamide [LSD] at the time of the suicide or defenestration of Frank R. Olson, a scientist working for the agency, who plunged to his death from the tenth floor of the Statler Hotel in New York City, on November 28, 1953, after having been tricked into drinking Cointreau laced with LSD.) Meanwhile, following a military coup that ousted him from power, Lumumba had placed himself under the protective custody of a United Nations peace-keeping force. It was a sanctuary from which the CIA feared he would be able to "sway events to his advantage," so two agents (both of them foreign nationals with criminal backgrounds) were dispatched to the Congo to penetrate his UN guard and contaminate his food or toothpaste with the virus. Before they could accomplish the mission, however, Lumumba was persuaded to leave his UN sanctuary and was taken prisoner by Congolese troops. He was then sent to Elizabethville, in Katanga Province, and turned over to his arch enemy Tsombe, who promptly had him killed. The CIA subsequently denied any part in luring him to his death, but a telegram sent two days later to the Leopoldville station by the base chief in Elizabethville left little doubt about the Agency's involvement in the matter. "THANKS FOR PATRICE," it read. "IF WE HAD KNOWN HE WAS COMING WE WOULD HAVE BAKED A SNAKE." Meanwhile, an official of the CIA's Office of Medical Science had been given a box of Fidel Castro's favorite cigars with instructions to treat them with a botulinum toxin so lethal that, according to the Assassination Report issued in 1975 by the Senate Select Committee to Study Governmental Operations with respect to Intelligence Activities, "a person would die after putting one in his mouth."

During John F. Kennedy's time in office, the use and contemplated use of the CIA as an assassination tool reached such proportions that Lyndon Johnson subsequently declared that the United States "had been operating a damned Murder, Inc., in the Caribbean." Johnson could have been talking about the assassination of Rafael Trujillo, the ruthless long-time dictator of the Dominican Republic, who had been ambushed and killed in May of 1961 by dissidents armed with weapons that included some that had been supplied by the CIA, but he must also have been referring to the fury directed at Castro by the Kennedy brothers, who were smarting at the humiliation he had inflicted upon them at the Bay of Pigs. In early November of 1961, President Kennedy asked Tad Szulc, a reporter for the Washington bureau of the *New York Times*, who had met at length with the Cuban leader during a recent visit to the island, "What would you think if I ordered Castro to be assassinated?" Szulc says he told the president that the United States should not be a party to murder, to which Kennedy responded, "I agree with you completely." According to Szulc's notes of the meeting,

Kennedy then declared that "he was under terrific pressure from advisers to okay a Castro murder," but that he was resisting this pressure.

It seems likely that the president was dissembling. If not, he soon changed his mind. Before the end of the month, he had authorized Operation MONGOOSE—a covert action program to overthrow and kill Castro, which was vociferously promoted by his brother Robert and directed by Brigadier General Edward Geary Lansdale, a psychological-warfare expert, who had become a CIA legend during the early 1950s, when he helped Ramon Magsaysay defeat the Hukbalahaps insurgency in the Philippines. At the time, a favorite ploy of the men Lansdale commanded was to puncture the neck of a captured Huk guerrilla with a pair of holes, hang his body upside down until the blood drained out, and then put the corpse on a jungle trail so that the Huks would think they were operating in a region inhabited by vampires.

In 1955, Lansdale became the CIA station chief in Saigon, where he helped his close friend Ngo Dinh Diem consolidate power by directing pacification programs in the South Vietnamese countryside. In this role, he served as the model for Alden Pyle, the murderously righteous American foreign service officer, who initiates a counterinsurgency operation that kills and maims innocent civilians in Grahame Green's prophetic novel *The Quiet American*. He also served as the model for Colonel Edwin Barnum Hillendale, the folksy but frustrated military assistance officer, who wins over Vietnamese villagers by playing ragtime on his harmonica in Eugene Burdick and William Lederer's best-selling 1959 novel, *The Ugly American*.

Unfortunately for history, Kennedy ignored the first book in favor of the second. Indeed, he was such an avid fan of *The Ugly American*— a fictional polemic that decried the loss of American prestige and power in the Third World—that he not only saw the characters in it as providing an answer to the question of how the United States could win the Cold War in Southeast Asia, but also proceeded to recruit Hillendale's real-life counterpart Lansdale as one of his chief advisers on South Vietnam. He then approved Lansdale's plan to train and send South Vietnamese guerrillas into Laos and North Vietnam. Thus did a bad novel encourage the president to ignore Douglas MacArthur's dying advice against fighting a land war in Asia (as well as Charles de Gaulle's warning that if he did he would find himself in a "bottomless military and political quagmire"), and to embrace the absurd notion fostered by General Maxwell Taylor and others that elite Green Beret troops of the U.S. Special Forces could accomplish against the Vietcong what equally elite paratroops and Foreign Legionnaires of the French Expeditionary Force had failed to accomplish against the Vietminh, seven years earlier. The result, of course, was the beginning of a cruel ten-year conflict that ended in defeat and divided the nation as it had not been divided since the Civil War.

After Lansdale was put in charge of MONGOOSE, a CIA agent named William Harvey delivered botulinum toxin pills to the Mafia gangsters in Miami, who had been recruited by Robert Maheu to arrange for Castro's death. It soon became apparent, however, that the Agency's Cosa Nostra surrogates were not up to the task—perhaps because using pills was not their time-honored method of rubbing people out—so Lansdale was eased out of MONGOOSE, and the government's anti-Castro activities were taken over by Desmond Fitzgerald, another veteran CIA agent, who was brought in from Vietnam where he had been in charge of paramilitary operations. Under Fitzgerald's prodding, the Agency's Technical Services Division cooked up some new ways to get the job done. One plan consisted of planting an exotic seashell that had been rigged to explode on the ocean floor off Cuba where Castro was known to go skin diving. Another involved James B. Donovan, a New York lawyer, who was then negotiating with Castro for the release of prisoners taken during the Bay of Pigs operation. (A year earlier, Donovan had negotiated the exchange of Colonel Rudolf Ivanovich Abel—the Soviet spy who had been captured in 1957 by the FBI in Brooklyn—for the U-2 pilot Gary Powers, who had been shot down over Russia in 1960.) The CIA's idea was to have him act as an unwitting accomplice to mayhem by making Castro a present of a diving suit whose interior had been dusted with a fungus that would produce Madura foot—a horribly painful and deforming tropical skin disease—and whose breathing apparatus had been contaminated with tubercle bacilli.

As chance would have it, I interviewed Donovan during this period for a Talk of the Town story that appeared in The New Yorker under the title "Man in Havana." He was a stocky, pink-faced fellow in his late forties, with blue eyes, a prominent forehead topped by a receding thatch of prematurely white hair, and a soft-spoken manner that served to heighten the effect of some unusually frank pronouncements. He told me that in his opinion there had been far too much concern with the quid pro quo aspect of his negotiations for the release of the prisoners and too much worry about whether fifty-three million dollars' worth of drugs, medicine, and baby food that had been shipped to Cuba as part of the deal would strengthen the Cuban economy and Castro's government. "Most people seem to disregard, except in terms of the propaganda value for the United States, the extent to which these drugs, medicine, and baby foods have succored the sick, the young, and the elderly people of a nation that is in dire need of such supplies," he said.

Donovan spoke at some length about the Mercedarian Order—officially known as the Glorious, Royal, and Military Order of Our Lady of Mercy or Ransom—which was founded early in the thirteenth century by a group of Spanish noblemen for the express purpose of seeking the release of Christians who were being held captive by the Moors. "The Mercedarians went as far as to offer themselves as substitutes for prisoners who were slaves on Moorish galleys," he told me. "But what I find particularly interesting about them, especially in terms of my own mission, is that whenever it was possible, they tried to accomplish their objective by the performance of corporal works of mercy, such as feeding the hungry, clothing the naked, sheltering the homeless, and tending the sick."

Donovan went on to say that when he had visited Havana over the weekend of Palm Sunday, he had taken his eighteen-year-old son with him. "Castro, who has a thirteen-year-old son, seemed to be greatly impressed by this gesture of confidence on my part," he said. "He took my son skin-diving and spear-fishing, and I'm convinced that it was largely because I had brought the boy along that I was able, during that weekend, to obtain his permission to bring out thirty-five American prisoners, which I did at the end of April."

"Man in Havana" ran in the magazine in early July. Four and a half months later, John F. Kennedy was murdered in Dealy Plaza, in Dallas. Even as the bullets from Oswald's rifle were shattering his skull, CIA agents were in Paris delivering a fountain pen that had been rigged as a syringe for injecting poison to a longtime but mentally unstable associate of Castro named Rolando Cubela, who had been recruited to assassinate the Cuban leader.

# 14

## Another Perspective

Shortly before I met Donovan, my first novel was published by Atlantic–Little, Brown. Like the story upon which it was based, it was called *The Sick Fox,* and it described the adventures of an American counterintelligence agent who, by reporting a rabid fox to some local German authorities, triggers a chain reaction of events that brings ruin to an elderly shepherd whom he has befriended. Unlike in the story, however, the counterintelligence agent in the novel is clearly disaffected with the Cold War and his role in it, and he is stationed at an underground nuclear storage depot called Alpha Site, which was clearly modeled on North Point and described in some detail. The book was published during the first week of May, and it got nice notices in *Time* magazine and the *Saturday Review of Literature,* which occasioned some letters of congratulation from several classmates whom I had not seen since college, as well as from some classmates of the half brother I had never met. It also occasioned a visit from Bill Collins, whom I had not laid eyes on since the night I stole the captain's jeep and drove him to the hospital at Fort Dix.

Collins was sitting sound asleep on a threadbare sofa in the anteroom of the magazine when I arrived for work one morning, just after ten o'clock. The receptionist told me he'd been there since eight. Except for a receding hairline and a pronounced scar on his upper lip, he looked just as I remembered him looking back in basic training, almost ten years earlier. After I woke him up and we'd shaken hands and told each other that we looked the same, I remonstrated with him for not telephoning before he came.

"Hell, Bill, nobody ever gets to work at this place before ten," I said.

"That's okay," Collins replied. "I had to come up on business anyway, so I caught an early train."

After I had brought him to my office and sat him down, we asked each other the usual questions. He told me that upon graduating from

Counterintelligence School at Holabird, he had been sent to Japan, where he spent two years on Hokkaido analyzing the threat of Soviet infiltration from the Kuril Islands, and that when he returned to the States he had married the girl from Boston. They already had two children—a boy and a girl—and they lived in Alexandria, outside Washington, D.C., where he worked in a foreign aid procurement office.

When it became my turn to catch him up on my life, I told him that I was married and living on the Upper West Side, and I invited him to dinner that night so he could meet my wife. He declined, saying that he had to catch an afternoon train back to Washington, but that he would love to take a rain check. So I went on to tell him about Germany and what I'd done there and, of course, how I had ended up sending "Got Me" Ramsay out to pull guard duty on one of the coldest nights in all history. That triggered memories of Fort Dix and basic training and the dismantling and interment of Ramsay's Nash, and before we knew it we were carrying on over beer and hash at a restaurant near Times Square.

I forget what first alerted me to the possibility that Collins' visit was not as spontaneous as he'd led me to believe. I'd mentioned the novel, of course—he said he hadn't read it—and that got me going on some of the craziness that attended the red and green lights at Alpha Site (a.k.a. North Point, but by that time I had begun to confuse the two), when he asked me in an offhand way how "close to the bone" it was, by which I assumed he meant how close to reality. That seemed to be an odd question if he didn't know about the book to begin with, but we had been remembering old times, and we were on our third beer, and I was in too good a mood to place any great weight upon the matter. I went on to tell him how I'd once gone to the crafts and hobby shop at the post recreation center in Kaiserslautern, looking for some wood to make myself a bow and arrow, and when the grizzled master sergeant in charge said they were out of hickory, I said I'd settle for a "piece of ash," to which he replied that in that case I ought to hike over to the *Bahnhofstrasse* on Friday night and meet the train that brought the women in from Dusseldorf. Collins smiled and, bringing the subject back to North Point, said he was curious to know how I had felt about sitting on top of all those warheads. I told him that I had been scared witless at first, but, like everybody else, I had gotten used to it.

"Do you think it changed you?" he asked.

"In what way?" I said.

"How you feel about things?"

"What kind of things?"

"NATO, the Cuban missile crisis, things like that. How d'you feel about the doctrine of massive retaliation, for example?"

"I think it means mutual suicide," I said. "What do you think?"

Collins shrugged without reply and poured himself another glass of beer.

I watched the foam shoot to the top of the glass, and as he dipped his head to take a sip before it could spill over, I asked him exactly what it was he did in Washington.

Collins licked away some foam partly covering the scar on his upper lip. "Like I told you, I'm in foreign aid procurement. We have warehouses from one end of the country to the other. We stockpile all kinds of stuff."

"Such as?"

"Tractors, trucks, clothing, grain, food—"

"How about military gear?"

"That too," Collins said. "Sometimes."

I smiled at him. "What time's your train?"

"I'll probably try to catch the five o'clock."

"Only gives you a couple of hours to take care of business."

Collins glanced at his watch. "Hey, that's right!" he said. "I'd best be going."

I raised my glass. "You sonofabitch," I said. "I saved your life."

"So you did," Collins replied, and he reached across the table to touch his glass to mine.

"I saved your goddam life and this is the thanks I get."

"What do you mean?"

"I mean that you didn't just pop by my office for old time's sake."

Collins took a sip of beer and studied me over the rim of his glass.

"You came by to find out whether my politics have changed, and if this book I've written means that I'm about to become some kind of apostate."

"Look—" Collins began.

"Kindly remember you owe me for saving your goddam life," I told him.

"I remember," Collins said.

"So tell me the truth and we'll be even."

"Try to see things from another perspective," Collins said. "People are wondering why the nuclear storage site in the book is in the exact same place it is for real, and why you described it the way you did."

"The trouble is, nobody in that Washington procurement office of yours has ever listened to Bertha," I told him.

"Bertha . . . ?"

"Look, Bill, whoever you're working for must have an operation in Germany, or at least a sister agency that does. Just tell them to have someone tune in to Bertha. She broadcasts out of East Berlin around midnight, three times a week, and she'll tell you more about North Point than anybody'll ever get out of my book. She also plays great jazz and classical."

Collins was giving me a quizzical look, as if he thought I might be pulling his leg. Remembering the medical captain from Orlando and the business with Warshawsky, and how once the paper trail on this kind of thing got started it was liable to go on and on, I decided to try to put an end to the matter before it got out of hand. I looked Collins in the face and said, "Go back down to Washington and tell them that I'm a loyal American with an honorable discharge, presently writing fiction without any hidden agenda, because that'll be the truth. You got me?"

At that point, we had a good laugh. Then Collins paid the check, assuring me that he would be reimbursed for it, and we got up from the table and went outside on the sidewalk, where we shook hands, exchanged telephone numbers, and said good-bye. I never saw him after that, but fifteen years later, when something I had written would once again stimulate the curiosity of one of the nation's intelligence agencies, I would talk with him again.

That autumn, after two years of bloody strikes and riots fomented by the CIA at the direction of President Kennedy, British Guiana's Prime Minister Cheddi Jagan—an American-trained dentist with Marxist leanings—was removed from office in a rigged election and replaced by a corrupt demagogue named Forbes Burnham, who held power in the newly proclaimed Republic of Guyana until his death in 1985. By that time, he had run up a foreign debt of more than $2 billion and driven the nation into bankruptcy. In 1992, Dr. Jagan was elected president of Guyana in the first free election to be held there in thirty years, and in 1994, the Clinton administration, unaware of history—in part because the CIA and the State Department had refused to declassify secret documents detailing the Kennedy administration's earlier interference— nominated as its new ambassador to Guyana a man named William C. Doherty Jr., executive director of the American Institute for Free Labor Development. As it happened, Doherty and the institute—an organization that had been sponsored by the AFL-CIO and financed by the CIA—had played a major role in fomenting the strikes and riots that had toppled Jagan's government almost thirty years earlier. Not surprisingly, the Guyanese government protested Doherty's nomination, and once it was withdrawn Dr. Jagan called for the secret documents to be made public. "Maybe President Clinton doesn't know our country, but the people who advise him should at least know their own history," he told the *New York Times*.

Clinton was, of course, paying the price for the loss of memory that invariably results when official secrecy cloaks illegal acts—in this case, the act of President Kennedy who, like Eisenhower before him, did not hesitate to encourage insurrection as a means of getting rid of an unwanted foreign leader. Having succeeded in the case of Jagan, and obviously determined to succeed in Cuba, Kennedy must have thought it reasonable and wise to apply the same tactic in South Vietnam in the summer of 1963, when hard-line advisers, such as Averell Harriman, Roger Hilsman, and General Maxwell Taylor, became convinced that all that was necessary to get the American-backed counterinsurgency effort in that country on track was to remove President Ngo Dinh Diem from office.

Not that there wasn't good reason for disliking Diem. In early May, South Vietnamese troops had fired on Buddhists who were celebrating Buddha's birthday in the City of Hue, and during the ensuing protests that were mounted against the government several Buddhist monks doused themselves with gasoline and set themselves on fire in public places. Graphic photographs of these immolations troubled the conscience of the American public and that of our ambassador to South Vietnam, Frederick E. Nolting, who urged Diem to redress Buddhist grievances in order to regain public confidence. However, Madame Ngo Dinh Nhu, the wife of Diem's brother, who commanded an army of policemen trained by the CIA (one of them, the police chief of Saigon, appears in the famous photograph that shows him executing at point-blank range a Vietcong prisoner whose distorted features reflect the passage of a bullet through his brain), charged that the Buddhists were infiltrated with Communist agents—a conviction that was widely shared by CIA personnel in Saigon. Madame Nhu then declared herself ready to furnish mustard if the monks should undertake to hold additional barbecues.

In August, when Nhu's forces sacked pagodas throughout South Vietnam and arrested more than a thousand monks, Kennedy authorized the American commander General Paul D. Harkins to tell dissident Vietnamese generals that the United States would support a coup against Diem if it had a good chance of success and did not entail the use of American troops. The first attempt was called off for lack of preparation, but in early November a second coup, in which the CIA participated to the extent of providing money to its leaders, was successful. On November 1, three weeks before Kennedy was assassinated, forces loyal to the dissident generals surrounded the presidential palace in Saigon and called upon Diem and Nhu to resign, offering them safe conduct into exile. When Diem telephoned Henry Cabot Lodge, who had replaced Nolting as ambassador, and inquired about the position of the United States, Lodge told him that the United States did not yet have a position, and he expressed concern for Diem's personal safety. (A week later, Lodge sent a cable of congratulation to Kennedy, telling him that "the ground in which the coup seed grew into a robust plant was prepared by us" and that "the coup would not have happened as it did without our preparation.") That night, an air assault was launched on the barracks of the presidential guard, and early the next morning Diem and Nhu escaped from the palace through a tunnel and made their way to a church in Cholon, where they were apprehended by soldiers, who placed them in an armored personnel carrier before stabbing and shooting them to death.

In his book *Swords and Ploughshares*, Maxwell Taylor describes Kennedy as reacting to the news of the killings "with a look of shock and dismay on his face which I had never seen before." Whether

Kennedy could have been all that shocked seems somewhat surprising, in light of the fact that he had been trying to overthrow Castro for more than two years, and he had every reason to expect that during the execution of Operation MONGOOSE the Cuban leader would be assassinated. In his 1979 book about Richard Helms, *The Man Who Kept the Secrets*, Thomas Powers argues that the president and his advisers may not have understood the gravity of the course they had embarked upon in Cuba. "A national leader is not just another man or woman, an individual like any other," Powers wrote. "To some degree he embodies his whole country, and his murder necessarily inflicts the deepest and most general psychic injury. This is why assassination has a special name, and why it is wrong. The evidence strongly suggests that Kennedy, in his ignorance, tried to do to Cuba what his own murder did to us, and I can't help thinking that there was a kind of rough justice in the event. This is a harsh thing to say, but I think Kennedy himself might have agreed. To say that a man who lives by the sword shall die by it does not mean simply that he runs the danger of meeting a more adroit swordsman. It means that he has chosen the world of violence, and has no right to protest when violence chooses him."

The logic of Powers' argument seems incontrovertible today, but at the time the young president was struck down and in the years that followed the presumption of his innocence in such matters was sanctified, if only temporarily, by the overwhelming grief of an uncomprehending nation of people for whom the worst had come to the worst.

# 15

## The Stunt Man

Two and a half months later, during the first week of February, the worst came to the worst for my wife Malabar and me. We had spent the weekend at our cottage in the snowy Connecticut woods, and we were driving back to the city late on Sunday afternoon when our twenty-eight-month-old son Alan choked to death before our eyes. We had stopped at an antique store to look at a table, when the German au pair girl with whom we had left Alan in the car came running in, carrying him in her arms. He had turned blue, and we took turns banging him on the back and holding him under a cold water faucet—it was around the time the Heimlich maneuver became known, but we hadn't yet heard about it—and then we rushed off to the local fire station, where they tried to resuscitate him to no avail. An autopsy showed that he had kept a small piece of stew meat in his cheek after his lunch, and that it had lodged in his trachea and suffocated him. It is not possible for me to describe the horror of that afternoon, or the sorrow that lay upon Malabar and me in the years that followed.

Three days later, we put Alan's ashes into a stream that ran through a ravine behind the cottage. Some months after that, I wrote a story about a man and his wife who spend a week in Rome after the death of their child—she picking sprigs of ivy from ruined stones in the Forum, from chariot ruts in the Colosseum, and from beds in the Borghese Gardens; he endlessly tracing the course of trickles that become brooks that grow into streams that widen into rivers that empty into the sea, until it seems as if whole continents are draining through his head. The story was called "Hydrography," and Shawn, ever thoughtful, published it in the issue of *The New Yorker* that appeared in the week of the first anniversary of Alan's death.

Mercifully for Malabar and me, she was five months pregnant when Alan died, and in June she gave birth to a blue-eyed boy named Stephen, who together with his sister Adrienne (born sixteen months later) cried, gurgled, pooped, burped, laughed, crawled, toddled, walked, and grew before our astonished eyes in a series of frames that, as if taken by a roll of film we had forgot to turn, were superimposed in double exposure on the fainter images of memory, until, growing past the age of their older brother, they carried us along with them into a future in which we could resume our lives. But the several years it took for that to happen were full of despair and torment, and I find that I can only summon them up in bits and pieces—a month-old Stephen tucked into the bow of a borrowed skiff in which we motored out to Napatree Point from a house we rented in Stonington; Adrienne sitting in her crib and holding her first apple; the two of them smiling shyly in the doorway of a little house we bought on Cape Cod, in 1967. As for what was going on in the world during that time—the rioting that took place in the black ghettos of our cities, the escalation of the conflict in Vietnam and the antiwar demonstrations that accompanied it, and similar events that became indelibly seared in the memory of an entire generation—I have only fleeting recollections at best.

When I look back through my files, I find that I seem to have functioned professionally, at least to the extent that I cranked out Talk of the Town stories about subjects ranging from a dire warning delivered by the manager of a Cold War think tank that any agreement in nuclear disarmament talks would require the nation to be doubly on guard against the possibility of being hit by some secret "sleeper" (such as a devastating new wrinkle in chemical warfare) to the usual peripatetic adventure pieces that Talk was known for. Among the latter were an acrophobic ramble across the Verrazano Bridge that was under construction above the Narrows, a claustrophobic trip through the narrow confines of a water tunnel being carved through bedrock hundreds of feet below the surface of the harbor, and an exhilarating turn at Christmastime around the parapet of the Pan Am Building in the company of a man named Abe Feder, who was lighting the facades of the hexagonal edifice with floodlamps mounted on a setback far below. The parapet was eight hundred feet above the city streets, and it afforded a spectacular view of city lights that "stretched before us like baubles in an immense and fabulously glittering jewel case." It also provided an unnerving vantage point, because its circumference was surrounded by a curved steel plate that channeled powerful wind currents streaming up the sides of the building so that they blew flat across the rooftop, instead of creating dangerous turbulence in the air above the heliport, and beat unmercifully against one's knees. Still, I could have stayed up there for hours.

"In Manhattan, the lights were mostly laid out in straight lines and in geometric patterns, but on the periphery of the vast display, where boulevards curved through Queens, and where waterfront streets curled along the edges of black velvet rivers, they seemed to have been arranged in careless and luxurious profusion. The mercury-vapor lamps on the cables of suspension bridges looked like strands of sapphires; on Park Avenue, a stream of white headlights came toward us, as if from infinity, and on the other side of the festively lit center mall, a stream of red tail-lights moved endlessly away."

Even in those heady upper reaches, the Cold War was close at hand. Feder was using a walkie-talkie radio to instruct his assistants on the setback below in how he wanted the floodlamps to be placed, and his receiver was picking up word of other nocturnal activity in the vast canyons surrounding us. At one point, he passed the radio to me, and I listened to the conversations of two men who were clearly government agents involved in a surreptitious entry. One of them had broken into and was searching the office of a labor union for left-wing literature and documents, and was reporting his progress and findings to the other, who was acting as a lookout.

Two other Talk stories I worked on during that era come to mind. One was the report of a speech that the Reverend Martin Luther King Jr. gave in April of 1965 at the headquarters of the Association of the Bar of the City of New York, which was next door to the magazine. (During the same month, Attorney General Nicholas Katzenbach ordered the FBI to discontinue a wiretap on King's personal telephone that had been authorized by Robert Kennedy nearly a year and a half earlier, on the grounds that King was being influenced by Communist sympathizers.) The meeting hall was liberally sprinkled with Pinkerton guards wearing gray uniforms and packing .32 calibre revolvers beneath their jackets, and there was a standing ovation when Dr. King—a short man with a slender body topped by the large, noble head that had become so familiar—entered the room and, accompanied by Judge

Samuel I. Rosenman and a whole bevy of Pinkertons, made his way down an aisle to the speaker's platform. Judge Rosenman introduced King, drawing a gale of laughter when he thanked his guest for finding the time between jail sentences to come to speak to the Bar Association members, and then King took his place at the lectern and urged his listeners in his inimitably resonant voice to speak out in the "dangerous silence" that had come over the land. "Yours is the voice which can be heard, which will be respected," he told the sedately dressed jurists and their wives. "Yours is the ability to sound the alarm to alert the nation to demand a voting bill which finally redeems the hundred-year-old dishonored pledge of the Fifteenth Amendment. The time is now. I do believe that when your thundering voice of advocacy is insistently heard, it will be heeded. It will speed the end of our denial, the end of discrimination, the end of our second-class citizenship, the end of all inferior education. Yes, it will hasten the end of the whole rotten ugly system of racial relations which for three hundred and fifty years has degraded the doer as well as the victim."

At the end of his speech, King urged his listeners to acquire a divine discontent with physical vio-lence, with militarism, and with racial intolerance. "I still have faith in America!" he cried in a fervent voice. "I have faith that we Negroes will win our freedom because our destiny is tied up with America's destiny. I have faith that we will hew out of the mountain of despair the stone of hope, and that we will—all together—achieve a symphony of brotherhood."

The other story I remember is one that Shawn stitched together out of portions of the accounts that he asked us staff writers to set down of our impressions and experiences on the night of November 9, 1965—the night of the great blackout that stretched from New York City across nine northeastern states and into Canada. Dozens of people contributed to this piece, which ran to more than four thousand words in length and took up the entire Talk of the Town section. What most people remember of that night is where they were when all the lights went out, and what adventures they experienced as they made their way home through the city's somber streets. What many may have forgotten is the instant struggle between fear and fascination that raged in every breast. The fear came straight out of the Cold War, and it was posed in the Talk piece as a question: "Was there anyone whose mind was not touched, at least fleetingly, by the conviction that this was it—that the missiles were on the way, and Doomsday was at hand?"

Gradually, however, uneasiness gave way to enchantment with the shared experience of the predicament that had enveloped us all: "The moonlight drew us back to the window, and as we stared at the impossible, unimaginable loveliness of the moonstruck towers rising out of the blackness, and now just beginning to flicker with tiny bug-glimmerings from fellow survivors, we were abruptly and unaccountably elated."

A short while later, my colleagues and I groped our way "down our building's inky, endless stair well toward the street," lighting matches as we went, and then set out with millions of other New Yorkers to make our separate long walks home. On the way, we passed candlelit bars and cafeterias; talked to fellow travelers who would be walking across the city's great bridges that night for the first and last time in their lives; and listened to stories told by some of the tens of thousands of people who had been trapped for hours in the subways. Moonlight was our constant companion. At the corner of Fifth Avenue and Fifty-ninth, "we came upon the Plaza Hotel by moonlight—a gigantic, snowy iceberg riding the night sea, its sheer face split by the prowlike black shadow of the Sherry-Netherland."

My daughter had been born only three weeks earlier, and though I knew before setting out from the office on a forty-block walk home that Malabar was there with both her and our toddling son, I found myself anxious to be with them. As it happened, the conclusion of the blackout piece was the conclusion of my own account of what happened that night. It read as follows:

When, following our long walk, we arrived at our apartment building, the lobby door was opened for us by the superintendent. He is a Maltese, a sturdy, handsome man with liquid black eyes and a glittering smile, and he was holding a candle, in whose light his face seemed to reflect more vividly than ever before the years he had lived on his ancient native island of conquerors and colonists—of Phoenicians, Carthaginians, Romans, Greeks, Arabs, Normans, Swabians, Turks, and Englishmen. "You're one of the last," he told us, and there was relief in his voice. As he led us across the dark but suddenly congenial lobby, we remembered that our superintendent breeds rare birds—exotic finches and warblers—confining them in a small room at the rear of the building, which he keeps warm with an electric heater.

When we inquired about the birds, he told us that they were fine, and that when he had gone in to check on them, they had sung to his candle. He went on to say that there had been no mishaps in the building, that all the tenants were well, and that earlier in the evening a retired pediatrician living on the third floor—an elderly man who had practiced medicine for forty-five years—had climbed ten flights of stairs to examine a fretful infant and reassure its anxious mother. Bidding the superintendent good night, we began our own considerable climb, accompanied by the echo of our footsteps in the stair well, and again striking matches—two to a flight—as we went. On the fourth floor, we passed a candle that one of our fellow-tenants had set outside his service entrance, and from then on our eerie ascent was guided by the glow of other candles, on other landings. As we approached the seventh floor, we heard a woman's whispery voice calling down to us. "John?" she said, and then, more hopefully, "John?" She was standing in the doorway, wearing a housecoat, and as we passed by, the expression of worry on her shadowed face—an expression that seemed to epitomize all such vigils—changed to disappointment, and then, quickly, to a smile of greeting. A few moments later, we unlocked the door of our apartment, and on a table just inside the entrance, we came upon the last candle of the night. It welcomed us home.

It would be comforting to pretend that my thoughts of family were always this serene during the years that followed Alan's death, but the fact is I was filled with fury. As Alan lay dead or dying on the floor of the fire station where Malabar and I had sought help, a stricken fireman had pleaded on the telephone—will I ever forget his anguished face, which must have mirrored my own?—with a local doctor to come at once. The doctor refused. Later, I learned that he lived nearby, and I dreamed of killing him. Instead, I wrote a short story about a man, who takes his wife and infant son on a ski trip to Vermont a year after they have lost their first child in an accident, whose obsession with his living child's safety causes him to act with preemptive violence toward some hippie youths whose conduct he believes to be threatening.

Short stories are often autobiographical—not so much in their plot lines as in the triggering events and perceptions from which they flow— and the character, obsessions, and actions of the man in that story were a mirror of my own. It was one thing for me to complete a short story, however, and quite another to break through the roadblock I had encountered in a novel I had started the summer before Alan died. Short story writers and their braver brethren, poets, write from feelings that can be quickly carried to conclusion, whereas novelists must be the patient constructors of houses, mansions, and sometimes a whole city of mansions. To write a novel is to build an edifice that requires constant renovation as it is going up, and thus faith on the part of the carpenter that tearing out a rooftop with some intricately gabled dormer windows, or risking vital underpinnings in order to excavate a larger basement, will result in a sounder, truer structure. I had no faith in anything in those days and so my novel floundered.

I had written the opening scene over and over. It was a scene that, as in the case of my encounter with the old shepherd in "The Sick Fox," was based on something that had actually happened to me—a gratuitously violent act of which I had been a victim on a famous day in the history of the Cold War, the day the Korean War broke out. (How we writers love to cherish, brood over, and enlarge upon the insults that have been visited upon us!) I was nineteen years old at the time, had just finished my freshman year at college, and had begun a summer job as a combination bellhop and waiter in a drafty old barn of a hotel—one of several rambling wooden structures that sat like ancient shipwrecks on a rocky promontory above the sea, in York Beach, Maine. It took no more than a day or two for me to realize that the meager gratuities proffered by the aging pensioned ladies who made up most of this establishment's sparse clientele—they ordered ice water while sitting on the veranda in the afternoon, warm milk and crackers before retiring at night, and precious little in between—were not going to go very far toward making up the coming year's tuition. On my first day off, I hitchhiked thirty miles north along the coast to Old Orchard Beach—a garish, honky-tonk town that sported a dance pier and an amusement arcade—and got myself a job as a desk clerk in a waterfront hotel that catered to vacationers from Quebec and weekend lovers from Boston. Upon returning to York Beach, I gave notice to my employers, packed my clothes and other belongings in a duffel bag, and was hitchhiking back up the coast to my new position when the opening scene in the novel took place.

Following the advice of a driver who had given me a ride, I left the main road and took a shortcut across a causeway that traversed a salt marsh, and came to a bridge that spanned a deep tidal river. It was a hot and humid day, and when I reached the bridge I sat down to rest. I was not expecting to get a ride because the bridge, lacking curbs and guard-rails, was still under construction, and the causeway I had come across was closed with portable wooden barricades. So I was surprised when I heard a car coming over the route I had taken, and even more surprised when, after drawing abreast of me, it came to a stop at the far end of the bridge. I immediately jumped to my feet and started toward it at a hesitant hitchhiker's trot that became a dash of gratitude. The car was an ancient model whose once-black paint, pitted by long exposure to salt air, had turned an oily iridescent blue, and as I ran I looked through its oval-shaped rear window and saw a head slip sideways as the driver reached across the empty seat beside him to open the door. Assuming that this was an act of accommodation, I shouted a breathless "Thank you" as I swung my duffel bag in beneath the dashboard, planted my left foot beside it, and, sliding onto the seat, grasped the handle of the door to shut it. And it was in this moment of complete entanglement (for I had wrapped the cord of the duffel bag around my wrist) and of hasty motion based upon the assumption that my benefactor might be in a hurry that I opened my mouth and, even while framing words to announce my destination, received a tremendous blow on the side of my head that sent me flying.

Now the preceding order of things was reversed in ludicrous fashion as I was catapulted out of the car, with left foot following right and the duffel bag whose cord was still wrapped around my wrist coming last. And it was as I somersaulted through the air, or just after I landed and lay flopping on the concrete apron of the bridge like a fish swung out of water, that I had my first reaction, thinking (or, afterward, thinking that I remembered thinking) the phrase "ass-over-teakettle" to describe the parabolic arc of my ejection from the vehicle. So it was chagrin that I felt first of all at this absurd turnabout, which, in the fashion of a Keystone Kop film, seemed all the more comical for having been speeded up, and then I felt pain, because I had landed upon my side and then skidded along the rough, freshly poured concrete until the friction of my body had brought me to a halt. As a result, one whole side of me was bruised, and I was bleeding from a scrape on my cheekbone. Pain quickly gave way to outrage, however, as the car drew slowly away and I saw a hand reach out, grasp the handle of the door, and pull it shut. The lackadaisical gesture of that hand—the same hand that had so rudely unseated me to begin with—unnerved me completely. Untying the knot that bound me to the duffel bag, I tried to sit up, felt a stab of pain between my shoulder blades, and rolled over on my back. In this position, blinded by tears of anguish and rage, I saw nothing but sky, which was filled with harsh light. But when I struggled to my feet moments later, the road was empty.

That is what happened on Sunday morning, June 25, 1950, as I was hitchhiking to my new job in Old Orchard Beach. The incident stayed with me through the years, and when I described it to friends I often found myself trying to make rational sense out of the irrational act of my assailant by theorizing that he was either someone (a construction worker?) enraged to find a hitchhiker on a bridge that had been closed to public use, or (more likely) someone deranged by the chilling announcement coming over the radio that the army of Communist North Korea was attacking across the thirty-eighth parallel and driving toward Seoul. Thirteen years later, when I decided to use the incident as the opening scene of my novel, I wrote down what had happened exactly the way I remembered it happening, except that instead of finding the road empty the hitchhiker sees that the car has turned and is coming back toward him. At that point, he picks up a rock from the roadway and hurls it at the windshield "with all the detestation with which he might have driven home a knife," which sends the car off the bridge and into the river, where a diminishing froth of bubbles bursts the surface to mark its sinking.

The idea of having the car carrying the hitchhiker's unknown assailant go off the bridge and into the river was certainly the kind of fictional improvement on reality that is the stuff of novels. But the opening scene as written was so full of inconsequence that as I ploughed my way further into the book it seemed more and more of an appendage, and it made my hero's adventures in the beachfront hotel seem less and less relevant to the turmoil of the real world. As a result, the writing slowed and finally ground to a halt, and for a couple of years I found myself in the throes of total writer's block as I tried to figure out how to salvage the sequence on the bridge and make something of the story that followed.

The whole business got unstuck one afternoon in the summer of 1967 as I was driving to Hyannis to pick up a friend at the bus station.

The idea came in a flash, as ideas often do, and provided a simple solution to the quandary in which I had been mired. The hitchhiker became a newly inducted army recruit, who is sent for help when a bus taking him from an induction center to a training camp unexpectedly breaks down. Seizing the opportunity, he deserts. While in flight, he crosses a desolate bridge, walks unwittingly into the middle of a movie stunt, and, believing that he is acting in self-defense, kills a stunt man who is making a film. Afterward, the fugitive is tricked by the mad, omniscient director of the film into replacing the dead stunt man in a movie about a man who is fleeing from the army. The fugitive–stunt man then performs a series of hair-raising stunts, which, because they provide a cover for his true identity, lead him away from the real world and into the unreal world of the mad director's film. Naturally, I called the book *The Stunt Man.*

The idea of having the hitchhiker-hero walk into a movie stunt came out of the blue, but the character of Gottschalk, the mad movie director who is going blind with glaucoma, was based partly upon what I imagined Orson Welles must be like, and partly upon the briefly observed personna of an equally famous film director with whom I had a chance encounter. One afternoon a year or so earlier, I had been sitting in my office at the magazine banging out a Talk of the Town story, when there was a knock and I turned in my chair to find Shawn standing in the doorway. He was a notoriously shy and unfailingly polite man, who nonetheless ran his magazine with a firm hand. (Some staff members called him the "Iron Mouse.") First of all, he asked how I was, and when I said, "Fine, thank you," he asked if he was taking me away from anything important. When I said, "Not at all," he wondered if I might find time to do him a favor, and when I replied, "Of course," he came into the office and sat down in a chair beside my desk.

"I have a visitor," he confided in his characteristically soft voice, which grew even softer as he spoke. "A film director whom we profiled recently in the magazine. You may have heard of him. His name is Federico Fellini."

"Fellini!" I exclaimed.

"Yes, he's in New York on a visit, and when he came by my office this morning, he asked me if there might be someone here who could conduct him on a"—at this point, Shawn's rosy cheeks grew even rosier with a flush of embarrassment—"tour of a nearby district of the city. Most of the staff seems to have gone to lunch, but when I saw that you were still here, I thought . . ."

"I'd be glad to show him around," I said. "Honored, in fact."

"You're sure it won't be too much of an inconvenience?"

"Not at all."

Shawn gave a smile of relief and got to his feet. "In that case, I'll introduce you to him. He's right outside by the water cooler. I ought to tell you, he appears to be a somewhat boisterous person. Bursting with vitality."

Fellini was a heavyset man, and he was wearing the kind of porkpie hat you see carnival barkers wearing. When Shawn introduced us, he said "Allo!" and shook my hand. Then, without further ado, Shawn scurried off in the direction of his office, and Fellini and I started down a corridor toward the elevators.

"What part of the city do you wish to visit?" I inquired on the way.

"I want to see zee baby horse," Fellini replied.

I immediately thought of the Central Park Zoo, though I had never seen foals or even ponies there. "I beg your pardon," I said.

"Zee baby horse," Fellini repeated.

We had reached the elevator bank, and as I pushed a down button, I smiled and shook my head to indicate that I still did not understand.

"*Zee baby horse!*" Fellini shouted. "*Hates Haffanoo!*"

That's when I realized that he wanted me to take him over to Eighth Avenue and Forty-second Street to see the young teenage prostitutes, who were arriving daily from the Midwest and other outlying parts of the country to ply their trade in cheap hotels sandwiched between porno magazine stands, peep show arcades, and theater marquees advertising films that promised close-up views of every imaginable intimacy. The whole scene over there had been the subject of recent articles in the city's tabloids, which is how Fellini may have heard about it. In any event, the next hour or so was an unforgettable demonstration of the power of personal magnetism. I doubt that Fellini had traveled half a block before he had at least a dozen painted, booted, and miniskirted child whores dancing about him and chattering away like sparrows clustered at a feeding stand. Somehow, he had managed to communicate to them not only who he was but also that he was conducting some kind of audition, because the word spread like wildfire, and pretty soon he was surrounded by a gleeful horde of whores of all ages, sizes, shapes, and colors. As I watched from the outskirts of the crowd, I could see that he was having the time of his life, pantomiming the approach of johns, making jokes in broken English about pimps, complimenting the members of his audience on their outfits, and, above all, studying their faces. Yes, he was studying their faces so intently that you could almost see him imagining them in his other world of film—in pitiless light, in soft focus, dissolving, gone. . . . I watched him for another half hour or so, and then I went back to the magazine to finish the story I was writing, and when I was able to resume work on the novel a year or two later, it was that total absorption I remembered as I wrote about a deity-director who, while going blind, manipulates the destiny of the stunt man.

# 16

## The Secret Shared

In the winter of 1966, my father came to New York to visit Malabar and me and see his granddaughter Adrienne for the first time. He stayed three days before returning to Boston to resume work on a bas-relief portrait he had been commissioned to make of a trustee of a New England prep school. On the second night, Malabar had to work late at her job at Time-Life Books, so I took him to dinner at one of my favorite Italian restaurants down on Mulberry Street.

We spent several hours at dinner, had coffee afterward, and talked about the escalating war in Southeast Asia. President Johnson's campaign of bombing the cities of North Vietnam had been going on for a year; he had recently doubled our troop strength in South Vietnam to nearly two hundred thousand men; and he had just come back from a meeting in Honolulu with the U.S. commander in Vietnam, General William Westmoreland—surely the most overconfident American general since George Custer—whom he had exhorted to go back to Vietnam and "nail the coonskin to the wall." Meanwhile, de Gaulle had warned us again about becoming militarily involved in that part of the world, and he had spoken out strongly about the adverse economic consequences that the war was causing in Europe.

"De Gaulle stood by us on Berlin and Cuba," my father reminded me. "It's a pity we won't listen to him about Vietnam, because he's been right about such things before and he's going to be right again."

When I remarked that our bombing strategy seemed to be aimed at bringing the North Vietnamese to the negotiating table, my father shook his head. "The terrain is all wrong," he declared. "This isn't open country like the Stukas flew over in northern France in 1940, or a nation of highly industrial cities like Germany. This is jungle and it's going to swallow up our soldiers and soak up our bombs like a sponge. Kennedy and Maxwell Taylor forgot that the French got beaten in Indochina with one of the best armies in the world, and Johnson doesn't seem to realize that the Alamo, like Dien Bien Phu, was a defeat inflicted upon surrounded men. Instead, he used a phony pretext like the Gulf of Tonkin to pull the wool over people's eyes."

When I reminded my father that Congress had voted overwhelmingly to approve the Gulf of Tonkin Resolution, he gave me a baleful look. "Sheep," he declared. "A nation of sheep."

My father didn't live to see the student protests, which might have changed his mind about the character of at least some of the nation's young people, or the famous ambush known as the Tet Offensive, and he was dying at the Tufts New England Medical Center when the so-called Wise Old Men—Dean Acheson, Averell Harriman, Clark Clifford, Douglas Dillon, and Henry Cabot Lodge—met in the autumn of 1967 to urge President Johnson to stay the course in Vietnam. I know what he would have said about them, however, as well as what he would have said later about Robert S. McNamara and his belated mea culpa. He would have said that such men were lucky to be living in America, where every stupidity gets forgiven, because if they lived anywhere else they'd be in disgrace. Then he would have paused and gone on to amend this pronouncement by telling the story of how Field Marshal Douglas Haig, commander-in-chief of the British Forces during the First World War, who had maintained that the machine gun was an overrated weapon as he sent tens of thousands of young men to be slaughtered on the barbed wire at Passchendaele, had died peacefully in his old age while tending roses in his Sussex garden.

It was late when we finished dinner that evening, and as I was paying the check three men entered the restaurant, which, except for my father and me, had been empty of customers for almost an hour. The first man was a tall, tough-looking young fellow with slicked-back hair, who, like the guardians outside the money-counting room of Sammy Solitaire's *jai alai frontón,* was wearing a sport jacket with a perceptible bulge in the region of the heart; the second was an older, heavyset man, who was wearing a polo coat and smoking a cigar; and the third was a carbon copy of the first.

When they came in, the waiter—a roly-poly fellow from Menton, on the French-Italian border, with whom my father had been speaking

Italian—came out of a back room and told them that the kitchen was closed.

The three men paid him not the slightest attention as they sat down at a table in the corner near the door. At that point, the gravelly voiced owner of the establishment came out of the back room and greeted them with an effusion that went on and on as he fetched wine and glasses, and our waiter bustled back and forth from the kitchen with all manner of delicacies.

When we got up to leave a few minutes later, my father leaned close to the waiter and, speaking softly in French, remarked that the kitchen had not been closed, after all.

The waiter never missed a beat. "*Monsieur,*" he said, "*il y a des gens pour lesquels la cuisine n'est jamais fermée.*"

A couple of days later, I accompanied my father to Grand Central Station, where he bought a Pullman seat on the three o'clock train to Boston. Then, after checking his bag and agreeing to meet at the information booth twenty minutes before departure time, we separated; I going off to my office and he to some art galleries on Fifty-seventh Street.

When I arrived at the information booth at the appointed time, I caught sight of him approaching from the far end of the concourse. Tall, white-haired, elegant-looking in a black coat, he was walking slowly, using his cane. But as he drew closer, I noticed that his gait, which had slackened perceptibly in the years following his heart attack, was dissolving into a shuffle as he came across the marble floor, and that his face had, since morning, become ashen and gray. When he reached the booth, he leaned an elbow on the circular counter, smiled wanly, and, seeing the concern on my face, shook his head.

"I'm okay," he said ruefully. "I just walked too far against the wind."

"D'you want to sit down?" I asked.

"No, but I think I'll rest a moment."

My father unbuttoned his overcoat, reached into his vest pocket, and took out a small silver box containing his nitroglycerin pills. Then, with the shyness of a boy stealing candy, he slid back the lid of the box with his thumb, withdrew one of the tiny pills, and slipped it beneath his tongue. A moment later, still leaning on his elbow, he was nonchalantly examining the vast galaxy of the ceiling overhead.

"How are you?" I asked.

"I'm okay," he said. "Stop looking at me that way."

"Sorry. I'm a little scared, I guess."

"Me too," my father replied, glancing at the station clock. "Let's go have a cup of coffee."

We walked slowly across the concourse floor to a sandwich shop that sat against the wall of an adjoining corridor. The shop was a garish, glassed-in hodgepodge of chrome, plastic, and Formica. We sat on adjacent stools, ordered our coffee, and for some moments sipped it in silence. I stole a sideways glance at my father, and was relieved to see that color was flowing back into his cheeks and that the tiny muscles at the corners of his mouth had relaxed. Abruptly, he turned toward me.

"There's something I've been meaning to tell you for a long time," he said. "Years ago, before I met your mother, I was married and had a son. It's a part of my life I've almost forgotten. I've had to forget it because, for one reason and another, I haven't seen my other son for nearly thirty years. I'm telling you now because I consider you my oldest son, and someday, when I'm gone, I want you to tell David and Valjeanne."

I found myself suddenly and acutely embarrassed, as if I had regressed to that agonizing adolescent stage where nearly every parental statement seems to constitute an awful indiscretion. I almost felt like shrugging. Instead, I thought of the day years before on the river when I had started across the ice to confront him, but the loneliness that had animated me then was gone forever. I considered telling my father the truth—that I had known for a long time and that David and Valjeanne had known even longer—but suddenly I found myself flinching from the secret as if from a soft spot where shell ice masks a treacherous current. I had kept it too long. It had become part of me. I was afraid to know the denial that must have lain behind the reason he and my mother had given me the names of my older brother. "I'm glad you told me, Dad," I managed to say. "It doesn't matter, of course, and"—I took a deep breath—"it wouldn't have even if you had told me long ago."

"I know that," my father said quietly. "I figured that if you had found out when you were younger, you would have come to me. The reason I'm leaving it up to you to tell your brother and sister is—well, it happened forty years ago. I'm over seventy now. I'm too old to go raking all that up again."

I drank down the rest of my coffee. "We'd better be off," I said. "It's ten of three."

But as we went down the ramp to the platform and walked out toward the front of the train, I was overcome by profound depression. Here in this cavernous place with its infinity of gloom and darkness and its concrete pillars hanging like stalactites above some underground river, where the winking lantern of a trackman bobbed in the eerie distance like the light of a small boat; here, carrying an overnight bag whose lightness suddenly seemed appalling, walking beside this aging man whom I would always love, I forced censure from my mind as I would have suppressed myself from cursing in a church.

At the door of the Pullman car, I handed my father's bag to a porter with reluctance, as if by relinquishing that feathery vessel I was admitting that it contained far too little of all the love, hope, and misunderstanding that had ever passed between us. I felt the silence of my father tugging at me like my fear of his death. When we reached his seat, he removed his overcoat and handed it to me. I folded it carefully and placed it upon the rack overhead. Then we went off to the smoking section, where he sat down and filled his pipe.

"I had a fine time," he said. "It was wonderful to see the children. Be sure to tell Malabar how much I enjoyed it."

I nodded and looked down at my father, who was applying a lighted match to the tobacco in his pipe. A moment later, he was enveloped by a cloud of fragrant smoke that called forth familiar memories—the old house in Arlington, his easy chair. "Ring us up when you get home tonight so we'll know you got back okay," I said.

"Take care of yourself," my father said.

I started to leave then, but I had only taken a step or two when I heard him call my name. I turned in the narrow passageway between baggage shelves that flanked the doorway of the Pullman car.

"I hope you're not bothered by what I told you," my father said. "It doesn't change anything between us, you know."

"Of course it doesn't," I said.

My father had removed the pipe from his mouth. "I wonder if I was right not telling you before."

Twice in the moment of silence that followed came the most inexorable cry I thought I would ever hear—the boarding cry. Then, as the shout died away, I found myself thinking that surely in all these years the sheer exercise of will involved in the attempt to forget and to displace must also have been a curious and merciful antidote to suffering. My father was watching me, waiting.

"Sure, Dad," I said. "You were right."

As I walked back across the station concourse, I glanced at the clock on top of the information booth. It was three minutes past the hour. Even now the train was pulling away from its pier, a sinister vessel, swaying, rocking, and then coasting easily through the Stygian darkness. In a few minutes it would emerge from that gloom and glide, as if through a walled canal, past the tenements of Harlem to another river. There would be a whole series of rivers—the Housatonic, the Connecticut, and the Thames—and I found myself breathing easier as I imagined my father looking out at them.

Now the train, gathering speed, was arrowing across Rhode Island. Night was falling and the orange windows of the coaches were flashing through the blackness with the implied continuity of the dashes that connect electrified headlines moving across dark facades. Westerly and Providence went by, and then the trip (as it had always seemed to me on my way home) was a breathless downhill rush. There was a brief pause at the station on Route 128, where cartops glistened as if awash, and then at Back Bay. *Back Bay? Baack Bayuhh!* More rocking and swaying now, and some not so gentle shunting back and forth. Yet can the seas of a harbor be choppy on a windless night? In any case, passengers are moving toward the rail to disembark. South Station. Home.


My father died in December of the following year. I knew that summer that he was going to die, because when I was home on a visit I drove him to Dr. Levine's office in Boston for a checkup, and while he was getting dressed after the examination, Levine came into the waiting room to talk to me. "Your father's heart is wearing out," he said.

During the winter that followed my father's death, I became depressed. His dying had a lot to do with it, but so did the fact that Malabar had become unhappy in our marriage, as did my inability to go forward with the novel, in spite of having figured out how I could make it work by centering it on the adventures of the fugitive stunt man. In the spring, I saw a psychiatrist, who helped me become aware that, like the man in my story who took his wife and infant son on the ski trip to Vermont, I was spending an inordinate part of every day imagining all the terrible accidents that might befall my living children. It was no wonder I couldn't write or be a loving husband. When I sat down at my typewriter in the morning, or at dinner in the evening, I saw a Madison Avenue bus lose its brakes on the hill just before Ninety-sixth Street and bear down upon the helpless au pair girl, who was leading our children across the avenue on her way to the park; I heard the telephone ring and watched the girl go to answer it, leaving the children unattended in the bathtub; and, of course, I pictured the two of them swallowing all manner of unsafe objects.

So inured had I become to such fantasies during the years since Alan died that I had come to accept them as a natural part of my life—a constant dread that it would be my lot to endure for as long as I lived. Once I described them to the psychiatrist, however, and was able to see them for what they were—a terrible form of self-punishment—they receded like the memory of a bad dream, and within a few weeks they ceased recurring altogether. As soon as that happened, I was able to get back to work on the novel, which I finished a year later, in the spring of 1969. However, my marriage to Malabar was beyond repair.

*The Stunt Man* was published in 1970, and it got good reviews in most of the major magazines and newspapers. Ten years after that, it was made into a movie of the same title with Peter O'Toole and Barbara Hershey. What was important at the time, however, was that it enabled me to put some degree of closure to the death of my child, and to do so by stating in dramatic terms the basic conviction that I held about life at that time—that we were all stunt men in one of God's bad movies.

# 17

## Digging in Your Garden

During the spring of 1968, Martin Luther King was shot to death in Memphis, and Robert F. Kennedy, who had just won the California Democratic primary and become the odds-on favorite to win his party's presidential nomination, was assassinated in Los Angeles. Late on the evening of Kennedy's death, Shawn called and asked me to write about the service that was going to be held the next morning at St. Patrick's Cathedral. I went to the church at daybreak and found myself sitting behind Edward Kennedy, whom I had not seen since we had lived in Eliot House at Harvard during the early nineteen-fifties.

. . . At six o'clock, a priest in red vestments began to intone the words of the Mass, and many of the mourners took seats in the pews and stayed on to listen and to pray. Very few appeared to notice that Edward Kennedy, who had stayed near the bier of his brother throughout the night, was sitting on the aisle in the eleventh row, looking straight ahead. Half blinded as they emerged from the darkness of the nave and into the merciless brilliance of the television lights, the mourners seemed to pass numbly through a corridor of total exposure. They included—white and black—nuns, girls in slacks and miniskirts, workmen in shirtsleeves, matrons and children, and businessmen wearing three-button suits and carrying briefcases. The words of the priest continued to echo through the vast cathedral: "Lord have mercy, Christ have mercy, Lord have mercy . . ." At quarter to seven, Edward Kennedy stood, drew himself erect, and, as if relinquishing himself to a river, joined the line of mourners, walking slowly into the searing light, looking at the casket containing the body of his brother. Then, following the others, he walked through the south transept of the cathedral and out on to Fiftieth Street, where, in the rising sun, the tall buildings, trees, awnings, and other gnomons of this perpendicular city were beginning to cast the shadows that would mark the passage of the day.

By the time of Robert Kennedy's death, I had just finished the first of a dozen articles that would appear in the magazine about the massive

142

public health hazard posed by asbestos inhalation. The initial piece, which was titled "The Magic Mineral," marked a major turning point in my professional life, because during the next twenty-five years I would devote myself almost exclusively to chronicling environmental and occupational hazards, and in doing so would uncover and expose the secrecy and callous disregard for life that informed corporate conduct at almost every level in the United States. In the process, I would discover that the manufacturing sector of the vaunted private enterprise system, which most Americans seemed to consider an essential bastion of democracy in the Cold War being waged against Communism, was squandering the lives of thousands upon thousands of workers, and that the captains of industry who presided over it were the wholesale purveyors of a hideous legacy of disease, disability, and death.

Shawn, who had published Rachel Carson's "Silent Spring" in *The New Yorker* six years earlier, played a major role in encouraging me to embark upon this new path, but the most influential figure I encountered at that time was Professor Irving J. Selikoff, the great chest physician and epidemiologist at New York City's Mount Sinai School of Medicine, whose pioneering study of the causes of mortality among New York and New Jersey asbestos insulation workers had shown that asbestos was not only deadly to inhale, but had also become one of the most important industrial causes of cancer in the world.

A white-haired man with intense blue eyes, Selikoff had participated in the basic research on isoniazid—the antibiotic drug that, by effectively killing tubercle bacilli, had provided a cure for tuberculosis—and late in 1953, he had founded a medical clinic in Paterson, New Jersey, where, by chance, seventeen of his early patients were men who had worked in a nearby asbestos insulation factory owned by the Union Asbestos and Rubber Company, which manufactured asbestos pipe insulation for the navy. At the time, all seventeen were working and apparently able-bodied, although fifteen of them showed some evidence of pulmonary defects resulting from their inhalation of asbestos, and when the factory closed down in 1954, Selikoff decided to continue observing them with X-ray examinations and lung function tests, in order to determine the effect of previously inhaled asbestos in the lungs of men who would not be further exposed.

By 1961, six of the seventeen had died, and by 1974—twenty years after he had begun to study them—only two were alive. Fourteen of the fifteen who had died had succumbed to asbestos-related cancer of the lungs or stomach, or to scarring of the lungs caused by their inhalation of asbestos fibers. By then, however, Selikoff had studied thousands of asbestos workers and had demonstrated to the world that they were dying in droves of asbestos disease.

When I first met him in the winter of 1968, he and his initial studies of the asbestos hazard were almost unknown to the public, and officials of Johns-Manville and other leading asbestos manufacturers were hiring consultants to dispute his findings, and sending representatives to harass him at medical meetings. "The Magic Mineral," which appeared in *The New Yorker* in October of the same year, changed all that. It described the extent of the asbestos hazard and the investigations of it that had been conducted by Selikoff and other scientists around the world, and it ended with some personal observations on my part and a warning about how the spraying of asbestos fireproofing material on the steel girders of high-rise buildings—a practice that had been going on for more than twenty years and was contaminating the ambient air of the nation's cities with trillions of highly respirable asbestos fibers—was posing a massive threat to the health of millions of unsuspecting urban dwellers:

> I walked on to the corner of Sixth Avenue, where a forty-four-story office building had been under construction for several months. During that period, I had passed the building nearly every day, but now, for the first time, I looked up and scrutinized it carefully. About halfway up its side, I saw some tarpaulins billowing in the wind. Above the tarpaulins, the steel girders and beams were reddish brown; between the tarpaulins and the ground, however, they had been sprayed with asbestos insulation, which clung to them like gray frosting. Then, all at once, I saw wads of the same gray stuff falling out of the area that had been curtained off by the tarpaulins. Some of the pieces were carried away on the wind; others that were heavier came tumbling down around me. One fell on the sidewalk at my feet. I picked it up, crumbled it between my fingers, and saw dozens of tiny fibres float away. It was the same color and texture as the stuff Dr. Selikoff had showed me half an hour before. The sidewalk was covered with it, and even as I stood there more of it came showering down. A woman hurrying to make the light with a friend brushed some off the sleeve of her coat, and said, "What the devil is

this stuff?" I watched her cross the avenue, and saw asbestos insulation blowing over the pavement like thistledown across a field. The wind was southerly, and most of the asbestos was traveling north, in the direction of Mount Sinai Hospital, where Dr. Selikoff and his associates are still following the trail Dr. Cooke set out on in 1924. But I was not thinking about Dr. Selikoff or the difficulties of epidemiology just then. I was thinking about the children who play in Central Park, and about all the other children who live in this city and breathe its air.

Public response to "The Magic Mineral" was extraordinary and demand for the article so great that the magazine reprinted it in a special booklet, and also put out a brochure containing a selection of editorial comment and letters from around the world that had been generated by the piece. More than three years would pass, however, before anything would be done about the dreadful peril posed to city dwellers by the spraying of asbestos fireproofing material on high-rise buildings. Meanwhile, during my research for "The Magic Mineral," I had run across a peculiar phenomenon that, after it had been repeated several times, persuaded me there was something else afoot. In Washington, D.C., I interviewed a physician, who was in charge of studying the asbestos problem for the navy. He informed me over lunch at the Army-Navy Club that asbestos was an essential ingredient in the construction of all warships—especially the nuclear submarines that had given the nation a major advantage in the Cold War—and that while a health hazard might exist for a few heavily exposed asbestos workers, it was important to keep the matter in perspective.

"Just remember," he told me, "you can get chest disease from digging in your garden."

A week later, I went to Cincinnati to talk about the asbestos hazard with the chief of asbestos field studies for the United States Public Health Service's Division of Occupational Health. He had come highly recommended. He was a fellow of the American Public Health Association, a past chairman of its Occupational Health Section, a past chairman of the American Conference of Governmental and Industrial Hygienists, a member of the Committee on Asbestosis and Cancer of the International Union Against Cancer, and an adjunct professor of environmental health at the University of Cincinnati.

"Keep in mind that practically everyone is susceptible to chest disease to some extent," he told me, "and that you can get chest disease even from digging in your garden."

Toward the end of the month, I received a telephone call from a man in the public relations department of Johns-Manville, who had heard that I was investigating the asbestos problem and wanted me to have the industry's viewpoint on the matter. After telling me about a number of industry studies that had found no evidence of any unusual incidence of lung disease among asbestos workers, he said that the whole business was being blown out of proportion by a few scientists who were seeking headlines.

"Don't forget," he assured me, "it's a well-known fact that you can get chest disease from digging in your garden."

At that point, I began to put two and two together, and during the next few years undertook to chronicle the massive cover-up with which industry and government was trying to hide the asbestos hazard from the American people.

It was too late, of course, for tens upon tens of thousands of asbestos workers and other unsuspecting victims, who had developed incurable lung disease as a result of their exposure to asbestos. In 1976, at the Nineteenth Navy Occupational Health Workshop in Charleston, South Carolina (to which I had been invited as a speaker), a captain at the Naval Medical Center, in Bethesda, Maryland, confided in me that the navy was "sitting on" thousands of X-rays showing irreversible lung damage in personnel who had been exposed to asbestos while serving onboard ships. The navy could do this with impunity, of course, because federal law does not allow service personnel to sue the armed forces for negligence.

That same year, Selikoff and some associates gave X-ray examinations to a thousand workers at the General Dynamics Corporation's Electric Boat Division, in Groton, Connecticut, where the navy's nuclear submarines were being built. They found that almost half of these workers had developed irreversible scarring of the lungs or the pleura—the delicate membrane that encases the lungs—or both. Some idea of the navy's attitude toward the problem at Electric Boat came from the comments of the director of the Division of Occupational Health and Preventive Medicine of the navy's Bureau of Medicine and Surgery, in

Washington, D.C. In an interview published in *Connecticut Magazine* in 1979, he answered the question of whether the navy bore any responsibility for working conditions at Electric Boat by observing: "If I order an automobile and the way they make automobiles is to throw people into a furnace, I am not responsible for that."

Some idea of the government's attitude toward the asbestos problem had come two years earlier during a deposition that was taken in connection with a lawsuit brought by diseased workers at a factory in Tyler, Texas, who had been engaged in the manufacture of asbestos pipe insulation used in the navy's nuclear submarines. The deposition was given by the chief of asbestos field studies for the Public Health Service, who had previously called upon me to remember that one could develop chest disease from working in one's garden. While under oath, he admitted that during the 1960s, when he had been in charge of the government's investigation of working conditions at the Tyler factory and other asbestos factories across the nation, he had struck a deal with company officials. In return for being allowed to inspect their plants, he had guaranteed not to give out any details about the asbestos dust levels to which the workers toiling in them were exposed, or to make any recommendations to the workers or their union leaders about how they might protect themselves.

"You can get chest disease from digging in your garden. . . ." If I heard that phrase once as I set out on the trail of the asbestos tragedy, I must have heard it a dozen times, and always used in the same way—to minimize the dreadful consequences of inhaling asbestos, which had already killed more than half a million American workers, and which will kill several hundred thousand more over the next thirty to forty years. Meanwhile, not content with trying to deflect inquiry with euphemism, asbestos industry officials and their paid hacks were not above trying other methods.

One day in 1970, my friend Frank Modell, *The New Yorker* cartoonist, came into my office at the magazine and remonstrated with me for not telling him that I had put in for membership at the Overseas Press Club, where he had taken me for lunch on several occasions.

"What're you talking about?" I said. "I haven't put in for membership at the Overseas Press Club."

"Don't kid me," Frank replied. "A guy I've known there for years came up to me yesterday and told me you had. He asked me all kinds of questions about you."

"Frank, I haven't a clue about this."

"Don't worry, I recommended you highly. I told him you were honest, reliable, good for the dues, and a swell lunch companion. In fact, I laid it on thick—that is, until he asked me a couple of personal questions which I declined to answer."

"What kind of questions?"

"Oh, you know. Were you married? Did you run around? Have a girlfriend? That kind of thing."

As it happened, I was in the middle of a divorce at the time, and engaged in some delicate negotiations with my wife about the custody of our two children, so the thought occurred to me that the inquiries made of Frank might have something to do with that. "Who does this guy work for?" I asked.

"Some big public relations firm."

After Frank left, I picked up the telephone and made some inquiries of my own. It took me about twenty minutes to find out that the man who had been asking about me worked for Hill and Knowlton, and that one of Hill and Knowlton's leading clients was Johns-Manville—the world's largest asbestos manufacturer.

Some months later, while I was researching a sequel to "The Magic Mineral" about the special hazard of spraying asbestos fireproofing materials in high-rise buildings, the vice president and director of public affairs for Johns-Manville invited me to visit company headquarters, in Manville, New Jersey, to hear the corporate side of things. The town is about fifty miles southwest of New York City, and I drove down there with him in a company limousine. The asbestos factory complex in Manville was almost half a mile square, and it was located smack in the middle of town, and since most of the twelve thousand people who lived there had worked for the company at one time or another, it should come as no surprise that they included one of the largest concentrations of asbestos-disease victims in the entire world.

The meeting took place in a conference room at the headquarters building. Just before it started, I saw the vice president reach into his open briefcase and turn on a tape recorder, so I was careful to listen and say little. I have forgotten the names of the half dozen or so company officials who were present. One of them was the corporate manager of industrial health, who assured me that the company had been striving diligently to lower dust levels in all its factories. A year or so later, his wife, who had worked at the Manville complex as a secretary, died of mesothelioma, an invariably malignant, always fatal tumor of the pleura or of the peritoneum—a similar membrane that lines the stomach—which rarely occurs without some, even if slight, history of exposure to asbestos. A few years after that, he himself died of the same disease.

Another official at the meeting was the director of corporate research and development. On the way to lunch, he told me that he and his colleagues had been impressed with "The Magic Mineral."

"You really know how to write about asbestos," he said.

"Thanks," I replied.

"We could use someone like you in our public relations department. Matter of fact, I understand there's an opening there right now."

I looked at him and said nothing.

"Don't know what your present position pays, of course, but this one starts at forty-five thousand."

I looked straight ahead and pretended I hadn't heard him. The sum he'd mentioned was more than three times what I was making at *The New Yorker.*

# 18

## Murder in the Workplace

The piece about the hazard of spraying asbestos on the steel girders of high-rise buildings was published in the autumn of 1971. Shortly beforehand, Mayor John Lindsey announced that asbestos spraying would be banned in New York City after February of 1972, and he held a press conference crediting "The Magic Mineral" with bringing the problem to public attention. Some of the asbestos manufacturers issued statements claiming that asbestos was irreplaceable as a fire retardant, and that without its protection fires could melt the girders of skyscrapers, causing them to topple over. At the time, the steel frame for the first fifteen stories of the World Trade Center had been erected and sprayed with asbestos, but once the ban went into effect the girders in the remainder of the building were protected with mineral rock wool—an equally effective and nonrespirable fire retardant that had been available for most of the century. Other major cities followed the example of New York, and in 1972 the fledgling Environmental Protection Agency imposed a nationwide ban on the spraying of asbestos on high-rise buildings, which many researchers believe has saved the lives of thousands of unsuspecting people, who might otherwise have developed malignant mesothelioma and other asbestos-related diseases.

Meanwhile, I had begun to write about other environmental and occupational health hazards. In January of 1971, *The New Yorker* had run a seventeen-thousand-word piece of mine about the disease potential of the stain-eating proteolytic enzymes that had recently been introduced into detergents being used in fifty million American households. The story contained the usual elements—denial by the leading detergent manufacturers that the enzymes posed any health hazard; warnings by independent medical scientists that they could cause pulmonary disease, such as asthma, and skin rashes; and indecision on the part of various government agencies about how to deal with the problem. Toward the end of the article, I predicted that speculation about the harmful effects of the enzyme-containing detergents would probably go on for some time, and tried to address the larger public health issue posed by their swift introduction into the marketplace. "If no problem develops in the coming months or years, it seems safe to conclude that it will not be because any intelligent decision has been made by anyone in a position of responsibility for the public welfare," I pointed out. "It will be luck. And even if the public should be lucky on this occasion, the question remains whether it will be similarly fortunate the next time a substance with unknown biological effects finds its way into practically every home across the land within a few months."

One of the leading sources for the enzyme piece was Professor René Dubos, the famous bacteriologist and director of the Department of Environmental Biomedicine at Rockefeller University, who had conducted early experiments showing that the strains of bacteria from which the enzyme preparations were produced had the ability to destroy red blood cells. Dubos was one of those rare scientists who, like Irving Selikoff, was not afraid to speak his mind, and I quoted him at some length in my piece:

> I predict that if there is going to be consumer trouble with enzyme detergents, we won't know it until sometime in the future, and I believe we simply can't afford this kind of attitude any longer. There must be an essential philosophy in our society that prohibits the introduction of any technical innovation until one has tested, insofar as one can, the consequences of its introduction both in the environment and upon the human beings who will come in contact with it. This, of course, has not been the case with enzyme detergents. Millions and millions of people are using them, and we have no idea what the result will be. It is criminal to have such a situation. At the very least, it is criminally stupid.

As things turned out, I was wrong to suggest that speculation about the disease-producing potential of the enzyme detergents would drag on into the future. The article in *The New Yorker* produced an immediate outcry of concern from one end of the nation to the other, and within a few weeks the three leading detergent manufacturers—Procter and Gamble, Colgate-Palmolive, and Lever Brothers—quietly withdrew the enzymes from their products. Some months later, Dubos wrote a gracious introduction for my first book of nonfiction, which contained the enzyme piece and the two articles *The New Yorker* had published on the asbestos hazard, saying that it demonstrated "how a skilled and intelligent reporter, working with exacting intellectual criteria, can build a bridge between the scientific community and the general public."

Earlier in his introduction, Dubos wrote a paragraph that not only described in wonderfully human fashion the insidious nature of the environmental threats facing mankind, but also drew a map of the road that I would follow as a journalist for the next twenty years. "Technology is constantly introducing new substances into our lives, but our bodies have not changed significantly since the Stone Age," he declared. "We have no instinct to warn us against the dangers lurking in a new beam of radiations, a new almost invisible kind of dust, a new innocent looking white powder. We are no better equipped by nature than were our caveman ancestors to recognize the environmental threats which are not perceived by our senses, and which do not produce acute effects readily linked to their causes. And yet, there is no doubt that some of the most common and most destructive medical problems of our time are caused or at least influenced by environmental factors."

In the winter of 1972, the asbestos-insulation factory in Tyler, Texas, was shut down by its owner, the Pittsburgh Corning Corporation—a joint venture of the Pittsburgh Plate Glass Company (then called PPG Industries) and the Corning Glass Works. This occurred after a survey conducted by hygienists from the newly formed National Institute for Occupational Safety and Health (NIOSH) showed that dangerously high levels of asbestos dust were present everywhere in the plant. Indeed, asbestos was so thick in the air at the factory that a person could scarcely see from one side of either of its two fabricating buildings to the other, and the NIOSH survey showed that nearly half of the men who had worked in those buildings for ten years or more had developed irreversible scarring of the lungs as a result of inhaling the stuff. The situation at the Tyler factory provided me with the starting point for a five-part series of articles titled "Annals of Industry: Casualties of the Workplace"—subsequently published as a book called *Expendable*

*Americans*—which exposed hazardous working conditions in asbestos factories and other industrial facilities across the nation. The articles also uncovered the existence of a medical-industrial complex consisting of company physicians, industry consultants, and key occupational health officials at various levels of the state and federal governments, who were trying to prevent workers from finding out about the disease hazards to which they were being exposed and to discourage government health agencies such as NIOSH from doing anything to remedy them.

"Casualties of the Workplace" was one of the longest series of articles that ever ran in *The New Yorker*, and it reflected Shawn's determination to keep the magazine in the forefront of major environmental issues. It alerted the American people once again to the pervasive public health hazard posed by asbestos, and it helped launch the greatest toxic tort litigation in the history of world jurisprudence, which eventually drove Johns-Manville and several other leading asbestos manufacturers to seek refuge in bankruptcy, and resulted in the de facto ban on the use of asbestos that exists in the United States today. It also won the National Magazine Award.

"Casualties of the Workplace" was edited by Charles Patrick Crow, who I considered to be the most prodigious and proficient nonfiction editor on the staff of *The New Yorker*, and who I was fortunate to have as my friend and editor for the rest of my career at the magazine. The articles were painstakingly checked for accuracy by Anne Mortimer-Maddox of the magazine's fabled fact-checking department, and they pulled no punches, because they named dozens of companies involved in the wholesale infliction of disease upon workers, as well as the names of many company physicians and medical consultants who were doing little or nothing to prevent it. What I will always remember are the eloquent and angry words of Anthony Mazzocchi, director of the legislative department of the Oil, Chemical, and Atomic Workers International Union (OCAW), which represented the workers at the Tyler factory. A blunt-spoken man, Mazzocchi had long brooded over what he considered to be the gross immorality that attended the plight of men who were either dying or being disabled early in life as a result of exposure to toxic substances such as asbestos, whose adverse health effects had long been known and ignored by the members of the medical-industrial complex. This is how he explained his reasons for making a cause célèbre of the Tyler factory:

> I wanted the whole country to know in detail what had happened at that factory, and to understand that what had gone on there—the fruitless Bureau of Occupational Safety and Health inspections, the lack of enforcement by the Department of Labor, the whole long, lousy history of neglect, deceit, and stupidity—was happening in dozens of other ways, in hundreds of other factories, to thousands of other men across the land. I wanted people to know that thousands upon thousands of their fellow citizens were being assaulted daily, and that the police—in this case, the federal government—had done nothing to remedy the situation. In short, I wanted them to know that murder was being committed in the workplace, and that no one was bothering about it.

When the first installment of "Casualties of the Workplace" appeared in *The New Yorker*, the magazine's advertising department took out a full-page ad in the *New York Times* quoting Mazzocchi's statement, and a few months later a lawsuit was brought in federal district court, in Tyler, on behalf of the men who had worked at the factory. The case was called *Yandle* v. *PPG Industries*. (Herman Yandle was the local union chairman, and he had worked at the factory for eleven years.) The evidence that the Tyler plant was a death trap was overwhelming, and the culpability of its owners was hardly in doubt. Supervisors there had told the men that asbestos was safe enough to eat, and the medical director of PPG Industries had told NIOSH officials, who estimated that some workers at the plant were inhaling more than a billion asbestos fibers each working day, that there wasn't much of a health problem at the factory because people didn't stay there long enough to get sick.

In the end, the lawsuit was settled out of court for $20 million. The major defendants who contributed to the settlement were PPG, Pittsburgh Corning, two English asbestos companies that had sold raw asbestos to Pittsburgh Corning, and—thanks to the sweetheart deal that had been made by the chief of the Public Health Service's asbestos field studies program—the United States government. It sounded like a lot of money until one stopped to consider that after attorneys' fees the average share for the men who had worked at the factory came to less than

$30,000 apiece, and that fully one third of the 895 men who had been employed there during the seventeen years it had been in operation were expected to die of asbestosis or asbestos-related cancer.

It is not known how many of the wives, children, and other relatives of the Tyler factory workers will develop asbestos disease as a result of household exposure. (Several studies have demonstrated that approximately one third of all family members living in the same house as a heavily exposed asbestos factory worker show X-ray evidence of irreversible lung damage caused by their inhalation of asbestos.) It is known, however, that Herman Yandle's mother died of mesothelioma in 1983. Her only known exposure to asbestos occurred during the 1960s, when she washed the work clothes worn by Herman and his brother, who were living at home while they worked at the Tyler plant.

Some of the most serious revelations in "Casualties of the Workplace" concerned Johns-Manville, but one in particular stands out in my memory. It was made by a man named Thomas Callahan, who had been a foreman at the Union Asbestos and Rubber Company factory, in Paterson, New Jersey. He had later helped set up machinery at the Tyler factory, which Union Asbestos subsequently sold to Pittsburgh Corning. When I called upon Callahan in the summer of 1972, he told me about some unsuccessful efforts by his employers to improve working conditions at the factory.

"Believe me, the company did everything it could in those days, but there was no way it could improve the ventilation system," he said. "In any case, we were a lot more humane than other people in the business. I remember going one day in the early fifties with Edward Shuman—he was then the general manager of the plant—to see some Johns-Manville people in New York. We asked them if they knew of any way we could improve the dust situation in our factory. My God, they were brutal bastards! Why, they practically laughed in our face! They told us that workmen's compensation payments were the same for death as for disability. In effect, they told us to let the men *work themselves to death!*"

As one might imagine, an assertion of this nature was likely to garner the close attention of almost any libel lawyer, and when "Casualties of the Workplace" was being prepared for publication in *The New Yorker* in the autumn of 1973, the magazine's attorney insisted that Callahan's story be checked for accuracy not only with Callahan, but also with Shuman. Contacting Callahan, who readily corroborated the way I had quoted him, posed no problem, but Shuman was another matter. He had long ago moved from Paterson, and none of his former associates knew whether or where he was living. We were less than an hour away from closing the piece and having to exorcise the entire passage in question when someone on the checking staff, who had refused to give up, located him by poring through telephone books for the greater metropolitan area. He was living on Long Island, and I remember listening in on an extension phone when the checking editor read him Callahan's quote and asked him if it provided an accurate description of what had happened. "Oh, yes," Shuman said in a quiet voice. "That's exactly what happened. I'll never forget it as long as I live. It was one of the worst days of my life."

# PART THREE

# 19

## In the Context of the Cold War

By this time, Richard Nixon's cover-up of the Watergate affair was beginning to unravel in earnest. On October 12—two days after Spiro Agnew resigned the vice presidency and pleaded guilty to tax evasion in order to escape indictment for bribery and extortion—a court of appeals upheld Judge John J. Sirica's order for the president to turn over the incriminating tapes that would lead to his own resignation the following summer. Meanwhile, federal prosecutors had learned that E. Howard Hunt had broken into the office of Daniel Ellsberg's psychiatrist with the technical assistance of the CIA, and that Nixon had been partly successful in enlisting CIA and FBI support in his attempt to deflect investigations into the Watergate burglary. In addition, the chairmen of several House and Senate committees with oversight authority for the CIA had begun to learn for the first time about the true nature of some of the covert activity the Agency had been engaged in since the Cold War began.

Revelations about misconduct on the part of the intelligence agencies continued during 1974, and in December the *New York Times* published a front-page story by Seymour Hersh about the CIA's domestic intelligence program, including the fact that the Agency had been intercepting and opening first-class mail from abroad for more than twenty years. Early in January 1975, President Gerald Ford formed a commission headed by Vice President Nelson Rockefeller to investigate such activities, and on January 27 the Senate established a Select Committee headed by Senator Frank Church, of Idaho, with the broad mandate of investigating all of the intelligence activities of the United States government with respect to whether any of them had been illegal, improper, or unethical. At that point, the floodgates holding back the nation's Cold War secrets gave way, and a deluge of disclosure about the dirty tricks that had been perpetrated in the name of preserving freedom came gushing forth.

Not surprisingly, murder was given first priority as the CIA was implicated in assassination plots involving Fidel Castro, Patrice Lumumba, Rafael Trujillo, Ngo Dinh Diem, and General Rene Schneider, of Chile. (Not included in the Senate investigation was the Agency's involvement in plots aimed at discrediting Achmed Sukarno of Indonesia, disabling Abdul Kassem of Iraq, and killing Gamal Abdel Nasser of Egypt.) The members of the Select Committee learned that between 1953 and 1973 more than twenty-eight million letters were made available without authorization to CIA agents in New York City by officials of the United States Postal Service. The CIA photographed the exteriors of nearly three million of these letters and opened and photographed more than two hundred thousand that were going to or coming from the Soviet Union. Such efforts were puny, however, compared to those of the National Security Agency that—courtesy of RCA Global, Western Union International, and ITT World Communications—received copies of millions of international telegrams that were sent to or from or were transiting within the United States between 1952 and 1975.

The members of the committee also found out that in clear violation of the CIA's statutory charter, Agency officials had spied on thousands of American citizens. The most extensive of the domestic spying programs was a seven-year operation called CHAOS, which had begun in 1967 in response to President Lyndon Johnson's request for intelligence about foreign influence upon dissenters of the Vietnam War. The CHAOS program also spied on Americans overseas at the request of the FBI. As a result, the CIA amassed thousands of files on Americans and indexed hundreds of thousands of Americans into its computer records.

As for the FBI, its most blatant transgression against civil liberty was the infamous COINTELPRO, an acronym for "Counterintelligence Program," under which agents of the Bureau set out both to "neutralize" target groups it considered to pose a threat to national security and to "disrupt" the lives of American citizens it deemed to be engaged in activities inimical to the existing social order. COINTELPRO was in operation from 1956 to 1971, when dissidents broke into the FBI field office in Media, Pennsylvania, and stole documents bearing a "COINTELPRO" caption—a word unknown outside the Bureau—which blew the operation's cover and resulted in its cancellation. To begin with, COINTELPRO target groups had been the Communist Party, the Socialist

Workers Party, and the Ku Klux Klan. During the 1960s, black nationalist organizations such as the Black Panther Party and SNCC were targeted, as well as Martin Luther King's nonviolent Southern Christian Leadership Conference, which FBI officials saw fit to characterize as a "Black Nationalist hate group." In 1968, following the student demonstrations at Columbia University, the FBI began to operate against a vague category it described as the "New Left," which included groups ranging from Students for a Democratic Society (SDS) to the whole of Antioch College.

In testimony given before the Senate Select Committee in November of 1975, William C. Sullivan, a former assistant to J. Edgar Hoover, described COINTELPRO as a "rough, tough, dirty business" in which "No holds were barred." That turned out to be something of an understatement. FBI agents routinely sent out dozens of anonymous letters, known as "snitch jackets," which engendered internecine strife in black and student target groups by falsely labeling leading members as police informants. Another favorite ploy of COINTELPRO operatives was to accuse targeted individuals of sexual misconduct. Typical was a letter signed by "A God-fearing klanswoman" and sent in 1966 by agents of the Richmond (Virginia) field office to the wife of a Grand Dragon of the Ku Klux Klan, telling her that her husband was committing adultery with a woman named Ruby, who has "lustfilled eyes and smart aleck figure." A letter signed by "A Soul Sister" and sent in 1970 by agents in the St. Louis field office to the husband of a woman who was an officer in a biracial activist group, suggested, "your old lady doesn't get enough at home or she wouldn't be shucking and jiving with our Black Men. . . ."

Some equally distasteful methods were used on Dr. Martin Luther King Jr., whom the FBI had been keeping a watch on since 1957 and had designated as a person who was to be rounded up and detained in the event of a "national emergency." King was under heavy FBI surveillance from the autumn of 1963 until his assassination in March of 1968, and was the target of an FBI smear campaign during that whole four-and-a-half-year period. Wiretaps, initially approved by Attorney General Robert F. Kennedy on the grounds that some of King's advisers might be communists, were maintained by the Bureau on King's home telephone, and FBI agents routinely installed microphones in King's hotel and motel rooms in what Bureau memoranda acknowledged was an attempt to obtain information about his sexual activities that could be used to discredit him as the leader of the civil rights movement. Around the time the wiretaps were installed in October of 1963, the FBI distributed a monograph containing a personal attack on King's moral character to the attorney general, the White House, the CIA, the State Department, and the Defense Department and its intelligence agencies. In December of 1963, shortly before *Time* named King as its "Man of the Year," FBI agents at Bureau headquarters in Washington, D.C., discussed ways of gathering information to discredit him, which included "placing a good looking female plant in King's office."

In testimony before the Select Committee on Intelligence Activities, some of Robert Kennedy's associates—among them former attorney general Nicholas Katzenbach, former assistant attorney general Burke Marshall, and Bill Moyers, a former special assistant to President Johnson—tried to deny that Kennedy had known about the microphone surveillance of King's hotel rooms. Their denials were disingenuous, to say the least. Particularly disingenuous was the testimony given to the committee in 1976 by Moyers, who claimed not to have known that the FBI was bugging King's hotel rooms, but admitted that he should have assumed this was the case "unless there was an informer in Martin Luther King's presence a good bit of the time." In any event, an eight-page "Top Secret" summary of King's hotel-room conversations, which the FBI had sent to Kennedy in March of 1964, made it perfectly clear that microphones could have been the only source of such information.

In November of 1964, Hoover stepped up the FBI vendetta against King by describing him to a group of women reporters as the "most notorious liar" in the nation. Shortly thereafter, he ordered Alan Belmont, one of his chief assistants, to see that a tape recording of King's hotel conversations was mailed to Coretta King, in order to precipitate a marital rift and separation that might diminish King's stature in the civil rights movement. A few days later, a tape that had been sterilized to prevent its being traced to the Bureau was sent to King himself at the Atlanta headquarters of the Southern Christian Leadership Conference. A letter accompanying it began by saying, "King, look into your heart," and ended by telling him that "there is but one way out for you" and, "You better take it before your filthy fraudulent self is bared to the nation." Not surprisingly, King and his associates—among them Andrew Young—concluded that the letter was not only a threat to expose King just as he was about to receive the Nobel Peace Prize, but also an attempt to prevail upon him to commit suicide.

Because the authors of the Select Committee's report felt obliged to protect the privacy of hundreds of citizens whom the FBI had smeared, the document has an ambiguous and sterile tone. Take, for example, the following passage from the section that describes how the Bureau operated against Hollywood entertainment personalities who spoke out in favor of the Black Panther Party or associated with its members: "When the FBI learned that one well-known Hollywood actress had become pregnant during an affair with a BPP member, it reported this information to a famous Hollywood gossip columnist in the form of an anonymous letter. The story was used by the Hollywood columnist."

Those two sentences are the only reference in the entire report to the Bureau's campaign to discredit Jean Seberg, whom Donald Stewart, the son of Donald Ogden Stewart and a colleague of mine at *The New Yorker,* brought to our apartment for drinks around the time that Bill Collins paid his unexpected but not impromptu visit to my office, in 1963. She was a small, lovely woman in her middle twenties, with wide-spaced blue-green eyes and sandy, close-cropped hair—a leftover from her much heralded film debut in the title role of Otto Preminger's *Saint Joan*—and she wore a fashionably short skirt, a sweater, flats, and almost no makeup. She had recently appeared with Jean-Paul Belmondo in *Breathless*—a film in which she played a flaky expatriate girl who sells the *Herald Tribune* on the streets of Paris—and when Malabar and I complimented her upon her performance in it, she murmured a few words of thanks and seemed relieved when the conversation shifted to another topic. During the hour or so of her visit, she said very little, though when she did speak it was with intelligence and charm, and we were left with the impression of a tentative woman—unsure of herself and uncertain of her future—someone who seemed slightly misplaced.

Stewart married an Italian photographer soon after that, and I never saw Jean Seberg again, not even in the movies. Nor did I hear of the rumor that FBI agents succeeded in planting in Joyce Haber's gossip column that ran in the *Los Angeles Times* on May 19, 1970, or read the updated version that appeared in the "Newsmakers" section of *Newsweek* on August 24. The story in *Newsweek* had it that Seberg, who was expecting her second child, had not been made pregnant by her husband, Romain Gary—the French novelist and diplomat from whom she had been separated for nearly two years and was in the process of divorcing—but by a high-ranking member of the Black Panther Party, whom she had met in Los Angeles, where she and Gary had lived off and on for a number of years, and where she had become active in raising money for black organizations, including the Panthers. As it happened, the FBI hounds had their facts askew. The truth of the matter was that Seberg was not pregnant by the black activist Hakim Abdullah Jamal, a COINTELPRO target with whom she had fallen in love in 1969, but as the result of a brief fling with a young Mexican student revolutionary she had met while making a film in Durango in the winter of 1970.

The first I remember hearing about any of this was in September of 1979, when I read Seberg's obituary in the *New York Times*. The obituary said that the actress, who was forty years old and suffering from depression, had killed herself with an overdose of barbiturates. Her decomposed body had been found some ten days after she had disappeared, in the backseat of her car, which had been parked in a fashionable district of Paris. According to the *Times,* Seberg and Gary had separated following reports in a "gossip magazine" that Gary was not the father of the child she was expecting.

The discovery of Seberg's body was followed by a series of stunning disclosures. A day or two later, Gary held a press conference in which he charged that her life had been destroyed by the FBI. Gary said that when Seberg had read the rumor planted by the Bureau in *Newsweek,* she had become distraught, gone into labor, and delivered a premature baby girl, who had died two days later. He went on to say that the baby was his—he knew it was not, of course, but had assumed fatherhood in order to protect his wife—and that Seberg had tried to commit suicide every year on the anniversary of its death. Fifteen months later, he committed suicide by shooting himself in the head.

Following Gary's press conference, William H. Webster, the Bureau's director, acknowledged that the FBI had planted the rumor to discredit Seberg. He offered no apology, but stated that "the days when the FBI used derogatory information to combat advocates of unpopular causes have long since passed," adding, "We are out of that business forever." His admission and other statements made the front pages of the *New York Times,* the *Los Angeles Times,* and other major newspapers across the nation. Many of the accounts said that FBI officials had sought to destroy Seberg's reputation because they believed her to be supporting black nationalist groups, and most of them quoted from an FBI memorandum, dated April 27, 1970, which had been sent from the Bureau's Los Angeles office to the Washington, D.C., office of its director, J. Edgar Hoover. The memo requested Hoover's permission to plant the rumor about Seberg's pregnancy with gossip columnists in the Los Angeles area, declaring that this would "cause her embarrassment and serve to cheapen her image with the general public." It went on to assure Hoover that if the smear campaign were approved, the "usual procedures" would be taken by the Los Angeles division to preclude identification of the Bureau as its source. A responding memo from the director's office not only approved of the plan, but also suggested a refinement, recommending that "it would be better to wait approximately two additional months until Seberg's pregnancy would be obvious to everyone."

As might be expected, a flurry of stories and editorials followed on the heels of Webster's belated 1979 disclosures. Most of the editorials inveighed against the Bureau's misconduct and called for reform, but none of them called for punishment of the responsible officials. Indeed, an editorial in the *New York Times* placed the whole business in the context of the Cold War by pointing out that the FBI had "suspicions that black nationalism and student radicalism were subject to foreign manipulation."

# 20

## Complicated Issues

By the time of Jean Seberg's suicide, I had been specializing for nearly a decade in stories about occupational and environmental health hazards. The five-part series on asbestos had been followed by an article about the depletion of the earth's ozone layer by man-made chlorofluorocarbon chemicals that had achieved widespread use as aerosol propellants and as coolants in refrigerators and air conditioners, and by a two-part series on the hazard of exposure to microwave and radio frequency radiation. In both instances, the industries involved had concocted public relations slogans similar to the one that had been invented by the asbestos manufacturers to convince people that inhaling asbestos was no more dangerous than "digging in your garden."

Officials of E. I. du Pont de Nemours, the world's leading producer of chlorofluorocarbons for more than forty years, insisted that nothing should be done to protect the ozone layer until there was actual proof that chlorofluorocarbons were destroying it—a convenient prerequisite considering the fact that there was then no way to measure the ozone layer, which is situated in the stratosphere some thirty miles above the earth. Du Pont officials assured the Congress, however, that if "credible evidence" should be developed to show that chlorofluorocarbons were depleting the ozone layer (thus allowing increased levels of ultraviolet radiation to reach earth and pose a threat to human health), then du Pont would cease to manufacture them.

What these officials were suggesting, of course, was that du Pont's chemicals should be considered innocent until proven guilty beyond a reasonable doubt. Not surprisingly, no one in Congress had the temerity to tell them that the chemicals had not been granted constitutional rights and were thus not entitled to the presumption of innocence. As a result, du Pont was allowed to conduct a futile search for "credible evidence" until satellite measurements conducted by the National Aeronautics and Space Administration showed that the chlorofluorocarbons had caused staggering losses of ozone above the Antarctic subcontinent and over the entire Northern Hemisphere. By that time, fourteen years had passed and some fourteen million additional tons of chlorofluorocarbons had made their way into the atmosphere, joining the ten million tons of the stuff already estimated to be there, all of which will continue to deplete the ozone layer throughout the twenty-first century and well into the twenty-second, causing tens of millions of excess cases of skin cancer here on earth and God only knows what other problems.

The two-part series on microwave and radio-frequency radiation focused on the health hazards created by the emissions from radar, various military weapons systems, television and radio broadcast transmitters, and other communications equipment, whose proliferation since the Second World War had been such that by 1971 electromagnetic radiation levels in New York and other cities were estimated to be one hundred to two hundred million times as great as the natural radiation background provided by the sun. (These urban background levels have been elevated considerably since then by the installation of tens of thousands of cellular telephone towers and other microwave-emitting devices in and near cities throughout the nation.) Not only was there considerable medical and scientific evidence on hand to suggest that such radiation might pose a serious public health hazard, but also an advisory council established by the President's Office of Telecommunications Policy had warned that the levels in and around American cities might "already be biologically significant." To counter any apprehension this assessment might create, officials and paid consultants of the electronic industry had gone about insisting to the press and Congress that the danger was "about the same as the likelihood of getting a skin tan from moonlight."

The articles about the microwave hazard were published in *The New Yorker* in December of 1976. The first one went into the history of microwave radiation and its capacity to cause cataracts and other injury. It described how the three branches of the armed services and several large electronics companies had for more than twenty years financed and directed virtually all of the research into the biological effects of microwaves, and how the military and industry had gone about suppressing medical and scientific evidence that such radiation could be harmful to human health. The second article, which appeared the following week, dealt in detail with the situation at the American Embassy on Tchaikovsky Street, in Moscow, into which the Soviets had been beaming low-level microwave radiation since the early 1960s, in an apparent effort either to activate listening devices that had been secreted in the walls of the old Chancery building or to alter the behavior of the diplomats who worked there.

The Moscow Embassy story had broken during the previous winter. It had been covered extensively in the press, which reported at the outset that Ambassador Walter J. Stoessel, who was said to have developed a mysterious blood ailment resembling leukemia, had warned embassy staff members that exposure to microwave radiation might result in leukemia, skin cancer, pregnancy problems, and psychological disorders. The staff members, who had never been told by their employer, the State Department, that they were being irradiated with microwaves, were understandably upset. They were scarcely reassured when President Gerald Ford, who was campaigning in the New Hampshire presidential primary, refused to discuss the situation at the embassy, or when a State Department spokesman, who declared that stories about Ambassador Stoessel's health were inaccurate and misleading, insisted that it would "not be appropriate to comment specifically on the Ambassador's health or on that of any other individual." Nor were their spirits lifted when they learned that two former ambassadors to Moscow—Charles Bohlen and Llewellyn Thompson—had died of cancer in recent years, and that Llewellyn had succumbed to leukemia. Or when they discovered that their medical records and those of their families were under review, that their white blood cell counts were going to be taken, and that two children living at the embassy had been sent to the United States because of abnormal blood conditions. Or when they were told that the aluminum screens being installed in the middle of the winter on the windows of the Chancery were supposed to deflect microwave radiation and prevent it from penetrating the building. Indeed, they sent a bitterly worded telegram to Secretary of State Henry Kissinger demanding to know why they had not been informed of the microwave hazard earlier; why the screens had not been installed sooner; and whether any previous medical tests conducted on embassy employees had played a part in the State Department's belated acknowledgment of the situation.

During the spring of 1976, the State Department held a series of closed briefings that were designed to allay the anxiety and soothe the anger of its Moscow employees. In April, a reporter for the Associated Press obtained a copy of a confidential paper used in these briefings, which stated that the Department had not informed its employees about the situation because it wished to avoid "unwarranted apprehension on the part of those assigned to Moscow." In May, newspapers across the nation reported that during the late 1960s the Advanced Research Projects Agency—a secret organization in the Department of Defense—had directed "Project Pandora," a highly classified study of the low-level radiation that was then being beamed into the embassy. In June, it came to light that as part of Project Pandora physicians under contract to the State Department had secretly tested female employees returning from the Moscow Embassy for genetic damage—all the while misleading them into thinking that the tests were being conducted for other reasons—and had found serious chromosomal abnormalities in a number of women, who were never informed that their condition might be linked to their exposure to microwave radiation.

Later that summer, the State Department signed a $300,000 contract with Johns Hopkins University for an epidemiological study to determine whether the irradiation of the embassy had caused any adverse health effects in the employees there. In September, Ambassador Stoessel left Moscow because of ill health and was reassigned as ambassador to the Federal Republic of Germany, in Bonn. When he was nowhere to be seen at his new post, there was a rumor that he had gone to Zurich to undergo special treatments and have his blood replaced.

My own article on what had taken place at the Moscow Embassy suggested that the State Department's handling of the affair was part and parcel of a cover-up that had been going on for years. During the week of its publication, I received a letter postmarked "Washington, D.C.," which bore no return address but contained a copy of a confidential cable sent to the embassy by Secretary of State Kissinger, who had earlier refused to comment on the situation there, saying that it involved "many complicated issues." The text of the cable consisted of nine questions that the secretary and his colleagues at the State Department thought embassy staff members might ask, should they read the article, followed by nine answers that were to be given by a State Department spokesman, should the questions be asked. Suffice it to say, the questions were self-serving and the answers a mixture of denial and obfuscation. For example, if asked about Ambassador Stoessel's health and whether it had improved since he had left Moscow, the spokesman was instructed to reply that "Ambassador Stoessel is on duty in Bonn and I have nothing to add to my earlier comments."

A day or two after receiving the copy of Kissinger's cable, I received telephone calls from several people in Washington, D.C., whom I had interviewed for my article. Among them were an official of the AFL-CIO, a congressional staff member, and a scientist working for the Food and Drug Administration's Bureau of Radiological Health. All of them wished me to know that they had been interviewed by agents of the FBI, who wanted to know if they knew the names of other persons to whom I might have spoken concerning the microwave-radiation problem. Since the involvement of the Bureau made it obvious that my article had touched some official nerve, I concluded that there must be more to the story than what I had written. For that reason, I arranged to send my articles and the Kissinger cable, as well as word of the FBI's curiosity, to half a dozen publishers to see if they might be interested in bringing out a book on the subject. When several of them turned out to be so inclined, I accepted the best offer and, after signing a contract, resumed work on the story.

While I was conducting research during the winter and spring of 1977, a number of people who had either read or heard about my articles came forward to give me additional information about the cover-up of the microwave hazard that had been carried out over the years by the military, the intelligence community, and various defense contractors. At the same time, a slew of documents bearing upon the same subject came over the transom or, more precisely, were sent through the mail by anonymous donors. In short order, I learned that in 1966 scientists working on Project Pandora at the Walter Reed Army Institute of Research, in Washington, D.C., had found that monkeys irradiated with microwaves of the same frequency as those beamed into the Moscow Embassy exhibited significantly diminished ability to perform simple lever-pressing tasks. I learned that in 1969 the navy had secretly performed blood studies and other tests on crew members of the aircraft carrier USS Saratoga, in an effort to determine whether they had suffered biological damage as a result of their exposure to the microwave radiation emitted by the ship's radars. I also learned that an extremely high rate of birth defects had occurred during the late 1960s and early 1970s among babies delivered by women at the Lyster Army Hospital at Fort Rucker, Alabama, where thousands of helicopter pilots training for service in Vietnam were heavily exposed to microwave radiation emanating from dozens of ground-controlled approach radars. In addition, I discovered that during this same period there had been an outbreak of leukemia and other cancer among a handful of technicians, who had been employed by the Air Force Weapons Laboratory and the Boeing Company to test the effects of electromagnetic pulse—a term to describe the burst of radiant energy known to accompany a nuclear explosion in the atmosphere—on the guidance-and-control systems of Minuteman intercontinental ballistic missiles that had been buried in underground silos in Montana.

Some of the stuff I learned during my research for the book seemed pretty far-out at the time. One fine morning in the spring of 1977, I drove from Manhattan to Moorestown, New Jersey, where the navy operated a huge fifteen-story experimental radar that was situated within sight of the New Jersey Turnpike. The radar, which had been built by RCA, was covered with a white plastic faceted dome that made it look like a giant golf ball. I spent the rest of the day talking with residents of the area, who told me that signals emanating from the device not only were interfering with reception on television sets and impeding the operation of record players, tape recorders, garage-door openers, and radio-controlled model airplanes, but also were disrupting cardiac pacemakers, with the result that a number of elderly people had collapsed at the wheel and gone off the road while driving past the radar on the turnpike. The navy denied everything, of course, but that was before commercial airline pilots found it necessary to instruct their passengers not to use cellular telephones or lap-top computers on take-off or landing, because the weak signals emitted by such gadgets can interfere with the operation of vital electronic equipment on aircraft.

Even stranger were stories I heard about the navy's experimental use of a high-voltage transmission line in Oregon as a giant antenna for broadcasting extra-low-frequency (ELF) electromagnetic fields into the ionosphere—a region of electrically charged particles in the upper atmosphere. The experiments were conducted under the cover of darkness to deceive the public, and they enabled the navy to test the theory that ELF fields, which were known to be capable of penetrating seawater, could be reflected into the oceans from the ionosphere and used to communicate with deeply submerged nuclear submarines. They are said to have caused dozens of dazed citizens living in and around the city of Eugene in homes equipped with cable-ceiling heating to come bolt awake in the middle of the night with their hair standing on end.

In retrospect, I realize that the reason I happened with such apparent ease upon so many classified Cold War projects was because my research was aimed at finding out what I could about the biological effects of microwave and other electromagnetic radiation—an indirect approach that the guardians of the nation's secrets, who had geared themselves to detect and thwart the efforts of Soviet and Eastern European spies, had not thought to defend against. What I should have realized at the time was that the inquiries made by government agents following the publication of my revelations about the Moscow Embassy were prelude to the higher level of scrutiny I would come under after learning that high-power electron-beam weapons thought to be capable of destroying incoming missile warheads at great distances had been under development at the Naval Weapons Laboratory in Dahlgren, Virginia, for nearly a decade, and that high-energy laser weapons had been under development at the Lawrence Livermore Laboratory for even longer, and that both of these programs posed serious health risks to the scientists who were working on them.

The health hazard at the Livermore Laboratory, which was managed for the Department of Energy by the University of California, subsequently provided a classic story of Cold War cover-up. A year or so later, when I was in San Francisco on a promotional tour for my book, unconfirmed reports from Livermore indicated that an unusually high number of scientists there had developed and died of malignant melanoma—a virulent and often fatal form of skin cancer usually caused by exposure to ultraviolet radiation from the sun. At the time, a spokesman for the laboratory suggested that the cancer outbreak had been caused by ultraviolet rays pouring through a hole in the ozone layer above Livermore, which had been opened up by ozone-depleting chlorofluorocarbon chemicals. The idea that the chlorofluorocarbons could have acted so selectively was, of course, absurd, but when the melanoma cluster was widely reported in the press some years later—together with word that the widow of one of the dead scientists was suing the laboratory for several million dollars—laboratory officials continued to blame the intense California sunshine. Several years after that, a British physicist who had worked at Livermore told me that the dead scientists had been exposed to ionizing radiation emitted by the highly classified X-ray laser that Edward Teller and his colleagues had made the centerpiece of Star Wars, and that the government had made large out-of-court settlements with their survivors in return for their silence.

# 21

## A Phrase with an Echo

By the time I heard that electron-beam weapons were under development at Livermore, the military had embarked upon a concerted campaign to convince Congress that the bomber gap of the Eisenhower years and the missile gap of the Kennedy era had been supplanted by a gap in the development of directed-energy weapons, which is what electron-beam weapons were called before Ronald Reagan persuaded a legion of fellow filmgoers to assist the nation's slide toward bankruptcy by financing the $36 billion Rube Goldberg scheme known as Strategic Defense Initiative, or Star Wars. Reports that the Soviets had used high-energy lasers to "blind" the infrared sensors of the air force's early warning satellites—the sensors were, in fact, simply reacting to some large fires that had broken out on a trans-Siberian gas pipeline—were followed by dire warnings that the Reds were developing orbital laser weapons capable of knocking out our intercontinental ballistic missiles even as they were being launched. A story in the *New York Times* reported that the Soviet particle-beam program was comparable to the Manhattan Project with which the United States had developed the atomic bomb during the Second World War. In May of 1977, the magazine *Science* ran a piece that described the revelations about the Soviet lead in the development of directed-energy weapons as "the sensation of the week in Washington," and it went on to say that "Congressmen have received secret briefings, the CIA has been moved to issue one of its infrequent statements, and there has even been a presidential assurance that the nation is not in jeopardy."

The Department of Defense was, of course, strumming the media as if they were a guitar, and all the hoopla was simply designed to drum up public apprehension and therefore continued congressional support for a directed-energy program that had been in full swing for at least a decade, as well as to fool the Soviets about how far it had progressed.

Ample proof of this could be found in the reports, memoranda, and research papers that were stacked in piles on the floor of the study and bedroom of my Greenwich Village apartment. By now, of course, my inquiries had taken me far afield from the realm of biology, where they had begun, and into the byzantine corridors of the technological paranoia that characterized so much of the Cold War. But having got this far into the maze, I could see no way out other than to finish the book for which I was under contract and submit it to the publisher. This I did during the month of May, and when it was done and handed in—I called it *The Zapping of America*—I got into my car and drove to Boston to see my children.

It was Memorial Day weekend. I had by then been divorced for almost seven years, and the mother of my children—a boy who was almost thirteen and a girl who was eleven—had remarried and was living with them and her new husband in Brookline, Massachusetts. My own mother and my stepfather lived not far away on the North Shore, and they owned a summer cottage in West Gloucester, at the mouth of the Essex River, where I had made arrangements to take the kids. The weather was unseasonably warm, and on Saturday we rowed up the river in my stepfather's skiff, found some wild asparagus growing on a hummock in the salt marsh, and caught and fileted a bunch of flounder, which we cooked for supper. On Sunday evening, I drove back to Brookline, and after dropping them off at their mother's house, I continued on down to New York City.

When I arrived at the brownstone in which I lived, on Twelfth Street, it was after midnight, and what with the sun and the rowing and fishing and driving and all, I was tired. Luckily, I found a parking spot almost in front of the building, and within a few minutes I had let myself in, using a set of hollow cylindrical keys that fit some burglar-proof locks that had been installed on the outer door and the foyer door by my landlord, who lived on the third floor. Once inside, I climbed some carpeted stairs, unlocked the door to my own apartment, which occupied the whole of the second floor, and entered my living room. As soon as I turned on the overhead light by the doorway, I had an impression that something was out of place, but as I stood there, facing a fireplace that was flanked by ceiling-to-floor bookshelves, I could not tell what it was. After looking about for a second or two, I walked into the bedroom and unpacked my bag; then I went into the kitchen and fetched a beer from the refrigerator.

When I entered the living room again, I was struck at once with the same impression—that something was not as it had been when I had left for Boston, three days earlier. Whatever it was, however, was vague, fleeting, almost imperceptible. I decided that I was perhaps more tired than I realized. I sat down on the sofa at my usual end, switched on the reading lamp, and, after taking a sip of beer, flipped through the mail. When I looked up a few moments later, I became aware that the bas-relief on the facade of the opposite wall—a bas-relief formed by the glossy, slightly convex book spines that lined the shelves on either side of the fireplace—was not reflecting light at the angles to which I had become accustomed during the half-dozen years I had lived in the apartment and had sat reading on that sofa, but was giving off a new and different lustre.

Since I was a housekeeper of decidedly average diligence, the cleaning lady, who came twice a month, was so busy with such remedial tasks as scrubbing the kitchen and bathroom floors and vacuuming the living room and bedroom rugs, that to my knowledge she had never dusted the books. Moreover, since I had not only read but also reread most of the volumes in my library, they had remained undisturbed for a considerable period of time. Therefore, it was not difficult for me to conclude once I had crossed the room and found fresh tracings in the layer of dust that coated the exposed surfaces of every shelf that the books had all been removed and replaced.

The possibility that someone had been in my apartment was profoundly disturbing. Why he or she had been there was something else again. Since nothing was missing, and since nothing except my books showed signs of having been disturbed, I reasoned that whoever might have entered the flat had been looking for something that could be hidden between the pages or bindings of books, which, of course, could only be money or papers. And since a gold watch and a pair of gold cufflinks were exactly where I had left them on the dresser of my bedroom, it seemed unlikely that money was the object of the search. As it happened, there was a false ceiling in the hallway that led from the living room to the bedroom and study, and a small compartment above it that was designed to store luggage, and, just as a precaution, whenever I left the apartment for any extended period of time that spring, I used it to squirrel away the manuscript of my book and the most sensitive of the documents in my pile of research. So I could rest assured that if people had, in fact, broken into my flat and searched through my belongings, they had probably not found anything compromising. With that comforting thought, I went to bed and fell asleep.

I awoke to find myself troubled by the idea that my home might have been invaded, but by no means convinced that this had actually happened. After all, the outer and foyer doors of the house were equipped with pick-proof locks, and I was almost certain that none of my fellow residents would have allowed any strangers to enter the premises. I knew them all, of course. My landlord, an elderly Viennese gentleman named Linzner, who was known to all of us in the building as Izzy, lived with his wife Maria on the floor above me; the basement apartment was occupied by her sister Roberta; the ground floor was rented by a couple who spent every weekend at their home in the Hamptons; and the fourth floor garret was lived in by a fellow who was a chef at a local restaurant, but had been working in Florida since the beginning of winter and, according to Linzner, had got himself into financial difficulty down there. This meant that only the Linzners or Roberta could have given access to the building that weekend, which seemed highly unlikely since it was they who had installed the pick-proof locks to begin with, and were constantly leaving notes on the foyer radiator reminding the rest of us to double-lock the outer door even if we were just popping out to the grocery store. But the significance of the tracery in the shelf dust was unmistakable, and when I heard the hallway stairs creaking as Linzner began his daily descent to fetch the mail, I opened my door as he passed on the landing, and said good morning.

He was a blue-eyed, white-haired man of nearly eighty, with an erect bearing that marked him as European even before his speech betrayed the accent of the city in which he had been born. As always, he returned my greeting with a formal nod that stopped just short of a bow.

"Izzy," I said, "were you and Maria here this weekend?"

"Except for Saturday when we haff gone to New Jersey to see Maria's nephew," he replied.

"Was anyone else in the house? I mean except for Maria's sister?"

"Nobody," Linzner said as he continued slowly on down the stairs holding tight to the bannister. He had taken only two or three steps when he stopped and turned around. "No, wait, I haff forgotten. There was somebody here. Two friends of the guy upstairs. They came in the morning just as we were leafing. They brought a letter from him with permission to use the flat and they haff had the keys. So I let them in. But why do you ask? Is something wronk?"

"Just curious," I said. "Do you know who they were?"

"They haff said they were with a steamship company, but I forget its name."

"And they stayed overnight?"

"One night only. They left in the morning yesterday. Tell me please, is there something wronk?"

"No, but if you remember the name of the steamship company, be sure to let me know."

"I am already remembering," Linzner said, tapping a forefinger against his temple. "It was the Norway—no, that is not right. But it was something like that. It was the Norwegian—yes, that was it—the Norwegian-American Steamship Line!"

The Norwegian-American Steamship Line. It rang a distant bell, but I could not immediately connect the sound with its source. When I went back inside, I sat for a while on the sofa, staring at the bookshelves and wondering who might have been so thoroughly curious as to remove and replace each of those hundreds of volumes. Then I looked through some old address books until I found Bill Collins' number, and picked up the telephone. However, no sooner had I put my finger to the dial than, seized by caution, I replaced the receiver in its cradle and went off to my office at the magazine to make the call from there.

It took me the whole day to track Collins down. The number he had given me belonged by now to someone who had no idea who he was, so I started calling all over Alexandria—the city hall, the newspaper, the library, the high school, places like that—in an effort to find him. Along the way, I made up a cover story. I told people that I was Collins' long-lost half-brother, and that I needed to locate him because I had some important news about our common past. That wasn't too far off the mark, and since it had the connotation of inheritance, most of the people I spoke with were friendly and cooperative. The trouble was none of them knew Collins. Then, in the middle of the afternoon, I got lucky. A lady in the Parent-Teachers Association remembered him because of the scar on his upper lip, and she also recalled that his wife had sung in the Methodist Church choir. The pastor at the time had since left for another parish, but the present pastor knew where he had gone—Dayton, Ohio—which is how I learned that Collins' wife had also sung with an amateur Gilbert and Sullivan troupe, and how, after a dozen more calls, I found Collins at home that evening in Bethesda, Maryland.

He was as surprised to hear from me as I had been to see him in the anteroom of the magazine fourteen years earlier, and, as we had then, we spent a few minutes catching up. He had suffered a heart attack several years before, but he had made a good recovery and was feeling well. Both of his children were in college, and his wife was working as a medical technician, and, shortly after his heart attack, he had retired from the military establishment (by then he had put in more than twenty years) and had gone to work for one of the large security consulting firms in the Washington area that sweep government offices and conference rooms for electronic bugs and such, known as "Beltway Bandits."

"Don't tell me you were working for the Counterintelligence Corps all those years?" I said.

"No," Collins replied. "Most of that time I was with another outfit."

From the tone of his voice, I knew better than to ask which one, so I told him a bit about myself—the divorce, my children, that kind of thing—and then I asked him if I could pass something by him.

"It's a phrase with an echo I can't quite place," I said.

"Sure," Collins replied. "Shoot."

"The Norwegian-American Steamship Line."

There was a pause, and then Collins started laughing.

I imagined him standing in the house in Bethesda with his head thrown back. "What's so funny?" I said.

"You've been out of circulation," he replied, when he had stifled his mirth. "Don't you remember the names of the covers we and the other agencies used to use?"

"No," I said.

"The big one was Hertz. Hertz U-Drive-It. That was in Havana, Caracas, and other parts of Central and South America."

"I seem to remember the *National Geographic*."

"Them, too," Collins said.

"And what about Norwegian-American?"

"That was the big one for North America," Collins said. "For years and years. But I don't think they're used all that much anymore."

# 22

## Pandora Redux

So now I had a pretty good idea of what had happened. Someone's agents had been keeping an eye on me and monitoring the progress of my research and had become concerned that I was on the track of something, and when they learned that the fellow who lived upstairs was working in Florida, they may have offered to sublet his pad for the weekend. Once inside the house, they could have picked the skeleton-key lock on my apartment door as easily as if they'd had the key itself, and with my landlord and his wife away, they didn't even have to worry about making noise as they searched the place. I imagined them going through the research papers stacked in piles on the bedroom and study floors, and then looking under the mattress and up the flue and in all the other obvious hiding places, before tackling the books on the shelves beside the fireplace. It must have taken them several hours, and the fact that what they had been looking for was right above their noses the whole time in the luggage compartment above the hallway ceiling gave me no little satisfaction. However, the fact that they had violated my private space rankled me no end, and as I rode home on the F train beneath Sixth Avenue, I found myself examining the impassive faces of my fellow passengers for a sideways glance, a furtive look, some small sign that would betray my surveillants' scrutiny and reveal them to me. They, their, them—that was the trouble, of course—I had no idea who "they" were. Nor could I have done anything about it even if I had known who they were. Their impunity was the last straw. By the time I let myself into my apartment, I needed to talk to someone, but even as I sat down on the sofa and reached for the telephone to call a friend, I was seized by the same caution that had sent me uptown to my office earlier in the day. After all, if they had not hesitated to break into my home, why would they think twice before tapping the telephone? On the other hand, if they had tapped my telephone, would they not be inclined to believe what they heard coming over it?

I spent the rest of the evening thinking of ways I might avenge myself upon the faceless inquisitors whom I now had good reason to believe had downgraded my service to the status of a party line. Among the schemes I toyed with was one in which cryptic messages hinting of conspiracy and espionage, and laced with constantly changing venues designed to send any interceptor off on the wildest of goose chases, would be telephoned to me from pay phones. But I soon got busy revising and polishing *The Zapping of America* for the publisher, and by the time that task was finished it was time for me to go to Cape Cod for the month's vacation I spent there each year with my children.

The kids and I had a splendid time—one of the best ever—fishing, sailing, playing tennis, and just hanging out together. What made it special was that I had started to build a modern house for us on some land I'd bought on the outer Cape a few years earlier—the kids would call it "the house that Zap built"—and soon we were so engrossed in our plans for the future that I forgot all about getting even with whoever had broken into my apartment and might now be listening in on my telephone. In fact, by the time I came back to New York I had decided that I didn't want to make any more forays with privileged glimpses into the congealed heart of the Cold War, or to joust any longer with its paranoid devotees, so I let the whole matter drop.

Shortly after my return, I received a telephone call from an aide to Kentucky Senator Wendell H. Ford. The aide berated me for criticizing his employer's failure to challenge the assertion of a physician under contract to the State Department who had testified at a committee hearing presided over by Ford that the only reason screens had been placed on the windows of the Moscow Embassy was to allay anxiety among the employees there. This same physician, who had also worked as a consultant for the CIA and the Defense Department's Advanced Research Project Agency, had been deeply involved in "Project Pandora," and Senator Ford's aide seemed unaware of the implication behind the fact that the criticism he was objecting to could only be found in a book that had not yet gone to the printer and must therefore have been obtained or purloined from the publisher.

In late October, the physician's named appeared on a telegram sent by the State Department to the press secretary at the Moscow Embassy. The telegram noted the impending publication of *The Zapping of America*, and it also instructed the press officer to inform embassy employees that there was no evidence to show that microwave radiation had caused any unusual incidence of cancer among them and to tell them that a forthcoming epidemiological study conducted by researchers at Johns Hopkins University would address this question in detail. A year later, the same physician met with the Johns Hopkins researchers to discuss the draft report of their investigation. He objected to their use of the word "disturbing" to describe their finding that eight out of the eleven deaths that had occurred among women who had worked at the embassy and fifteen out of thirty-one deaths among women in a comparison group had been due to malignant neoplasms. The word was nowhere to be found in the final report that was released a few weeks later. The final version said that "a relatively high proportion of cancer deaths" had been noted among female employees at the embassy and in the women who made up the comparison group, but that "it was not possible to find any satisfactory explanation for this."

There was no wonder in that, because the whole investigation was hopelessly flawed from the start. To begin with, the State Department's records of people who had served in foreign embassies were so poorly maintained that the the Johns Hopkins researchers encountered difficulty in even identifying the population they were supposed to study. In addition, they were unable to obtain death certificates for one third of the embassy employees who were no longer alive, and only a third of the living employees responded to a health questionnaire they were sent in the mail. Even after conducting an extensive telephone survey, the researchers were able to obtain health histories only on less than half of the people who had served at the embassy. Nor could they find any records to indicate where individual employees had lived or worked, so that individual levels of exposure to microwave radiation could be ascertained. To give some idea of what they were up against, a list compiled under "Project Pandora" of the names, dates of service, and estimated microwave exposure of more than three hundred people who had served at the embassy during the 1960s was withheld by the State Department until after they had completed collecting the data for their study, with the result that the crucial exposure data was not incorporated into it. But the chief flaw of the study lay in the fact that the members of the comparison group—people who were not supposed to have been exposed to microwave radiation—had worked at embassies in other Eastern European countries where microwave surveillance was conducted as a matter of routine.

This meant that instead of comparing apples with oranges, as any decent epidemiological study should be designed to do, the Johns Hopkins researchers had ended up comparing apples with apples. They were not unaware of this. In their draft report, they noted that there had been reports of microwave surveillance at some of the comparison embassies, and that they had been denied access to the data. The State Department physician insisted that this was hearsay, however, so all reference to it was deleted from the final report. Meanwhile, the thirty-two-year-old wife of a thirty-five-year-old Foreign Service officer—he had died that autumn of a brain tumor, she had recently been diagnosed with breast cancer, and both had been stationed at the embassy during the early 1970s—had drawn up a list of more than twenty men and women who had developed cancer after living or working during the late 1960s and early 1970s in the north or central wings of the embassy, which were two areas the State Department had previously acknowledged to be the chief targets of microwave surveillance. The Foreign Service officer's wife had retained an attorney with the idea of filing a lawsuit for damages against the State Department, but after the Johns Hopkins study was released and newspapers across the nation ran articles stating that its results were inconclusive, the attorney was unable to find any expert medical witnesses to testify in her behalf, and she was forced to drop the case.

In the spring of 1979, the lawyer for a twenty-nine-year-old marine guard, who had been stationed at the embassy during the late 1960s and was now suffering lymphoma, invited me to meet with his client, who was not expected to live much longer. The attorney was hoping that I might be able to provide information that would help with a lawsuit he was hoping to bring against the State Department. I told him what I could. His client told me that he remembered seeing technicians wearing silver-colored radiation-hazard suits with full hoods, face masks, and wire-mesh goggles on the eighth floor of the embassy, just below Ambassador Llewellyn Thompson's office. When I asked him what was up there, he said he had no idea, because he was never allowed inside. His lawsuit was thrown out of court because of the Feres Doctrine, under which servicemen are not allowed to sue the government, and he died around the time the obituaries of Jean Seberg appeared in the newspapers. Before he died, he put me in touch with two other marines, who had become ill after serving as guards at the embassy during the late 1960s and early 1970s. One of them was suffering from Hodgkin's disease, and the other had developed cancer of the bowel. The one with Hodgkin's also remembered seeing people wearing radiation-hazard suits on the eighth floor.

The fact that two different marines recalled such a thing brought to mind something my sister had told me two years earlier, when she had read the article about the Moscow Embassy I had written for *The New Yorker*. She told me that during the two years she had worked for the CIA at the Paris Embassy in the early 1960s—a time when, coincidentally, Walter Stoessel had been first secretary there—she had been assigned the task of retrieving special coded material that was transmitted from the Moscow Embassy under the code name "Pandora." The coded material consisted of five-digit numbers on waxy brown paper, and it was printed out by a large machine with many dials that had been installed solely for that purpose in a windowless, sponge-lined vault situated off the office of the assistant chief of station, who was also deputy director of Western Intelligence.

After my sister retrieved the material, it was relayed to Washington by a special channel. Her recollection of the experience was heightened by the fact that she was always locked inside the vault when she gathered the Pandora transmissions from Moscow, and that there was a small fan in there to keep the place from becoming too stuffy. When I asked her why she had been assigned this task, she told me that she was one of the few employees at the station who had been given a "Q" clearance—the kind granted by the Atomic Energy Commission for access to classified data relating to nuclear secrets.

# 23

## Editorial Control

While the government was keeping a lid on what had gone on at the Moscow Embassy, plaintiff attorneys armed with court-issued discovery orders were delving into the secret history of the asbestos industry. As a result, juries across the nation soon learned that asbestos manufacturers had conspired with one another as early as the 1930s to keep their employees in the dark about the hazard of inhaling asbestos. They also learned that it had been Johns-Manville's policy for more than forty years not to tell its workers when their chest X-rays showed evidence of lung scarring, but to let them continue working until they had to quit either as a result of inability to breathe or as a result of death from asbestos lung disease. For example, a memorandum written back in 1949 by Johns-Manville's medical director acknowledged that the lung scarring caused by asbestos inhalation was "irreversible and permanent," but it went on to say that "as long as the man is not disabled it is felt that he should not be told of his condition so that he can live and work in peace and the Company can benefit by his many years of experience."

Not surprisingly, jurors were appalled by the callousness of such deception, and during 1981 and the first half of 1982 no fewer than ten juries in various parts of the nation found Johns-Manville liable for more than $6 million in punitive damages, which are awarded for outrageous and reckless misconduct. By then the company and its insurance carriers had paid out $50 million in compensatory damages to settle 3,400 asbestos-disease lawsuits out of court, and a dozen or so other major defendant insulation manufacturers and their insurers had spent some $550 million in compensation and legal fees. However, thanks to corporate bias on the part of the nation's leading newspapers, the asbestos litigation—the greatest toxic tort litigation in the history of world jurisprudence—had received little coverage. As a result, the American people were largely ignorant of the appalling record of renegade behavior toward workers that had been exhibited by the manufacturers of asbestos insulation—a record that deserves a place in the annals of industrial infamy second only to that of I. G. Farben and other German firms that employed slave labor during World War II.

When any major corporation within the private enterprise system runs into trouble—for whatever reason and no matter how nefarious its conduct—it can almost always count on the economic support or leniency of the Congress and the government. During the Cold War, this was especially true if the corporation in question was deemed to be making a contribution toward the waging of the struggle against Communism. Witness the alacrity with which the government bailed the Lockheed Aircraft Corporation out of its financial difficulties in 1984—a year in which the company admitted to bribing a prince of the Netherlands and the premier of Japan—and the meager fines dished out by the Pentagon to Boeing, Emerson Electric, Fairchild Industries, General Electric, General Motors, Grumman, GTE, Hughes Aircraft, Loral, LTV/Sierra, Northrup, Raytheon, Rockwell, Teledyne, and dozens of other leading military contractors for offenses that included overcharging for weapons systems, fraudulent testing of weapons systems and parts, contract kickbacks, and illegally obtaining classified Pentagon documents. Nothing, however, comes close to the leniency that was accorded Johns-Manville (now known as Manville Corporation) after August of 1982, when the company sought refuge in Chapter 11 of the federal bankruptcy code from the product-liability and negligence lawsuits that had been filed against it by thousands of diseased, disabled, and dying asbestos workers, and by the survivors of dead asbestos workers, who had been exposed to the company's asbestos insulation products.

Thanks to the Bankruptcy Reform Act passed by Congress in 1978, Chapter 11 is a no-fault system that operates in a manner similar to those that have been designed to deal with dented automobile fenders. Under its provisions, Manville was shielded from further asbestos-disease claims, which not only allowed the company to survive but also to thrive. The sixteen thousand asbestos disease victims who had filed lawsuits against the firm prior to August of 1982 were considered by the bankruptcy court to be merely creditors of the company, and they had no more standing in the bankruptcy proceedings, which dragged on in Dickensian fashion for nearly five years, than did the banks, trucking firms, and suppliers that made up Manville's commercial creditors. In fact, when all was said and done, they had less standing, because Manville's commercial creditors received nearly one hundred cents on the dollar for the monetary debts they were owed, while the asbestos-disease claimants, who now number more than two hundred thousand, are being compensated for their lost health and lives at only about one tenth of the amount they had been receiving in out-of-court settlements and jury verdicts during the years when Manville and other asbestos manufacturers were forced to answer for their conduct in the nation's courts.

Considering the length and breadth of Manville's malfeasance, the outcome of the bankruptcy proceedings must rank as one of the greatest miscarriages of justice against workers in the nation's history, and since more than ten years had passed since I had written about the asbestos tragedy, it seemed appropriate to bring matters up to date. I did so in a four-part series of articles titled "The Asbestos Industry on Trial," which ran in *The New Yorker* in June of 1985, and was published later that year as a book called *Outrageous Misconduct*. The articles and the book not only chronicled the misdeeds of the asbestos manufacturers, but also exposed the gross lack of responsibility that had characterized the actions of some of the nation's leading insurance carriers, who had known all along about the ravages of asbestos disease. As early as 1918, an official of the Prudential Life Insurance Company—now the nation's wealthiest life insurance company—had acknowledged in a Labor Department publication that it had become the standard practice of many carriers not to issue life insurance policies to asbestos workers because of the "assumed health injurious conditions" that existed in the asbestos industry. In 1934, the Aetna Life Insurance Company—now the nation's largest publicly held multiple-line carrier—ignored a warning about the long-term disease hazard posed by asbestos that was issued by its own surgeon general. In 1935, the medical director of Metropolitan Life—then the largest life insurance company in the United States—bowed to pressure from the asbestos industry and softened the conclusions about asbestos disease in a report he had written for the United States Public Health Service.

Suffice it to say, if at any point along the way, Aetna, Travelers, Commercial Union, Liberty Mutual, INA, Hartford, Home, Lloyd's, or any of the other major product-liability insurers of the asbestos industry had gone public with their inside knowledge, they might have been able to save tens of thousands of lives and untold suffering and pain. Such disclosure, however, would have encouraged claims and damage suits and run counter to basic insurance company practice, which is to write as much coverage as possible and as cheaply as possible, in order to reap a rich harvest of policy premiums that, when invested, will return enough money to pay for future claims and make a profit for the company. So the insurers of the asbestos industry decided to say nothing, look the other way, and, when necessary, pay asbestos claims quietly out of court. This strategy, which they pursued for decades, enabled them to take in millions of dollars in premiums by selling billions of dollars' worth of product-liability insurance, and to remain confident as they did so that asbestos claims and underwriting costs could be kept to a minimum. At the same time, it helped to conceal behind a dam of silence a vast and ever-increasing reservoir of disease, disability, and death. Only after changes in tort law enabled the widow of an asbestos worker named Clarence Borel to prevail in a landmark 1971 failure-to-warn lawsuit against the leading manufacturers of asbestos insulation did the dam give way and the deluge of litigation that would ultimately cost insurance carriers tens of billions of dollars come cascading down upon their heads.

Not surprisingly, the medical profession also bears a large measure of responsibility for the asbestos debacle, which has already claimed the lives of more than half a million American workers, and which will kill another three hundred thousand over the next thirty years. If a significant number of the physicians who knew about the asbestos-disease hazard had spoken out in timely fashion, they might have blown the lid off the cover-up and spared thousands of lives. Instead, most doctors remained silent, thus acting in the time-honored tradition of the medical profession, whose members by and large continue to avoid speaking out on important matters of occupational and environmental health out of elitist deference to an old-boy network that precludes them from voicing criticism either of one another or of a private enterprise system that, by befouling the ambient air and drinking water supplies with toxic chemicals and other hazardous agents, has created public health problems of staggering magnitude for the entire nation.

In any event, because of timidity on the part of doctors, obtuseness on the part of public health officials, and collusion on the part of the insurance industry, asbestos manufacturers were able to conduct a highly successful cover-up of medical and scientific knowledge about asbestos disease during the forty-year period between 1930 and 1970. Only the uncompromising commitment of Dr. Selikoff, who worked tirelessly to make his findings known, and the hard work of a handful of dedicated trial lawyers, who proceeded to unearth a mountain of evidence to support the initial allegations of the cover-up that were published in *The New Yorker,* brought to light the truth about the suffering wrought by the manufacturers of asbestos upon hundreds of thousands of unsuspecting workers in the United States. It was a truth, like the truth Emile Zola wrote about in *J'Accuse,* that had for years been buried underground, where, growing and gathering force, it had been waiting to burst forth.

As the legal noose began to tighten around the necks of the asbestos manufacturers during the late 1970s and early 1980s, there was no shortage of politicians to help them out. In 1977, Representative Millicent Fenwick, an aristocratic, pipe-smoking Republican from New Jersey, whose congressional district included the town of Manville—home of the largest asbestos manufacturing complex in the nation, as well as the nation's largest concentration of asbestos-disease cases—introduced a bill in Congress that sought to bar victims of asbestos disease from bringing product-liability or other common-law tort actions against the asbestos industry. Fenwick's bill, which was said to have been written with the assistance of Johns-Manville's legal staff, proposed to compensate claimants from a federally administered central fund that would have provided an asbestos worker, with a dependent wife and two children who could prove that he was totally disabled by asbestos disease, with the grand total of $1,000 a month.

In 1980 and again in 1981—a time when juries were assessing punitive damages against Johns-Manville for its misdeeds—Senator Gary Hart, a Democrat from Colorado, where the company had moved its headquarters from New York City, introduced a bill that was even more favorable to the industry than Fenwick's. Hart's measure, which was drafted after consultation between his staff and Manville's Washington lobbyists, was widely known in Congress as "the Johns-Manville bailout bill." It not only proposed to bar victims of asbestos disease from filing lawsuits under the tort system, but also left the administration of asbestos-compensation claims with the states, which had always required diseased workers or the survivors of workers who had died to prove their claims in adversarial proceedings contested by the asbestos manufacturers and their insurance carriers.

Hart's involvement with Manville blew up into a brouhaha in March of 1984, when I happened to come across his name while glancing through a sworn deposition that had been given for the Manville bankruptcy hearings by John A. McKinney, the company's chief executive officer and board chairman. In his deposition, McKinney acknowledged that he had contributed to Hart's 1980 Senate reelection campaign, and that other Manville officials had been urged to contribute to Hart through the Manville Political Action Committee. This, of course, was not unusual. What was unusual was that McKinney went on to testify that he thought Hart had been a trustee of the Manville PAC.

At the time I came across this strange admission, I was in the middle of writing my series of articles about the travails of the asbestos industry, and Hart had just beaten Walter Mondale in the presidential primary elections in Florida, Massachusetts, and Rhode Island. With the crucial New York primary less than three weeks away, I went to Shawn and suggested that the information I had uncovered about Hart's connection with Manville was too important to hold for publication in the magazine—something that would not occur for many months—and got his permission to write an Op-Ed piece about it for one of the newspapers.

Over the weekend, I turned out a twelve-hundred-word article describing Hart's sponsorship of legislation that would have kept workers with asbestos disease from suing Manville. The piece was written almost entirely from the documentary evidence, which included the text of Hart's proposed bill, what he had told his colleagues when he took the Senate floor to introduce it, what the Federal Election Commission reports had to say about the Manville PAC contributions he had received, and what McKinney had said in his deposition. As for the senator's motive, I suggested that "it appears likely that Hart wanted to shed the liberal image that had followed him from his days as presidential campaign manager for George McGovern in 1972, and to show business interest in Colorado that he was not anti-business."

Once I finished the piece, I had to decide where to submit it. It was easy to eliminate the *Wall Street Journal*—hardly a friend to working men and women—and just as easy to eliminate the *New York Times*. Over the years, coverage of the asbestos saga in the *Times* had been almost nil, and the newspaper's editorial policy on the subject had been nothing short of obtuse. On August 27, 1980—the day after Manville filed for bankruptcy—an editorial writer for the *Times* had found himself sufficiently ignorant of the overwhelming evidence of fraudulent deception of workers engaged in by Manville and other insulation manufacturers to be able to compare the ghastly agony of asbestos lung disease with the manufacturers' fiscal uncertainties. "Asbestos is a tragedy," he wrote, "most of all for the victims and their families but also for the companies, which are being made to pay the price for decisions made long ago."

Having eliminated the *Journal* and the *Times,* I decided to try the piece on the *Washington Post*, only to learn that the *Post* had been running editorials calling upon Congress to step in and bail out the defendant asbestos manufacturers with a federal compensation scheme similar to the one proposed by Hart. In the end, I sent my article off to the Viewpoints editor at *Newsday*—the largest afternoon daily in the nation—and when she telephoned her acceptance I took a cab out to the newspaper's editorial offices on Long Island, where I met with a number of senior editors, including the editorial page editor, to whom I showed the documentary source material for the piece. After reviewing the source material, they told me that they would run the piece in the next day's edition. They also assured me that it would be sent out that same evening on the 250-paper national wire owned by *Newsday*'s parent company, the *Times Mirror* Corporation, which was pleasing news because it guaranteed that the piece would be widely read.

Because I believed the story to be highly sensitive and politically important, I had insisted on making any revisions or deletions in it that might become necessary, and for this reason I stayed at the *Newsday* offices until the piece was locked up and ready to go to press. As I was about to leave, a junior editor took me aside and told me something that, in retrospect, should have troubled me more than it did at the time. He said that the newspaper's Washington bureau chief had thrown a fit in an editorial meeting that morning, claiming that if my piece were published and Hart should receive the Democratic nomination and be elected, *Newsday*'s access to the White House could be severely impaired.

On Friday, March 23, the Op-Ed article appeared in *Newsday* under a banner headline that read, "Is Sen. Gary Hart for Workers or for Big Business?" It was accompanied by an illustration showing a pair of skeletal workers wearing hard hats on their death heads, who flanked a young child standing before a public school. In the piece, I pointed out that millions of Americans would be going to the polls during the next few weeks to vote in primaries in which Senator Hart would be a candidate, and that since hundreds of thousands of them would have been exposed to asbestos, or have relatives and friends who had developed asbestos disease, or children who attended schools that were contaminated with asbestos, they had a right to ask why Hart had sought to protect the companies that were responsible for covering up the hazard.

That same day, the Viewpoints editor wrote me a note thanking me for the piece and informing me that Hart had "made arrangements this very day to come to *Newsday* for lunch on March 27." That evening, she went off on a sailing vacation in the Caribbean, and a funny thing happened to my article on its way to the *Times Mirror* wire service. It never got there. The editorial page director later told *New York* magazine that "Brodeur didn't want his story on the wire because he couldn't have full editorial control over it."

# 24

## Telling It Like It Is

Whatever the real reason for *Newsday*'s failure to put the piece on the national wire, Hart's association with Manville never surfaced as a major issue until the very end of the campaign. Mondale brought the subject up briefly when he debated Hart in Philadelphia, and in passing on another occasion in Texas, but not until the New Jersey primary in June, when he desperately needed a victory to avoid a deadlocked convention in July, did he raise the asbestos issue in a significant manner. At that time, he made a two-hour stopover in Manville, where he met with a number of asbestos-disease victims and promised that, unlike Hart, he would seek to preserve their right to sue the manufacturers whose products had made them sick.

The meeting in Manville received extensive media coverage and gave Mondale's campaign in New Jersey a much needed lift. At the time, some of his supporters wondered why he had waited so long to take political advantage of Hart's link to Manville and his sponsorship of a compensation bill that would have bailed the asbestos industry out of its legal difficulties. What few of them knew was that three of Mondale's closest campaign advisers—people with unrestricted access to the candidate—worked for firms that represented asbestos manufacturers. Michael Berman—Mondale's campaign treasurer and trusted colleague—was a registered lobbyist for the H. K. Porter Company (of Pittsburgh), which was a defendant in thousands of asbestos lawsuits. Anne Wexler, a longtime political adviser to Mondale, and a former assistant to the president during the Carter-Mondale administration, was the chairman of a Washington consulting firm that had been retained by Manville to provide lobbying services for proposed and pending legislation affecting the company. And Richard Moe, a senior political adviser, who had been Mondale's chief of staff during his vice presidency, was not only a member of David Polk and Wardwell, Manville's principal outside legal counsel over the years, but also had lobbied in behalf of Manville in the Congress when changes in the Bankruptcy Reform Act were being considered during the winter and spring of 1984, while the primary elections were being held. During the course of the campaign, there was said to have been much discussion in the Mondale camp over whether to use the asbestos issue against Hart, especially in key industrial states, such as Massachusetts, Pennsylvania, Illinois, and New York. Caution prevailed, however—no doubt because of Mondale's vulnerability to counterattack—and the issue was allowed to lie dormant until a desperate Mondale decided to raise it at the eleventh hour in New Jersey.

What a difference a decade makes! This was the same Walter Mondale who not only had been a leader in the fight to pass the Occupational Safety and Health Act of 1970, but also had personally involved himself in the asbestos controversy three years later by reading my article about the infamous Tyler plant into the *Congressional Record*. At that time, he told his Senate colleagues that the piece deserved their attention "because it represents one of the most frightening accounts I have ever read of unsafe working conditions—in this instance, exposure to asbestos fibers on [the part of] workers." A few weeks later, speaking to the Society for Occupational Safety and Health at the Cosmos Club, he quoted from the same article when he exhorted the members of his audience to increase their efforts to promote workplace safety and health. He went on to declare, "I urge you all—doctors, lawyers, economists, everyone—to tell it like it is with respect to workshop dangers."

During his losing bid for the presidency in the autumn of 1984, Mondale scarcely mentioned the asbestos issue. As for Hart, he did not see fit to answer questions about the subject until early in the summer of 1985, when he appeared as a guest on CNN's "Larry King Live," shortly after the articles that revealed his involvement with Manville appeared in *The New Yorker*. When telephone callers to the show queried him about his acceptance of campaign funds from Manville and his sponsorship of legislation favorable to the firm, Hart responded by denying that he had ever had "any relationship whatsoever with the corporation." He went on to claim that the bill he had proposed was not a bailout measure, but had simply been intended to create a system of administrative remedy similar to workmen's compensation.

When an obliging King asked Hart if the writer of the articles in *The New Yorker* had called him, Hart said, "No, he did not," adding, "There was no effort made so far as I know by the author to verify the facts and information contained in it about my role."

On July 22, Hart wrote a letter to Shawn, complaining that I had made no effort to check my piece with him or his office, and denying that his proposed legislation had been written in consultation with Manville's lobbyists. Shortly thereafter, Martin Baron, chief of the magazine's famous fact-checking department, who had personally verified the accuracy of the material dealing with Hart, wrote a letter of reply in which he informed Hart that he had spoken at length on more than one occasion with members of his staff about his asbestos bill, and that he had had access to an extensive documentary record regarding its provisions. Baron quoted deposition testimony by McKinney that clearly indicated Hart had consulted with Manville's lobbyists prior to writing his bill. He told Hart, "It is unfortunate that your letter contains only the barest acknowledgment of what is perhaps the most important part of the story—the knowledge that the asbestos manufacturers, especially Johns-Manville, and the insurance companies had of the asbestos health hazard decades before it became a public health problem." He went on to remind Hart that this was "all the more unfortunate" because Hart had been informed of Manville's role in the cover-up in a detailed eleven-page letter sent to him in 1980 by the members of a prominent Boulder law firm.

The following month, Hart began to put out feelers that he might make another run for the presidency in 1988. On September 22, his office issued a press release describing a speech he had given in Denver in which he denounced the role being played by political action committees. In this speech, Hart declared that "special interest money is corrupting American politics and preventing the idealism of Americans from being translated into new policies," and that "PACs have made it more difficult for Congress to enact legislative remedies to many social problems." The press release was sent out to newspaper editors across the nation with a handwritten memorandum from Hart that invited their comments.

Most of the nation's newspapers praised Hart's PAC initiative. Only one of them—the *Charleston* (West Virginia) *Gazette*—denounced him outright for his prior ties with Manville. The *Gazette*'s publisher, W. Edward Chilton III, was so outraged by Hart's hypocrisy that he wrote him a letter asking why he had not apologized for sponsoring legislation favorable to Johns-Manville when he knew full well that its officials had been aware of the dangers of asbestos disease since before World War II.

The links that existed between the two leading Democratic candidates for president and the renegade asbestos industry were simply another indication of the extraordinary symbiosis that had taken root during the Cold War between the nation's political leaders and its corporate structure. That such connections could go largely unchallenged reflected the general unwillingness of the American people, who for forty years had been extolled to fear Communism above all else, to pass judgment upon a private enterprise system that they had been conditioned to perceive as providing an essential bulwark against the "evil empire" of the Soviet Union. In the end, a sanctimonious Mondale embarked upon a lucrative practice as a partner in a major Washington law firm (before being named ambassador to Japan), and a troubled Hart dared the *Miami Herald* to investigate his extramarital escapades. It was a telling reflection of what had become of the nation's political ethics that he would be forced to leave public life not for having conspired to deprive disabled and dying asbestos workers of the right to sue their corporate tormentors, but for having taken a blonde who was not his wife to Bimini.

# 25

## Takeover

Several months before the series of articles entitled "The Asbestos Industry on Trial" appeared in *The New Yorker*, the magazine, which had been founded in 1925 by Harold Ross and Raoul Fleischmann and controlled by the Fleischmann family ever since, was sold to Advance Publications, Inc., an $8 billion media conglomerate owned by S. I. Newhouse Jr. and other members of the Newhouse family, who already owned twenty-nine newspapers, several of the nation's largest cable television systems, Random House, Parade Magazine, and Conde Nast, Inc., which publishes *Vanity Fair, Vogue, Mademoiselle,* and several other magazines. It would be difficult to overstate the surprise and consternation that gripped the members of the staff when they learned in January of 1985 that Newhouse was out to buy *The New Yorker*. A few months earlier, he had purchased 17 percent of *The New Yorker*'s outstanding stock, while denying that he had any intention of adding the magazine to his family's communications empire, and staff members had been kept in the dark about the fact that secret negotiations had been under way to sell it to him. By the time the truth came out, the purchase of *The New Yorker* by Advance was virtually a done deal. No one seemed to have any clear idea of what was going on, let alone what to do about it, and the general confusion was enhanced when word trickled back from people who had talked with Shawn that he seemed to know little about the proposed buyout other than what he was being told by Peter Fleischmann (Raoul's son and the magazine's owner) and Fleischmann's lawyers, who were supposedly keeping him up-to-date.

A true and complete account of the takeover of *The New Yorker* and the role Shawn played in it will have to be pieced together by people other than those who were working there at the time. Suffice it to say, many of the staff members considered Shawn to be not only the embodiment of the magazine, but also the greatest editor who ever lived. For my part, during the thirty years I worked for him, I found him to be an extra-ordinarily brilliant, infinitely considerate, unbelievably well-informed, amazingly prescient, deeply secretive, and quintessentially controlling man, who read and gave his stamp of approval to every word and draw-ing that went into the magazine, while at the same time placing enor-mous trust in those of us whose work he deemed suitable for publication by allowing us to decide what projects we wished to undertake.

By the time of the takover, however, he was seventy-seven years old and, though seeming to be as indefatigable as ever, had begun to look his age and was obviously feeling the burden of his years. Moreover, he had either been unable or unwilling to develop a suitable successor. Be-cause of these factors, and in the absence of any clear direction from him, morale at the magazine declined sharply during the week that fol-lowed the news that it was up for sale. Indeed, some senior staff mem-bers were overheard discussing the names of writers by whom they feared they might be replaced if and when a new owner decided to clean house. Then word got out that the magazine's attorney had cau-tioned Shawn not to hold a meeting of the staff members for fear that it might be misunderstood by Newhouse. At that point, I sat down and wrote Shawn a note. I started out by telling him that the atmosphere at *The New Yorker* reminded me of the Fall of France in that there was much talk of capitulation and very little about resistance. I went on to say that this was no time for breast-beating and defeatism, but for "those of us who have been your longtime colleagues to come together, address the choices that loom before us, and speak our minds as con-structively as possible." I ended by calling upon him to hold a meeting of the senior staff as soon as possible.

Flushed and obviously upset, Shawn appeared in my office shortly after I had sent him the note by messenger. "I have no intention of be-coming Petain," he declared.

I assured him that by drawing an analogy with the surrender of the French I had not intended to suggest that he was an appeaser, but went on to tell him that if there were any countermeasures to be taken they had better be taken soon.

At that point, Shawn told me that he had been in touch with a wealthy admirer of the magazine, who he hoped might outbid New-house for it, but he seemed to have little conviction that this would happen. He then described what he had learned from Fleischmann and his attorneys about the status of the negotiations for the proposed sale. His understanding of what was taking place seemed rather vague, and when I asked him what advice he was getting from his own attorney, I was flabbergasted to learn that he had none. When I expressed surprise at this, he told me that he felt no need of legal counsel because he was hoping to persuade Fleischmann to change his mind about selling the magazine. At that juncture, I should have realized that the game was not just in the late innings but, for all intents and purposes, over. Instead, after persuading Shawn that he should have his own attorney, I accepted his invitation to join a twelve-member editorial council made up of senior writers, editors, and cartoonists whom he had designated to advise him on how the editorial department should deal with the proposed takeover.

During the next ten days, the editorial council met in Shawn's office on several occasions to discuss ways in which we could best preserve the magazine's editorial independence. Much of the talk revolved around just what editorial independence meant—a matter upon which agreement proved difficult to reach. Meanwhile, on February 11, Newhouse sent a letter to the magazine's board of directors, offering to buy *The New Yorker* for $125 million. "We recognize that the unique quality of *The New Yorker* is the product of its personnel and of their operating practices and traditions, including the tradition of complete editorial independence," Newhouse wrote. He went on to define editorial independence as "the editors' having total control of the magazine's editorial character, policies, procedures and content." He then assured the board members that "We wish to preserve its quality through maintaining its personnel and its traditions."

Newhouse's letter spurred the members of the council to decide that editorial independence could best be guaranteed if people on the senior staff were to have a say in the selection of the next editor. (The discussions that led to this decision were understandably delicate because no one on the council had ever been known to talk to Shawn about the possibility that he might one day no longer hold the post.) After more back and forth, it was decided that a letter be sent to Newhouse proposing that once the editorship became vacant he and the senior editorial staff should each have the right to nominate three candidates, and in the event that agreement between him and the staff could not be reached on any of these nominees the matter would be submitted to a designated third party for arbitration.

On Friday, March 8, the board of directors agreed to sell the magazine to Newhouse for $142 million. That same day, Shawn sent a terse message to the staff that made little secret of how he felt about the situation. "This morning, *The New Yorker*'s directors voted unanimously to approve a merger agreement with Advance Publications, which is owned by members of the Newhouse family," he wrote. "The editorial staff was not a party to these negotiations. Nor were the views of the editorial staff solicited during these negotiations. We were not asked for our approval, and we did not give our approval. When there are further developments, I will meet with you again."

That afternoon, the editorial council met with Shawn in his office and voted unanimously with his concurrence to send Newhouse the letter containing our proposal as to how the next editor should be selected. The council also decided that Shawn, who was scheduled to have lunch with Newhouse on Monday, should urge Newhouse to accept our proposal at that time, and should report back to the council on his reaction. At that point, I predicted to my colleagues on the council that our proposal would be rejected out of hand, and told them that when that happened we would either have to capitulate or go on strike.

Shawn's reaction to the second possibility was one of adamant disapproval, and as I sat there watching him shake his head in distress and saw discomfited expressions come over the faces around me, I realized that there was not going to be any support for a walkout.

I have no idea what took place over that weekend, except that Shawn obviously had a change of heart and decided on his own—certainly without informing any of the members of the council—that it would be best for him to acquiesce to what appeared to be the inevitable takeover of *The New Yorker* by Newhouse. What I know for sure is that before going to lunch with the new owner, he gave an interview to a reporter from the *New York Times*, which appeared in the newspaper on the following day under a headline that read, "Editor of New Yorker Seeks 'Mutual Trust.'" The article quoted Shawn as saying not only that he hoped to "establish a relationship of mutual trust" with Newhouse, but also that he would not consider drawing up any document for the new owner to sign. "You can make a magnificent document," he told the *Times*. "If the people who draw up the document, or even sign the document, want to get around it, they can. And if they want to live up to it they will. It isn't documents in the long run. It's what the people's real intentions are."

This was high sounding stuff, but it was not what Shawn had agreed to at the meeting of the council on the previous Friday. In the heat of the moment, I sat down and wrote him a note that I would come to regret. I told him that I had read the interview he had given the *Times* with "astonishment and dismay," and that by acting unilaterally to establish a relationship of trust with Newhouse, "you have gone against the unanimous advice that was given to you by the Council last Friday, and violated both the substance and the spirit of the solemn agreements you made with its members." I went on to tell him that he had "deserted those of us who stood firmly with you in a time of crisis," and I ended by informing him of my resignation from the editorial council.

In retrospect, I have come to believe that my reaction to what Shawn did was dictated to some extent by the fact that I had just completed an arduous two-year investigation of the half-century of betrayal of the nation's unsuspecting asbestos workers by their employers, and I was walking around with the short fuse for secrecy that had motivated me during much of my career as a journalist. Whatever the case, I soon realized that I had made a grave mistake. William Shawn had, indeed, become the embodiment of *The New Yorker*—the closest thing to a godhead that any of its staff members had ever encountered—and by criticizing him openly I had violated the aura of trust and affection that surrounded him. There was no question in my mind then—as there is none now—that he had broken the agreement he had made with the council. However, to have confronted him with it so starkly had not only been rash but, considering the reverence in which he was held by practically everyone at the magazine, well-nigh blasphemous.

Two days later, I sent him a note in which I apologized for having been intemperate. "You did what you felt was right and what you certainly had the right to do," I told him. "As for me, I regret having undertaken a role in this affair in which I felt compelled to voice disapproval of your action, for by doing so I have offended you and created division. In view of what I perceived to be at stake, however, the alternative of lapsing into silence would have been inadmissible."

I sent a copy of this note to Shawn to each of my colleagues on the council, together with a personal note in which I apologized for having done "violence to the concerned and constructive spirit in which you and other members of the council tried to grapple with a difficult problem that could not be resolved." I ended by saying that I believed the positions taken by the council to have been sound.

On April 9, a proxy statement was sent out to shareholders of *The New Yorker*, which set forth Advance Publication's plan of merger. In a section titled "Operations After the Merger," the new owners not only guaranteed to maintain the magazine's sixty-year-old tradition of total editorial independence, but also agreed that "when a new editor-in-chief of *The New Yorker* is being considered, the final decision will be made by Advance, but it will consult with, and seek the advice and approval of, a group of staff members to be selected and to function in a manner then deemed to be appropriate by the senior editorial staff of *The New Yorker*."

Twenty-one months later, Newhouse walked into Shawn's office and, without having consulted anyone on the editorial staff, dismissed him by handing him his letter of resignation. At the time, I was in southern California. I had just fallen in love with a charming, intelligent, and beautiful bookstore owner named Milane Christiansen, who would one day become my wife, and I declined the invitation of several colleagues at the magazine, who called and asked me to return to help protest Shawn's abrupt dismissal. I also declined to join more than a hundred and fifty of them in signing a letter that asked Robert Gottlieb, whom Newhouse had designated as Shawn's successor, to withdraw his acceptance of the position he had been offered. I understood that they intended this as a token of their love and respect for Shawn, but I felt that it was a futile gesture. The time for effective protest at *The New Yorker* had come and gone.

# 26

## Credible Evidence

Shawn's departure from *The New Yorker*, where he had been the editor for thirty-five years, took place on February 11, 1987. On that day he sent a poignant farewell message to the staff that reflected his essential nature:

Dear colleagues, dear friends:

My feelings at this perplexed moment are too strong for farewells. I will miss you terribly, but I can be grateful to have had your companionship for part of my journey through the years. Whatever our individual roles at *The New Yorker*, whether on the eighteenth, nineteenth, or twentieth floor, we have built something quite wonderful together. Love has been the controlling emotion, and love is the essential word. We have done our work with honesty and love. *The New Yorker*, as a reader once said, has been the gentlest of magazines. Perhaps it has also been the greatest, but that matters far less. What matters most is that you and I, working together, taking strength from the inspiration that our first editor, Harold Ross, gave us, have tried constantly to find and say what is true. I must speak of love once more. I love all of you, and will love you as long as I live.

Needless to say, a man with a capacity for such feeling was not someone who held grudges, and in spite of my criticism of his actions at the time of the takeover, Shawn and I maintained a friendly relationship during the rest of his tenure at the magazine. Following the publication of "The Asbestos Industry on Trial," he agreed that I should write a second article about the destruction of the earth's ozone layer by manmade chlorofluorocarbon gases. My first piece on the subject, which had been published in 1975, had won the Journalism Award of the American Association for the Advancement of Science. It described the findings of F. Sherwood Rowland, a professor of chemistry at the University of California at Irvine, who, with a colleague named Mario Molina, had calculated that the several million tons of chlorofluorocarbon gases that were floating about in the atmosphere of the earth—an amount about equal to the total amount ever manufactured—would eventually rise into the stratosphere. There they would be photolyzed by ultraviolet light, releasing atoms of chlorine that would initiate an extensive and complex catalytic chain reaction in which ozone would be destroyed in huge quantities. Since the ozone layer prevents harmful ultraviolet radiation from reaching the earth, Rowland and Molina had sensibly warned that the increase of ultraviolet light resulting from ozone depletion by the chlorofluorocarbons might cause a significant rise in the worldwide incidence of skin cancer, and might also result in widespread crop damage.

During the ten years that had passed since then, officials of the Environmental Protection Agency had banned the use of chlorofluorocarbons as aerosol propellants in the United States, but had taken no other measures to restrict them. Meanwhile, officials of I. E. du Pont de Nemours and Company, the chief manufacturer of the compounds, had continued to insist that unless "credible evidence" were furnished to show that they actually posed a hazard to ozone, government regulation was unwarranted. Throughout this period, I stayed in close touch with Rowland, an indefatigable giant of a man, who, in the face of doubt expressed by industry consultants, as well as vacillation on the part of many of his fellow scientists, had been urging that the use of chlorofluorocarbons as aerosol propellants be banned on a worldwide basis without further delay, and that all nations sharply reduce their use of the chemicals in all other nonessential applications. Rowland was convinced that mankind was faced with two alternatives. "We can continue the large-scale experiment on the stratosphere which is now in progress," he warned, "or we can discontinue the experiment, for the simple reason that its consequences may prove to be disastrous for mankind." As for the attitude of du Pont and the other manufacturers of chlorofluorocarbons, he had this to say:

> The chlorofluorocarbon industry has decided that it does not intend to consider any evidence credible as long as there is the slightest doubt about the validity of any part of the ozone-depletion hypothesis. Thus, credible evidence becomes impossible to achieve—simply because there will always be some degree of uncertainty in measuring atmospheric changes and there will always be discrepancies in the mathematical models that simulate chemical reactions in the stratos-

phere. For this reason, one can expect industry to keep on asking for more time to conduct other investigations. The tactic is known as studying the problem to death, and—considering what is at stake—it is a blatantly cynical one.

Rowland went on to point out that scientists had been studying the chlorofluorocarbon problem for more than ten years, and that during each of those years at least a million tons of chlorofluorocarbons, worth more than a billion dollars, had been sold throughout the world. "That's the bottom line as far as the chemical companies are concerned," he declared. "The bottom line for the rest of us is that during each of these ten years a million tons of chlorofluorocarbons, containing at least five hundred thousand tons of chlorine, have been added to the atmosphere, and that sooner or later all this chlorine will be unleashed in the stratosphere to attack the ozone layer."

Rowland's unusually strong words and harsh prediction caused something of a furor in scientific circles and elsewhere when they appeared in *The New Yorker,* in the late spring of 1986. By that time, a huge hole had opened up in the ozone layer over the Antarctic, and the problem of ozone depletion had once again begun to make headlines around the world. During the next few months, members of the scientific community woke up to the danger Rowland had been warning about for more than a decade. In December of 1986, the National Aeronautics and Space Administration (NASA) and the World Meteorological Organization (WMO) formed a special panel of leading atmospheric scientists to assess all aspects of the ozone problem, and in September of the following year, high government officials of more than thirty nations met in Montreal, under the auspices of the United Nations Environment Programme, and called for a drastic reduction in the production and emission of chlorofluorocarbons. (This was subsequently expanded to include a total worldwide ban.) Six months later, the panel of scientists formed by NASA and the WMO declared not only that the hole in the Antarctic ozone layer had been caused by chlorofluorocarbons, but also that a grave loss of ozone was occurring in the stratosphere above the populated areas of the Northern Hemisphere. Ten days after that, du Pont threw in the towel and made the belated decision to cease its production of the compounds.

In 1989, the United Nations Environment Programme named me to its Global 500 Honour Roll for writing the articles that had helped bring the problem of ozone depletion to public attention. As for Rowland, recognition of his discovery of the hazard and appreciation for his tireless efforts in insisting that it be dealt with would soon propel him into the front rank of the world's scientific community. In 1990, he was elected president of the American Association for the Advancement of Science, and in December of 1995 he, Molina, and a Dutch atmospheric scientist named Paul Crutzen shared a Nobel Prize for discovering the hazard of stratospheric ozone depletion and for helping to save the planet from catastrophe. It was the first time in history that a Nobel had been awarded for hazard research.

As might have been expected, the members of the editorial staff did not welcome Bob Gottlieb with open arms when he arrived at the magazine in the winter of 1987. However, by the end of his first year there, he had earned the respect of most of them, because he soon showed himself to be imaginative, intelligent, tasteful, tough-minded, and thoroughly professional. Not only did he improve the quality of the fiction that ran in the *The New Yorker,* but he also maintained the high quality of the nonfiction pieces for which the magazine was best known—a remarkable achievement for someone who had spent his entire career in book publishing, and who had never had any prior journalistic experience. In addition, though unable to prevent the advertising department from polluting the magazine with all manner of inserts, coupons, and other tasteless promotional junk, he was successful in maintaining the essential separation of church and state that had always marked the relationship between the editorial and business departments. For my part, I came to regard him as not just an adequate replacement for Shawn, but as a brilliant editor-in-chief of *The New Yorker* in his own right.

Gottlieb had admired the ozone-depletion pieces, and he wanted me to continue writing about environmental problems for the magazine. With his encouragement, I embarked upon the last and most controversial project of my journalistic career—a three-part series of articles that described the cancer hazard posed to hundreds of thousands of unsuspecting people by exposure to the electromagnetic fields (EMF) given off by high-voltage and high-current power lines. The pieces, which revealed some heavily financed attempts on the part of the electric-utility industry to cover up the problem, appeared in the magazine in June of 1989 and were published as a book entitled *Currents of Death* in the autumn. The response was extraordinary. Over the next several years, I received more than two thousand letters and telephone calls regarding the power-line health hazard, and, in spite of not having an assistant or secretary, did my best to respond to each and every one of them. During that time, I appeared as a guest on more than fifty television and radio programs, including the NBC "Today Show," ABC's "Nightline," CBS' "This Morning," and CNN's "Larry King Live." Meanwhile, dozens of citizens' groups were organized in states from one end of the nation to the other to protest the presence and/or construction of power lines near schools, homes, hospitals, and places of business. For their part, officials of the electric utility industry redoubled their efforts to convince the public that there was no cause for alarm. They were aided by the silence of state and federal authorities, who feared that if they were to acknowledge that exposure to power-frequency magnetic fields could cause or promote cancer, the American people would demand that the government do something about it.

By the late winter of 1990, I had begun to write the first of several sequel articles for *The New Yorker* about new studies that indicted power-line magnetic fields as a cause or promoter of cancer, and about unusual clusters of cancer that had occurred among children and adults living in communities in various parts of the nation in which dwellings and schools had been built close to power lines giving off strong magnetic fields. (These articles would subsequently appear as a book entitled *The Great Power-Line Cover-Up*.) At the time, officials of the Environmental Protection Agency released a detailed 367-page report in which they concluded that power-frequency magnetic fields were a "probable" cause of cancer in humans. Their conclusion was based largely upon the fact that five of six human case-control studies that had been published in the peer-reviewed medical literature showed that children living in homes near power lines giving off strong magnetic fields were developing cancer—mostly leukemia and brain cancer—more readily than children who did not live in homes near such power lines.

The authors of the EPA report pointed out that a majority of more than thirty occupational studies showed that workers exposed to power-frequency magnetic fields on the job were developing leukemia, brain cancer, and other malignancies at a rate that was higher than expected. "These cancer sites are found consistently across different geographic regions, age groups, industries, occupational classifications, and study designs," they wrote. "Given this diversity of studies, in addition to the likelihood that across broad job categories the exposure to various chemicals is not uniform, it is difficult to identify any single agent or group of confounding exposures that could explain the consistent finding of these same cancer sites." They also described a body of experimental research that included studies showing that magnetic fields could impair the immune system, and they declared that there was "reason to believe that the findings of carcinogenicity in humans are biologically plausible."

Within a few days, officials of President George Bush's White House Office of Science and Technology Policy ordered the EPA to delete the word "probable" and replace it with the word "possible." Thus began the official cover-up of the power-line hazard that inspired the title of my book, and that continues to the present day. The reason for the cover-up is undoubtedly fiscal. If government health officials were to acknowledge the validity of the epidemiological and experimental evidence indicating that exposure to power-line magnetic fields can either cause or promote cancer, the American people would surely demand that the government take preventive measures designed to protect their health and that of their children, and to preserve the value of their homes. And since close to a million dwellings may be situated dangerously close to power lines giving off strong magnetic fields, government officials might then be required to make great expenditures in behalf of the public health at a time when tremendous pressure is being brought to bear upon them to reduce the deficit and manage the national budget. Far easier, therefore, for them to question the existence of the power-line hazard and to suggest that the problem is emotional in origin—as they have done in the case of Agent Orange and the Gulf War syndrome—while at the same time calling for further studies of the hazard to be conducted.

In the late autumn of 1990, the director of the White House Office of Science and Technology Policy, who had been a professor of physics at Yale University, tried to persuade EPA officials to delay the release of their report, on the grounds that it might alarm the public. (The attempt failed when a junior researcher at the Agency informed the Associated Press about it, and the story found its way into newspapers across the nation.) However, in 1991, the members of an EPA scientific review committee, whose members included paid consultants of the electric utility industry, concluded that the human evidence was insufficient to establish a cause-and-effect relationship, and recommended that the report be rewritten.

Since then, much more evidence has been gathered to indict power-frequency magnetic fields as either a cause or a promoter of cancer in humans. Today, no fewer than nine of the eleven childhood residential studies that can be found in the peer-reviewed medical literature show that children living in homes near high-voltage or high-current power lines experience a statistically significant increased risk of developing leukemia and/or brain cancer. (In the most highly regarded of these studies, the risk is two to three times as great as that of other children.) Utility-industry consultants and scientists who claim that this is not a risk worth worrying about conveniently disregard the fact that because power-frequency magnetic fields are ubiquitous in modern society the residential studies do not compare the cancer risk of exposed children with that of unexposed children, but, rather, the risk of more heavily exposed children with that of less exposed children. This, of course, means that the true risk for children has been considerably understated, just as the risk of lung cancer for people who smoke cigarettes would be understated if one were to base it on a comparison of two-pack-a-day smokers with one-pack-a-day smokers.

The real nature of the childhood cancer risk can best be seen in the results of the extraordinarily thorough Swedish case-control study of 1992. This study investigated leukemia and brain cancer among all Swedish children who had lived for any length of time between 1960 and the end of 1985 in dwellings situated within a thousand feet of any of Sweden's 9300 miles of high-voltage transmission lines. It was conducted by scientists from the world-renowned Karolinska Institute, in Stockholm, who were able to estimate the magnetic-field exposure of each of these children with great accuracy, because they had been able to obtain records of the daily current loads on each of the transmission lines for the entire 26-year period of the study.

The Swedish scientists observed a clear dose-response relationship between increasing magnetic-field exposure and the occurrence of childhood leukemia. Indeed, they found that children living in dwellings in which they had been exposed to average power-line magnetic fields of more than one milligauss experienced twice the risk of developing leukemia as children living in homes in which they had been exposed to fields of less than one milligauss; children exposed to more than two milligauss had almost three times the risk; and children exposed to more than three milligauss had nearly four times the risk. (A gauss is a unit of measurement of the strength of a magnetic field; a milligauss is one thousandth of a gauss; and two milligauss is a level commonly found in homes across the United States that are close to power lines carrying high voltage or high current.) It stands to reason that if cancer risks of this magnitude can be found by comparing more exposed children with less exposed children, the true nature of the risk posed to children by exposure to power-line magnetic fields must be far greater. But no one in the utility industry has seen fit to acknowledge this aspect of the problem, and, incredibly, the members of last year's much-touted National Academy of Sciences committee, who claimed to have found no convincing evidence that exposure to power-line magnetic fields presented a human health hazard, did not even bother to address it in their deliberations.

Other industry consultants have tried to minimize the hazard by pointing out that the average strength of the magnetic fields given off by power lines is dwarfed by that of the earth's magnetic field. What they conveniently fail to note is that unlike the earth's steady-state magnetic field, the alternating-current fields emitted by power lines flow to and fro—first in one direction and then in the other—sixty times a second, and that a similar to-and-fro movement will occur in anything magnetic that is penetrated by such a field, including the molecules of the brains, blood-forming systems, organs, and tissues of human beings. This phenomenon is called entrainment, and a great deal of experimental evidence has been published in the medical and scientific literature to suggest that it can alter the normal activation of enzymes, hormones, and cellular immune responses in ways consistent with the promotion of cancer. One need not be a medical scientist to appreciate that chronic, long-term exposure to such a phenomenon, which has no counterpart in man's evolutionary history, may well prove to be hazardous to health, and particularly to the health of young children whose brain cells and blood-forming cells are in a state of rapid development.

As for adults, a majority of the fifty or so occupational studies that have been published in the medical literature demonstrate that workers more heavily exposed to power-frequency magnetic fields experience a statistically significant increased risk of developing cancer when compared with less exposed workers. Indeed, some studies show that heavily exposed power linemen run ten times the risk of developing brain cancer as their less exposed colleagues. A study in the United States and a companion study in Finland implicate exposure to power-frequency magnetic fields in the development of Alzheimer's disease. In addition, several epidemiological studies show that men and women working as electricians, electrical engineers, and in other jobs that expose them to power-frequency magnetic fields are developing breast cancer at rates significantly higher than less exposed workers. What makes these findings especially worrisome is that the incidence of breast cancer is vanishingly rare in men—only one in every 100,000 American men develops breast cancer in a given year—but almost epidemic among American women. (About one in every nine women will develop breast cancer in her lifetime.) Moreover, the epidemiological studies suggesting a link with breast cancer are substantiated by laboratory experiments showing that low-level power-frequency magnetic fields can interfere with hormonal control of human breast cancer cells, causing them to proliferate rapidly. The link is further substantiated by animal studies that demonstrate a correlation between exposure to power-frequency magnetic fields and a strong decrease in levels of the hormone melatonin, which is known to protect against breast cancer. Not surprisingly, some observers believe that the breast cancer connection may prove to be the "smoking gun" of the power-line health hazard debate.

In June of 1995, the eleven members of a committee convened by the National Council on Radiation Protection and Measurements (NCRP)—all of them recognized experts in electromagnetic-field research—concluded that the childhood studies provide clear evidence of a positive association between cancer and exposure to magnetic fields on the order of two milligauss. The NCRP committee members further stated that laboratory studies indicated that exposure to magnetic fields could reduce the natural defense response of the immune system, and interfere with critical steps in cell growth in ways consistent with tumor formation. As a result, they recommended that new day care centers, schools, and playgrounds should not be built where power-frequency magnetic fields exceed two milligauss; that new housing should not be built under existing high-voltage transmission lines, or in such close proximity to these lines that measured magnetic fields would exceed two milligauss; and that new transmission and distribution lines should not be built where they would produce magnetic fields exceeding two milligauss in existing housing. They also recommended a ten-year mitigation program under which the strength of magnetic fields emitted by power lines would be reduced in stages.

Perhaps because they appeared in a draft report that had been prematurely leaked and was subject to review, the findings and recommendations of the NCRP committee never made their way into the pages of the *New York Times,* which had by then published several articles questioning the existence of a power-line hazard. Nor were they reported by other major newspapers in the nation, or by any of the major television networks. Nor did any major newspaper or TV network reveal the decision by EPA officials to delay (supposedly for budgetary reasons) the release of their rewritten report on the cancer hazard posed by power-frequency magnetic fields until after the 1996 presidential election, let alone that their conclusions were in essential agreement with those arrived at by the authors of the NCRP report.

What did make headlines in the *Times* and other major newspapers was the announcement at a press conference in Washington, D.C., a few days before the election, that a sixteen-member committee of the National Research Council (NRC), an arm of the National Academy of Sciences, had found no proof that exposure to power-line magnetic fields was associated with the development of cancer or any other disease. Since the members of the National Research Council committee had reviewed the very same medical and scientific studies that had been reviewed by the members of the National Council on Radiation Protection committee, one had to wonder how two committees of scientific experts could possibly manage to arrive at such dramatically different conclusions. The answer to this question is simply that, unlike the members of the NCRP committee, the members of the NRC committee were willing to discount what they themselves acknowledged to be "multiple" epidemiological studies showing that children living in homes near high-current or high-voltage power lines were developing leukemia more often than other children. The chief reason they gave for doing so was their opinion that animal and cellular experiments had failed to show how power-frequency magnetic fields could trigger or promote the growth of cancer. In taking this position, they managed to overlook the fact that it took nearly half a century after epidemiological studies showed that cigarette smoking was a devastating cause of lung cancer in human beings for scientists to demonstrate how the compounds present in cigarette smoke cause cellular changes leading to lung cancer. They also managed to ignore the fact that more than thirty years after epidemiological studies demonstrated that asbestos workers were dying of lung cancer in droves, scientists still do not know how an inhaled asbestos fiber reacts in lung tissue to cause cancer, or, for that matter, how DDT and other toxic pesticides and chemicals cause cellular changes that lead to the development of cancer. More to the point, they dismissed recent experimental studies showing that exposure to low-level magnetic fields can play an essential role in tumor development by interfering with DNA repair.

Having absolved magnetic fields of any role in causing or helping to promote leukemia in children living near power lines giving off strong magnetic fields, the members of the NRC committee were faced with the quandary of having to explain their acknowledgment that the associations with childhood leukemia were based upon "statistically reliable and robust findings that must be considered carefully in drawing conclusions about overall risk." To solve this dilemma, they decided that the excess leukemia must be caused by something else connected with proximity to power lines, such as some unknown factor having to do with the age of the home in which a leukemic child has lived, some unidentified agent that had been used in the construction of the home, housing density, neighborhood traffic density, or the use of herbicides in and around power lines to destroy foliage. What they chose to ignore in their attempt to conjure up agents to blame other than the magnetic fields was that, except for herbicides and the vague suggestion about the age of homes, the other possibilities had been raised as potential confounders years ago by the electric utility industry, and had been considered as such in many of the studies that had been conducted. As for the suggestion that herbicides might have caused the findings of excess leukemia in the childhood studies, the committee members overlooked the fact that almost all of these studies involved children living near high-current lines in paved urban areas where herbicides were rarely, if ever, used to destroy foliage.

Perhaps because the committee members had been asked to review the research literature in order to determine whether residential exposure to power-frequency magnetic fields posed a health hazard, they chose to gloss over the findings of the great majority of some fifty occupational studies, which show that workers exposed to power-frequency magnetic fields on the job—for example, power linemen, telephone linemen, welders, electricians, electrical engineers, and electric railway operators—are developing leukemia and/or brain cancer at considerably higher rates than other workers. Moreover, as in the case of the childhood studies, they neglected to take into account the fact that the occupational studies have not compared exposed workers with unexposed workers, but, rather, more heavily exposed workers with less exposed workers. This crucial omission in their assessment of the human studies enabled them to minimize the true nature of the cancer risk experienced by workers exposed to power-frequency magnetic fields on the job, and by children living in homes near power lines carrying high current or high voltage.

When all is said and done, what was lacking in the NRC committee's assessment was common sense. After all, if multiple studies show that children who live in homes near power lines that give off strong magnetic fields are developing leukemia and brain cancer more often than other children, and if multiple studies show that workers exposed to strong power-frequency magnetic fields on the job are developing leukemia and brain cancer more often than other workers, wouldn't common sense tell one that exposure to magnetic fields ought to be considered a more likely suspect than some unknown factor having to do with the age or construction of a residence, the previously considered factor of traffic density, or a highly unlikely exposure to herbicides?

Another way to look at the power-line hazard is that never before has so much human and experimental evidence indicting an agent as carcinogenic been subsequently shown to be invalid, and the agent in question subsequently found to be harmless. In this connection, one ought to keep in mind that power-line magnetic fields do not have constitutional rights (and, therefore, the presumption of innocence until they are proved guilty), and that by prematurely conferring the presumption of benignity upon them the National Academy of Sciences may have done a disservice to the public health. It would not be the first time that academy committees have issued findings that turned out to be flawed. Between 1975 and 1985, the expert members of no fewer than four NRC committees adopted a ludicrously cautious wait-and-see approach to the global crisis posed by depletion of the ozone layer by manmade chemicals, even as the ozone layer was deteriorating above their heads. And in 1984, the members of an NRC committee managed to underestimate the environmental hazard of asbestos inhalation by twentyfold at a time when public health officials were trying to decide what to do about asbestos contamination in tens of thousands of offices and school buildings across the nation.

Toward the end of the committee's report about power-line magnetic fields, its authors recommend continued research into the power-line health hazard "because the possibility that some characteristic of the electric or magnetic field is biologically active at environmental strengths cannot be totally discounted." Considering that the great majority of more than sixty human studies strongly implicate power-frequency magnetic fields as a cause or promoter of cancer, and that the committee members themselves acknowledged that "positive human epidemiologic data are the strongest evidence in evaluating any human health risk," it is not surprising that they may have wished to cover their bets. In the meantime, the question many people may want answered is what they can do to protect themselves and their children while research yet to be conducted confirms or contradicts the already robust evidence that living near power lines carrying high current or high voltage, or working in jobs that entail exposure to power-frequency magnetic fields, results in an increased incidence of leukemia and other cancer among children and adults? There is only one sane answer to that question: avoid unnecessary exposure to power-frequency magnetic fields whenever and wherever possible.

During recent months, there have been reports that some members of the National Research Council committee believe that their findings were distorted at the October 1996 press conference, which was organized by officials of the National Academy of Sciences, and by the accounts that appeared in the newspapers and on television. Should that be true, one can only hope that some of them will summon up the courage to speak out about the matter, for there is nothing except the fear of offending the powers-that-be at the academy to prevent them from doing so. Which reminds me of an experience I had some twenty years ago, when I sat as a member of an NRC committee charged with deciding what the American worker should know about the multiple cancer risks to which he or she is exposed in the workplace. After deliberating for many months, the committee decided that workers should be fully appraised of cancer risks in the workplace, and I was assigned to write a portion of the final report that declared as much. A day or so after the committee approved the final report and disbanded, I was telephoned at my home by the National Academy staff member who had acted as an adviser to the committee. He asked my permission to soften some of the language I had written "in the interests of achieving consensus." When I inquired whether his request was being made in behalf of the full committee membership, I was told that it was an informal one. At that point, I declined to make any changes. When the academy staff member persisted, I told him that as far as I knew cancer did not operate by consensus, and that if any changes were made in the part of the report I had written without the concurrence of the committee, I would make public disclosure of it. Needless to say, I was never again invited to serve on a National Research Council committee.

Be all that as it may, public relations spokesmen for the electric-utility industry have been having a field day with the National Academy report and the wide and unquestioning coverage it received in the nation's press and on all the major television network news programs. Some years ago, they came up with a snappy slogan to deal with the power-line health hazard—a slogan that, like others before it, was designed to dampen public anxiety and convince everybody that there was no immediate problem. "The jury is still out," they kept claiming—a variation of the waiting-for-credible-evidence ploy with which the manufacturers of chlorofluorocarbons managed to delay for more than a decade the implementation of preventive measures to protect the ozone layer. Now, thanks to the National Academy review, industry officials are claiming that the jury is back and that their verdict exonerates the power lines.

Believe that and you'll be able to avoid getting a skin tan from digging in your garden in moonlight.

# 27

## Enemies of the People

Back in the spring of 1986, I was invited to deliver the commencement address at the Boston University School of Public Health. It was a liberating experience because it enabled me to speak my mind about the private enterprise system that had condoned and tried to cover up the industrial and environmental hazards I had been describing in the pages of *The New Yorker* for nearly twenty years. The magazine pieces, which had often taken many months to research and write, had to be constructed with painstaking attention to definition and detail, and they had afforded me little opportunity to express the contempt in which I held the captains of industry who had inflicted disease, disability, and death upon thousands of my fellow citizens.

I started out by reminding my audience of the anguish and isolation of Dr. Thomas Stockman, the hero of Henrik Ibsen's play *An Enemy of the People* who is publicly humiliated when he dares to place the public health of the spa town in which he lives above its economic health. I went on to describe the assault that the producers of toxic chemicals and their insurance carriers were (and still are) mounting against the laws of strict liability, which protect the public health by requiring a manufacturer to test his product, to know if it has any harmful effects, to be familiar with the medical literature relating to it, and to guarantee that it will not pose a threat to those who consume it or use it. I reviewed the fierce attacks that these manufacturers and insurers were mounting against the jury system, and pointed out that by attacking the integrity of juries, whose members are drawn at random from voter registration lists, they were practicing a dangerous form of Orwellian doublethink. "What they are really saying is that we must be protected from ourselves," I declared.

After describing the asbestos litigation as a triumph of common law against corporate misconduct, I told the graduating health professionals in my audience that industry was out to replace the concept of strict liability with a no-fault system that would, in effect, institutionalize occupational and environmental cancer and other disease as a way of life. I warned them that if and when that occurred they would find themselves as helpless as Ibsen's Dr. Stockman. In closing, I urged them to be on guard and to speak out freely.

> Only by listening carefully to the Orwellian voices of denial, darkness, and deception; only by jealously guarding our common-law rights; only by implementing them again and again; only by perpetually restating the truth and making it new for our time, just as Ibsen did 104 years ago when he wrote his great play, will you be able to carry out the mandate of your profession—to identify and prevent disease and educate your fellow citizens in how to do so. Then and only then will all of us—public health professionals, journalists, lawyers, teachers, factory workers, people of whatever station—be able to improve our society by bringing to justice and then rehabilitating those elements in it which truly deserve to be considered the enemies of the public health, and, therefore, of the people.

As things turned out, I not only got a few things off my chest in my commencement address, but also opened up a sideline as a public speaker. During the next few years, I delivered similar speeches at trial lawyers' meetings in more than a dozen states, at a number of universities, and before several civic groups. My respect for tort law and the concept of strict liability was not, however, always accompanied by admiration for those who made their living at it. This was particularly true in the case of some of the nation's leading asbestos litigators, whose early achievements I had celebrated in *Outrageous Misconduct,* but whom I later excoriated in public for having abandoned (for monetary reasons) the cause of future asbestos-disease victims at a crucial period during the Manville bankruptcy hearings.

By and large, though, I got along fairly well with the attorneys I met—no doubt because most of them were out to remedy the same injustices I had been writing about as a journalist—and on a number of occasions I took the opportunity (though never for money) to assist them in their endeavors. Back in 1968 and 1969, I gave information about the culpability of the makers of asbestos insulation to Ward Stephenson, the pioneering attorney in Orange, Texas, who represented the widow of Clarence Borel in the landmark failure-to-warn case known as *Borel* v. *Fibreboard*. This case triggered the avalanche of litigation that forced Johns-Manville and other asbestos insulation manufacturers to seek refuge in bankruptcy, and cost them and their insurers tens of billions of dollars. During the 1970s and 1980s, I was able to help a number of civilian radar operators and repairmen win lawsuits against the manufacturers of the equipment with which they had been working. These workers—relatively young men in their thirties and forties—had been heavily exposed to microwave radiation as a result of being required to align and adjust the beams of high-power radars while the radars continued to operate, and they were suffering from a wide variety of ailments, including blindness, deafness, memory loss, systemic hemorrhaging, heart disease, and cancer. In one of the cases, the United States Army Missile Command at Redstone Arsenal, in Huntsville, Alabama, came to the aid of some defendant radar manufacturers by refusing to declassify information about the equipment they produced on the grounds of national security. The tactic failed when I was able to provide the plaintiff's attorney with proof that the radars in question were being sold as surplus on the open market to countries in Latin and South America.

Fearful that the huge number of microwave injury cases among its personnel would come to public scrutiny, the army, navy, and air force intervened time and again in cases in which civilians tried to obtain compensation for radiation injuries. I did my best to thwart their intrusion whenever I could. On one occasion, I provided assistance that helped win a major workmen's compensation case for the widow of a New York Telephone Company technician, who had died of chronic brain disease after undergoing heavy exposure to microwave radiation as a result of maintaining the telephone company's transmitting and receiving equipment on the eighty-seventh floor of the Empire State Building. Her lawyer used the information I gave him to impeach the credibility of some of the telephone company's expert witnesses, including a United States Navy physician, whose efforts to cover up the disease hazard posed by exposure to microwave radiation I had exposed some years earlier in my book *The Zapping of America*.

On a January night in the winter of 1987, I received a telephone call at my Village apartment from a man named Robert Strom, a Boeing

Company technician who had fallen victim to another Cold War cover-up that I had written about in the same book. Strom started out by telling me that he had been a loyal Boeing employee for twenty-seven years, and that between 1983 and 1985 he had assigned to operate an electromagnetic pulser inside a shielded test chamber, where he had undergone daily exposure to powerful electromagnetic pulse (EMP) radiation. (Boeing was using EMP to simulate the flashes of radiant energy accompanying nuclear explosions, in order to determine their effect on electronic equipment carried in the bombers and other aircraft that the company was manufacturing for the air force.) Strom went on to say that his supervisors at Boeing had assured him repeatedly that there were no health hazards associated with exposure to EMP, and he informed me that almost no safety precautions were taken to protect him and other employees who worked in the test chamber from exposure to the radiation. After telling me that he had recently been diagnosed with chronic myelogenous leukemia, Strom said that he had just finished reading *The Zapping of America,* and that he had been surprised and troubled to find a chapter in it that revealed that Boeing had known about the leukemia hazard associated with exposure to EMP since the early 1970s. He also said he had reason to believe that Boeing had been secretly testing his blood for preleukemic changes during the time he had been working with EMP. He sounded puzzled and disturbed. He asked me what I thought he should do.

The chapter in my book to which Strom referred had been written more than ten years earlier. It described an EMP test program that Boeing had operated for the air force between 1968 and 1972, in which the effects of electromagnetic pulse radiation on the warheads and guidance-and-control systems of the nation's Minutemen intercontinental ballistic missiles were simulated by huge airborne pulsers that were called "big zappers" by the men who worked with them, and were carried aloft by army H-47 Chinook helicopters. In my book (as well as in *The New Yorker* articles that preceded it), I had written that "As early as 1971, Boeing was aware of two cases of leukemia and one case of skin cancer—all three occurring in men in their thirties or forties—among a group of seventeen technicians who had been conducting EMP tests at missile sites near the towns of Brady and Cascade, Montana."

In the course of researching the articles, I had flown out to Helena, Montana, in the summer of 1976. There I learned about the outbreak of leukemia that had occurred among people working at or living near the EMP test sites, and met the members of a ranching family who had suffered hair loss and blood abnormalities after being irradiated by the airborne pulsers. Later, I found out that at a 1970 conference on the biological effects of EMP, which had been sponsored by the Lovelace Foundation for Medical Education and Research, of Albuquerque, New Mexico, and attended by Boeing's director of occupational medicine, it had been recommended that test animals be subjected to the chronic long-term effects of EMP. Such studies were never conducted, however, and in my book I had written that "human beings, not rats and monkeys, were in effect used as test animals in experiments involving chronic, long-term exposure to electromagnetic pulses."

Now, eleven years later, one of those human beings, Robert Strom, was asking me what I thought he should do. I had no qualms about telling him that I thought he should retain a good attorney and sue Boeing for fraudulent concealment.

Strom replied that he was having trouble finding attorneys in Washington who were willing to bring an action against the state's corporate giant, so I contacted a friend of mine in Seattle named Susan Lee, who owned a litigation consulting firm. For several months, she tried without success to obtain legal representation for Strom on the West Coast. Finally, she managed to bring his plight to the attention of officials at Trial Lawyers for Public Justice—a nonprofit organization founded by Ralph Nader—and they persuaded Michael Withey, of the Seattle firm of Schroeter, Goldmark and Bender, to take the case.

In June of 1988, Withey filed suit against Boeing, Boeing Medical Service, and the Lovelace Biomedical and Environmental Research Institute. The lawsuit alleged that exposure to EMP radiation had caused Strom's leukemia, and it charged the defendants with using EMP to conduct human medical experiments upon Strom and some seven hundred other Boeing employees without obtaining their informed consent. During painstaking discovery, Withey and some colleagues dug up proof that Boeing had, as Strom suspected, conducted a secret study to determine the health effects of EMP upon him and his coworkers. They were also able to obtain evidence that the company had suspected all along that exposure to EMP could result in serious biological damage. Among this evidence was a memorandum written in 1979 by Boeing's chief of Radiation Health Protection, which acknowledged that "the whole chemical balance within the body is disturbed by the electromagnetic fields of the peak [EMP] radiation."

Not surprisingly, Boeing settled the case in the summer of 1990, two weeks before it was scheduled to go to trial. The company paid half a million dollars to compensate Strom and his family, and also agreed to conduct annual medical examinations of Strom's coworkers for ten years. In addition, Boeing and Lovelace paid more than $200,000 into a class fund to be used by an independent medical administrator, who would oversee the medical examinations, evaluate and report their results, and conduct any additional diagnostic tests that might be necessary.

The Strom case reaffirmed the right of workers to be informed by their employers about health hazards to which they are exposed, and it brought the problem posed by exposure to electromagnetic radiation to public attention again. This right had been violated time and again during the Cold War for reasons of presumed or falsely claimed national security, and this health problem—thanks largely to the government's failure to deal with the power-line hazard—is growing by leaps and bounds.

# 28

## An Epidemic of Traitors

A month or so after Strom called, the American Embassy in Moscow found its way into the headlines again, in much the same way as it had nearly forty years earlier, when *Life* magazine ran its story about the young army sergeant who had fallen in love with a *"Mozhno"* girl named Galina. This time, a twenty-six-year-old marine sergeant named Clayton J. Lonetree from St. Paul, Minnesota, who was the son of a Winnebago father and a Navajo mother, and a guard at the American Embassy in Vienna, turned himself in to the CIA and confessed that two years earlier, while stationed at the embassy in Moscow, he had taken up with a Soviet woman named Violetta Sanni, who worked at the embassy as a translator. Lonetree also confessed that he had later sold documents and information to a man whom Sanni had introduced as her Uncle Sasha. Since the CIA suspected that Uncle Sasha was a KGB agent named Aleksiy G. Yefimov, Lonetree was brought to the United States, placed in solitary confinement in the brig at the marine base at Quantico, Virginia, and charged with espionage for having given the Soviets the names of American agents stationed at the embassy in Moscow, and for having provided them with its floor plans. The charge about the floor plans aroused my considerable interest, because ten years earlier I had encountered little trouble in acquiring a set of floor plans for the Moscow Embassy while doing research for *The Zapping of America*.

Soon after Lonetree's arrest was made public, the State Department announced that twenty-eight marine guards at the Moscow Embassy were being recalled to the United States, where they would be given polygraph tests to find out if they had consorted with Russian women. In late March of 1987, the Marine Corps announced the arrest on suspicion of espionage of a second guard at the Moscow Embassy. He was a twenty-one-year-old corporal from Queens named Arnold Bracy, who was the son of a minister. Two days later, the Corps brought a second charge of espionage against Lonetree, which was based upon Bracy's confession (subsequently retracted) to agents of the Naval Investigative Service that he and Lonetree had allowed Soviet agents to enter sensitive areas of the embassy, including the eighth-floor communications room, where secret messages were encoded and transmitted. According to an article in the *New York Times,* Lonetree had let the Soviets into the restricted areas, while Bracy, who had also been accused of consorting with a Russian woman, was suspected of turning off cameras and alarm systems that monitored those areas. The *Times* said that marine embassy guards were always unmarried, so that the government could save money by not having to ship and support dependent wives and children overseas. The *Washington Post* quoted Defense Secretary Caspar W. Weinberger as saying that the United States had suffered "a very great loss" as a result of the two marines having allowed Soviet agents to root through secret areas of the embassy.

By early April, three more marine guards had been accused of socializing with Russian women. Administration officials speculated that security at the Moscow Embassy may have been so compromised by the misconduct of the guards that Secretary of State Schultz might not be able to hold conversations safe from eavesdropping during his forthcoming visit to the Soviet Union. Intelligence analysts speculated that the full extent of the damage might not be known for years. Pentagon officials announced that they had begun to investigate the conduct of marine guards at embassies elsewhere in the world. The *Times* noted that the marines already accused of espionage could, if convicted, face the death penalty.

Vice President Bush was reported to be furious at what he considered to be the State Department's resistance to tougher security measures at the embassy. Several members of Congress called for stricter supervision of marine embassy guards, and recommended that they be given random lie-detector tests. An editorial in the Sunday *Times* railed against an "epidemic of traitors" and declared that "the Marine guards who let the KGB roam the Embassy may have compromised almost everything done there." An article in the daily *Times* pointed out that the Moscow affair was "only the latest example of the extent to which this country has put its faith in the trustworthiness of individuals."

In the middle of April, lawyers for Lonetree acknowledged that their client had had an affair with a Soviet woman, but said that he was being made a scapegoat for State Department negligence. On April 20, a *Time* magazine cover story declared that one of the other accused marines, twenty-six-year-old Sergeant John Joseph Wierick, of Eureka, California, had "spread the contamination to the U.S. consulate in Leningrad," to which he had allegedly given the KGB access at the "urging of a Soviet woman." According to *Time*, no fewer than seventy agents of the Naval Investigative Service were hard at work "grilling and polygraphing every one of the more than 200 marines who have served at the Moscow and East European embassies in the past decade," and "all but a few of the first 50 they quizzed flunked questions about fraternizing with local women." High-ranking marine officers were described as being deeply chagrined at the tarnished honor of the Corps. White House officials criticized the Soviets for their blatant use of sexual entrapment. It was said that since Lonetree's arrest, embassy personnel had been communicating secret information in writing, often on the kind of erasable slates used by children.

In May, the Marine Corps announced that for lack of evidence it was dropping the most serious charge against Lonetree—that he had allowed Soviet agents to enter the embassy—but that the espionage charges involving the sale of classified documents remained against him. (According to Lonetree's attorneys, who included William Kunstler, these documents consisted mainly of an unclassified telephone book that was easily accessible to anyone, and a fire-escape schematic similar to the diagrams that were posted next to embassy elevators.) In June, the Corps announced that it was dropping all charges against Corporal Bracy, who was freed from the brig at Quantico, after being confined there since March. Upon his release, Bracy said that agents of the Naval Investigative Service had coerced him into making a false confession by telling him that he would lose his rights as an American citizen if he did not.

When Lonetree was put on trial in August, two CIA agents who gave closed-session testimony for the prosecution acknowledged that when they had taken his confession a year earlier, they had not advised him of his Miranda or Article 31 rights, or told him that they were turning over the transcript of his statements to members of the Naval Investigative

Service, or warned him that he might face charges as a result. Nor had they undertaken to disabuse Lonetree of the naive but apparently real conviction that he was being interrogated for recruitment as a potential double agent against the Soviets. Several other witnesses for the prosecution, who had known Lonetree in Vienna, testified that he had expressed a desire to leave the Marine Corps when his enlistment was up, become a foreign service officer, and return to Moscow, where he had a girl-friend. The prosecution introduced some of his love letters to Violetta Sanni into evidence. Lonetree wept as he listened to an expert on Soviet intelligence operations testify for the prosecution that the KGB made frequent use of sexual seduction in recruiting potential spies.

Over the vigorous objection of his lawyers, the navy captain who was the court-martial judge allowed the prosecution to call one of Lonetree's high school teachers to the witness stand. She had kept Lonetree's civics class notebook for more than ten years, and had turned it over to the government investigators upon learning of her for-mer student's arrest on espionage charges. In it, at the age of fifteen, Lonetree had doodled swastikas and a hammer-and-sickle, and had written "Hitler Lives" and "Jews are our misfortune." Lonetree's attor-neys contended that he had been deeply in love with Violetta Sanni and had been unable or unwilling to believe that she was a spy, even after she had introduced him to Uncle Sasha, who had paid him thirty-five hundred dollars for the floor plans. They described their client as an immature and gullible loner and borderline alcoholic, who clung to adolescent antisocial ideas that had been spawned in part by ethnic dis-crimination he had experienced as a Native American. In his summa-tion to a jury of eight marine officers, the chief prosecutor, who was a marine major, compared Lonetree to Benedict Arnold.

On August 20, after deliberating for nearly four hours, the jury found Lonetree guilty of all the charges that had been brought against him. These included two counts of espionage, two of conspiracy, four of providing a KGB agent with the names and photographs of several American agents in Moscow and Vienna, three of giving the Soviets floor plans of the embassies in Moscow and Vienna, and two of failing to report his contacts with Soviet civilians to his superiors. He was sen-tenced to thirty years in prison. This was later reduced to twenty-five years, in return for his cooperation in providing details of his recruitment by the KGB. According to the *Times,* Lonetree was the first marine ever to be tried and convicted of spying.

Lonetree's attorneys, who vowed to appeal the verdict, claimed that he had received a highly prejudicial trial. Among other things, they pointed out that the trial judge had barred witnesses who could have testified that all or most of the information that he admitted passing to the Soviets was available from public sources. They also accused the chief prosecutor of falsely portraying Lonetree as the first marine ever tried as a spy, pointing out that during the 1980s several marines who had been charged with attempted espionage had been allowed to plead guilty and given light sentences.

Ten days after Lonetree was convicted, a marine jury at Camp Pendleton, California, found the only other marine who was brought to trial in the Moscow Embassy affair guilty of two counts of dereliction for consorting with a Russian prostitute while on duty, but acquitted him of charges that he had lied to government investigators who suspected him of spying. Three months later, the *Times* reported that American intelligence officials were far less certain than they had been six months earlier that Soviet agents had ever been allowed into sensitive areas of the Moscow Embassy. One official speculated that the whole affair may have been an attempt by the CIA to shift the blame to Lonetree and other marine guards for secrets that had already been compromised by Edward Lee Howard, a CIA officer who had eluded FBI surveillance and defected to the Soviet Union in 1985, after having been trained by the Agency to work on a major technical eavesdropping project that was to be operated out of the Moscow Embassy, and then fired by the Agency for stealing money and using cocaine.

As things turned out, this official had the right idea but the wrong man. Secrets had certainly been compromised during Lonetree's tour of duty in Moscow. Indeed, the greatest intelligence debacle of the entire Cold War had occurred during the last half of 1985 and 1986, when, thanks to the efforts of Aldrich Hazen Ames, KGB counterintelligence officers had arrested ten of the CIA's most valuable Soviet informants and proceeded to roll up virtually every major espionage operation that the Agency had been conducting inside the Soviet Union. As things turned out, the old boys in the CIA's clandestine service, who seemed less anxious to find the culprit than to determine that it wasn't one of them, soon realized that the disaster could not be laid at the doorstep of Howard, for the simple reason that Howard had not known the identity of any of the blown agents. So the lovesick Lonetree became a convenient scapegoat, even though by the end of 1987 the CIA and just about everybody else, including the editors at the *Times,* had come to realize that his indiscretions and those of his marine colleagues could not possibly have constituted a major breach of security.

Shortly before Christmas, the *Times* decided that the embassy guards had not been part of a treasonous epidemic, after all, and ran an editorial that accused the navy of trampling the lives and careers of several marines. The editorial called for a congressional investigation not only for the sake of the marines whose reputations had been sullied but also to determine whether the deplorable conduct of the Naval Investigative Service was prompted by embarrassment over its failure to uncover the Walker family spy ring, which had gone undetected for years before its belated discovery, in 1985. This investigation was never conducted. Two months later, a report issued by the Congress' General Accounting Office accused the State Department of failing to report more than five hundred instances of possible wrongdoing by marine guards at embassies around the world. A month before that, a four-man presidential panel that included Richard Helms—the former CIA director, who had pleaded guilty to the charge of lying to the Senate Foreign Relations Committee about the Agency's role in the overthrow of President Salvador Allende of Chile, and who had been fined and given a two-year suspended jail sentence for doing so—declared that former Ambassador Arthur Hartman should be held responsible for the Moscow Embassy affair, pointing out that he "knew or should have known of the Marine security guard misconduct." Appointing Helms, whose cronies in the clandestine service had toasted him at lunch and paid his fine on the very day of his sentencing, to sit on a panel charged with investigating the relatively minor security lapses caused by the misconduct of some marine guards at the embassy in Moscow appears to have been a brazen stroke designed to divert attention from the Agency's responsibility for the catastrophic security breach that had occurred in Moscow as a result of Ames' treason.

Considering the culture of cover-up that has dominated the CIA for decades, it should come as no surprise that during his nine-year career as the most important KGB spy ever to be installed in the Agency's innards, Rick Ames was able to breeze through polygraph tests with flying colors, get himself transferred to the supersensitive Soviet/East European Division, fly with impunity all over the world to meet his Russian handlers, casually deposit into various bank accounts the more than two million dollars they paid him for betraying the Agency's deepest secrets, and arouse no suspicion while paying for a half-million-dollar house with cash, driving a Jaguar, sporting an expensive wardrobe, and wearing a Gucci watch. Indeed, so deep ran the vein of secrecy and deceit within the CIA that William Webster, the former head of the FBI, who was the Agency's director between 1987 and 1991, was never told during his entire four-year tenure that the Soviet/East European Division's operations in the USSR had been totally compromised, and that the most extensive molehunt in the Agency's history was underway. Nor was Bob Gates, who was director of Central Intelligence between 1991 and 1993, any better informed. He first heard about Ames when he read of his arrest in the newspapers.

Like the hapless Lonetree, Ames was compared at the time of his sentencing to Benedict Arnold. Considering that he has since been characterized by virtually all of his CIA colleagues as a lazy drunkard, one can only imagine what might (and may well) have been wrought by a mole who was both industrious and sober. Meanwhile, in the summer of 1989, Marine Brigadier General M. E. Ruth, who reviewed Lonetree's petition for clemency, recommended that his sentence be reduced to fifteen years. General Ruth declared that the impact of Lonetree's misconduct upon national security was "probably minimal," and that he should be given time off for turning himself in. Ruth also pointed out that Lonetree's sentence was unusually harsh, compared to the sentences of other service members and government employees who had been convicted of espionage, and that the motive for his misconduct was "not treason or greed but rather the love-sick response of a naive, young, immature, and lonely troop in an isolated and hostile environment."

Four years later, a Court of Military Appeals upheld Lonetree's conviction by a slim 3–2 margin, but set aside his twenty-five-year sentence on the grounds that he might have been inadequately represented by his civilian lawyers with regard to his plea-bargaining options. (Some observers believe that this was an attempt on the part of the military to get back at Kunstler and his colleagues for having vigorously attacked the military system of justice during Lonetree's trial.) Whatever the case, a military judge soon reduced Lonetree's sentence to twenty years, and since he had already served a third of it, he became eligible for parole. His attorneys urged that he be released from prison, alleging that he had been pilloried in order to divert attention from the debacle caused by the betrayal engineered by Rick Ames. Even the prosecutor was said to believe that Lonetree's case should be reexamined in light of the Ames affair. But reexamination might have opened the whole business to potentially embarrassing scrutiny, and so Lonetree, who had been a model prisoner, was set free on February 27, 1996, with additional time off for good behavior. His mother was on hand to greet him at the prison gate.

"My son is a victim of Ronald Reagan's Cold War," she said.

# 29

## A Good Soldier

Back in 1987, when blame for the marine-guard affair was being dished out right and left, I met a man who worked for a firm that installed copper sheathing in hospital rooms to deflect stray voltage that might disrupt the myocardiographs that monitor heart signals during by-pass and transplant surgery. He introduced me to a colleague who had installed steel-plated panels on the eighth floor of the Moscow Embassy during the early 1970s, in order to shield classified communications equipment. When I asked him if he had ever seen anyone wearing a radiation-hazard suit on the eighth floor, he shook his head, and when I asked him if he knew why anyone might have been wearing one up there, he gave a shrug.

Not long afterward, I bumped into a fellow who had worked for the Army Signal Corps at Fort Monmouth, New Jersey. When I asked him if he knew anything about radiation-hazard suits, he said that he'd heard that such a garment had been developed by a company that had been a contractor in the installation of the huge ballistic-missile-early-warning-system radar at Thule, Greenland. He said he'd also heard that the suits were designed to be worn by people working around powerful microwave transmitters, such as the Distant-Early-Warning radars and the radar-suppression pods that are mounted under the wings of air force B-52 bombers, but that he had never seen anyone wearing one of them. He went on to explain that radar-suppressors are designed to pick up an enemy signal, analyze its frequency, and nullify it by sending back a signal that was equal and opposite in phase, thus enabling a bomber to penetrate into enemy air space undetected.

When I asked him if such a device could be set up in a building, in order to squelch an incoming signal, he said it was possible but not something he thought anyone would be likely to do because the radiation emitted by countermeasures equipment was so powerful it would be like swatting a mosquito with a flamethrower.

We may never know for sure—at least not in my lifetime—what really went on at the Moscow Embassy. As for why they were wearing radiation-hazard suits on the eighth floor, anything is possible. For example, in 1961, when President Kennedy returned to Washington from his Viennese summit meeting with Nikita Khrushchev, he was full of stories about Soviet intrigue, including the possibility that the Russians had smuggled a small atomic bomb into the attic of their embassy on Connecticut Avenue. In light of Kennedy's own fondness for intrigue and his capacity for disingenuousness—consider the questions he posed to Tad Szulc of the *Times* when he knew perfectly well that the CIA was trying to kill Castro at his express order—it seems entirely possible that he may have been ascribing to the Russians a scheme of the CIA's own making. This appears all the more likely in light of the fact that we were then aware that the Russians were planning to deploy an extensive anti-ballistic missile system around the periphery of Moscow, and that during the early 1960s the Project Pandora transmissions from Moscow to Paris could only be handled by someone with a "Q" atomic clearance.

One thing is certain: From the beginning of the Moscow Embassy affair almost no one—certainly not the people in the State Department—has told the truth. Back in 1976, when Ambassador Stoessel was reassigned to Bonn, the State Department denied that he had leukemia, and subsequently refused to comment on his health. But a few years after I read his obituary in the *New York Times*—he died of leukemia at the age of sixty-six, in December 1986, just as the marine guards were being recalled for lie-detector tests—I received a letter from his daughter, Katherine. She told me that he had been fighting the disease that killed him for more than a decade.

As might be expected, Stoessel's obituary contained accolades from some of his former colleagues in the State Department. Henry Kissinger, who continues to remain silent about "the many complicated issues" surrounding the radiation hazard at the embassy in Moscow in 1976, described him as "one of the most distinguished Foreign Service officers in the best tradition of the Foreign Service." Lawrence S. Eagleburger, who had also served as under secretary for political affairs, said that Stoessel was "one of the real experts we had in the Foreign Service."

On November 19, 1975, while serving as deputy under secretary of state for management, Eagleburger had written a letter that was classified "SECRET" to William E. Colby, director of the Central Intelligence Agency, in which he expressed deep concern about the potential health hazard posed by a new and more powerful microwave beam (known by the code name "MUTS," an acronym for Moscow Unidentified Technical Signal), which had been directed at the embassy since May and had recently been altered. Eagleburger concluded his letter to Colby by saying, "I believe the Soviet changes in the MUTS signal deserve the earliest attention from both our agencies, and I look forward to hearing from you soon." Eight months later, shortly before Stoessel (whom Eagleburger surely knew was suffering from leukemia) left his post in Moscow, Eagleburger wrote to John D. Hemenway, president of the American Foreign Service Association, assuring him that the State Department's expert consultants "have concluded that at present there is no cause for concern regarding health hazards and that there is no evidence of any causal relationship between these microwave transmissions and any health problems experienced by those serving in Moscow now or those who have served there in the past."

Katherine Stoessel is a delicately boned and beautiful woman in her late forties, who is a dancer, dance teacher, and choreographer in a Hudson River valley town outside of New York City. As an infant during the time her father served as second secretary at the American Embassy in Moscow, she was cared for by a Russian nanny named Klava, whom she called "Mama." She attended the American School in Paris during the early 1960s, when he was first secretary at the American Embassy there, and she was sent to a school in Lausanne, when he was reassigned to the Embassy in Moscow as minister-counselor, in 1963. During the time her father served as ambassador to Poland, she graduated from New York University, taught kindergarten, and pursued a career in modern dance in New York City, and by 1974, when he was made ambassador to the Soviet Union, she and her two younger sisters had been living away from home for several years.

In a recent letter, Katherine told me that her father first became ill while serving as ambassador to Moscow, in 1976, and that he and her mother decided then not to discuss his leukemia or the revelations that were unfolding about the radiation hazard at the embassy with her or her sisters or anyone else. (In 1977, a journalist at the *Washington Post* told me that when the subject of leukemia and radiation was broached to Stoessel at a cocktail party in Washington, D.C., Stoessel had declared stoically that he intended to be "a good soldier.") Katherine believes that as a result of their pact of silence, her parents "became an even stronger and closer unit than before." She also remembers that during the years that followed, "when Dad was having a 'sick spell,' Mom would cancel family events, but not tell us why."

Katherine recalls that in the summer of 1984, she and her youngest sister stayed with their parents near Avignon, in the southern part of France, where the elder Stoessels had often vacationed together. "I knew Dad was dying," she wrote. "I was overwhelmed off and on with grief. But I couldn't express it to my parents. I remember crying alone. And then holding my sister and crying. We knew, but we couldn't, or felt we couldn't talk about it. It was taboo—we were to pretend that 'everything was O.K.' And he did rally again, but at this point, deep down, I knew, and so did my sister to some degree."

Katherine Stoessel says that after her father's death "a spell was broken and the family grew much closer." In her letter, she writes, "My mother opened up, the 'taboo' was gone, we talked openly about the microwaves, our feelings etc. . . . our mother was more accessible and open than she had ever been." In 1987, Katherine and her mother and two sisters took Walter Stoessel's ashes to a lake in New Hampshire that he had loved, having spent summer vacations there as a child. "We took a canoe out and scattered the ashes on the lake, and buried some on the land in a grove of trees, where he had spent his summers. Of course, we swam in the lake, cried together, laughed together, and were closer as a family than we'd probably ever been. I'm not implying that my mother or that any of us were radically transformed. But his death and the airing of the 'secret' did change our relationship with each other, I think for the better. My mother, by making a pact with him, in a way sealed us (the children) from them for ten years. That's why I was left with an overriding sense of aloneness by the whole affair."

In 1991, Katherine Stoessel choreographed and performed a solo dance titled *Picture Album*. The text for the dance, which she also wrote, reads in part as follows:

> This is the Russians microwaving the American Embassy
>     on Tchaikovsky Street
> This is Klava my Russian mother
> This is the CIA
> This is the CIA microwaving the Russians in return
> This is my father sick
> This is my parents leaving Moscow
> This is the lake he loved as a boy
> This is a lie
> This is the government not talking
> This is us not wanting to know

# 30

## Soiled Laundry

Now that the Cold War has ended, more and more of its dirty secrets are coming out. In the last few years, we've learned that the CIA made a rich man out of General Manuel Antonio Noriega, the dictator of Panama who is currently serving a forty-year prison term in the United States for drug trafficking, by paying him millions of dollars for providing the Agency with political and intelligence information. We've learned that during the early 1980s, the CIA formed a special counter-insurgency battalion in the Honduran Army, known as Battalion 3-16, and that with the Agency's full support and knowledge the members of this battalion acted as a death squad by kidnapping and murdering hundreds of their fellow Hondurans. We've learned that the CIA created a special intelligence unit among the Haitian police, which became notorious for torturing and murdering hundreds of suspected opponents of the military regime, and that while acting as a paid agent of the CIA Emmanuel "Toto" Constant, the chief of the infamous paramilitary death squad called Front for the Advancement and Progress of Haiti (FRAPH), is suspected of having helped plan the killing of Haiti's minister of justice. We've learned that the CIA has long given financial support to Vladimiro Montesinos, the military intelligence chief of Peru, who is suspected of having masterminded several massacres of government opponents. And we've learned that Colonel Julio Roberto Alpirez, of the Guatemalan military intelligence service, who, like Panamanian dictator Manuel Noriega, Nicaraguan dictator Anastasio Somoza, and the late Roberto D'Aubuisson, leader of the death squads in El Salvador, was a graduate of the United States Army School of the Americas at Fort Benning, Georgia, had been a paid informant of the CIA since 1988. Indeed, Alpirez was on the Agency's payroll in 1990 when he ordered the machete murder of Michael DeVine, an American citizen who was an innkeeper in the Guatemalan rain forest, as well as in 1992 when he is alleged to have supervised the torture and killing of the insurgent leader Efrain Bamaca Velasquez, who was the husband of the American lawyer Jennifer Harbury.

All this just in Central and South America.

Since the Cold War ended, we've heard a lot about how much the CIA is going to change. Robert M. Gates, who was director between 1991 and 1993, was supposed to have set the Agency on a radical new course of reform by calling for the abolition of all its paramilitary capabilities and for greater openness toward the public. Gates also declared that the CIA should redefine its enemies and concentrate henceforth on combatting terrorist nations, international terrorist organizations, drug kingpins, and illegal arms vendors. "I think that the government of a country and its leader that will brutally and ruthlessly destroy a passenger airliner in flight is an enemy of civilized nations," he told an interviewer in 1992. He could have been referring to the Iraqi government and to Saddam Hussein, to whom the CIA gave sensitive intelligence information about Iranian military capabilities and arranged to have supplied with cluster bombs by a Chilean arms dealer, even as it participated in the illegal Iran-Contra affair in which the Reagan White House was secretly selling weapons to Iran. Not included in his assessment of dastardly conduct was the destruction of Korean Airlines Flight 007 over the Sea of Japan by the Soviet Air Force in 1986, or the downing over the Persian Gulf in 1989 of an Iranian airliner filled with women and children by a missile launched on the order of the captain of the United States Navy cruiser *Vincennes,* presumably because these acts were the honest mistakes of well-intentioned military officers who were carrying out military missions.

Gates was succeeded in the job of director by R. James Woolsey Jr., who also set out to redefine the role of the CIA. According to Woolsey, the principal missions of the Agency should not only be to combat terrorism and the proliferation of nuclear, chemical, and bacteriological weapons, but also be to ensure that American business firms get to compete on a level playing field abroad by conducting economic intelligence to determine whether trade officials in other nations were accepting bribes to give contracts to foreign companies. (Some idea of the playing field the Agency had in mind came in early 1995, when the French government deported five CIA agents who had been caught red-handed as

they tried to bribe French officials in an effort to learn France's negotiating position in the world trade talks.)

Woolsey soon alienated Congress by fighting against cutbacks in the
intelligence community's secret budget, which is estimated to be about
$28 billion a year. He also alienated the old boys in the Agency's clan-
destine service by vowing to investigate their blatant sexism and alcohol abuse. But nothing tarnished the luckless Woolsey as much as the
fact that Aldrich Ames' long career as a spy at the heart of the CIA
came to an end on his watch. In an apparent attempt to salvage his diminished prestige, he tried to find some middle ground between congressional demands for severe sanctions against the officers who had
been responsible for the Ames debacle—the Agency's inspector general
had issued a four-hundred-page report that recommended disciplinary
action against twenty-six of them—and the need of the old boys in the
clandestine service to keep their reputations unsullied. In the end, he issued severe reprimands to four officers (three of whom were retired)
and lesser reprimands to seven others. This action satisfied no one. It
enraged the old boys, infuriated Congress, and brought Woolsey's troubled tenure at the Agency to an end. He was replaced as director by
John M. Deutch, a former provost at MIT and deputy secretary for defense, who, not surprisingly, vowed to clean house and sweep out the
Cold War culture that has dominated the twenty-thousand-member
agency for nearly half a century.

Deutch soon found himself faced with a spy scandal of his own
when Harold J. Nicholson, the highest-ranking CIA officer ever arrested for espionage, was indicted by a federal grand jury and charged
with selling classified information to Russian intelligence agents. He
was then forced to defend the CIA against charges that it had encouraged the sale of crack cocaine in South Los Angeles as part of a secret
scheme to help finance the contras in Nicaragua—an allegation fueled
by the fact that the Agency had for years maintained close ties with
Nicaraguan and other Latin American drug traffickers. As for sweeping
out the Cold War culture, one of Deutch's last acts before being replaced by the fifth CIA director in just over five years was to revoke
the security clearance of the State Department official who had blown
the whistle on the Agency's relationship with the murderous Colonel
Alpirez, thus sending a chilling signal to the American people that the

CIA intended to protect the secret identities of its informers even when they were implicated in the killing of American citizens.

As for the FBI, its soiled laundry has also been given a more thorough airing since the Cold War ended. This has occurred largely through disclosure of some of the vendettas carried out by the Bureau against American citizens during its three-decade-long witch-hunt for suspected subversives. The best known of these, of course, was the Bureau's breath-takingly unwarranted intrusion into the private life of Martin Luther King Jr., but there were many others, such as the case of Professor Dirk Struik, a mathematician at MIT, who was recently honored by MIT on the occasion of his one hundredth birthday. In 1926, Struik, an avowed Marxist, emigrated with his wife to the United States from the Nether-lands, in order to accept a lectureship at the institute. In 1934, he became an American citizen, and in 1940 a full professor at MIT. In 1951, he was indicted by a Middlesex County grand jury on three counts of conspiring to overthrow the federal government and the Commonwealth of Massa-chusetts by force and other illegal means. The indictment stemmed from testimony given to the grand jury by an FBI informer named Herbert A. Philbrick, who had been recruited by the Bureau to report on suspected Communists in the Boston area. Philbrick, who became a national hero as the result of a best-selling book about his exploits titled *I Led Three Lives*, testified that while attending a Communist study group meeting in 1948, he had heard Struik voice support for the efforts of Indonesian nationalists to overthrow Dutch colonial rule of their country. As a re-sult, Struik found himself described in a *New York Times* headline as a "Teacher of Red Revolution" and was suspended from MIT for five years while he awaited a trial that never took place.

Another FBI informer of the late 1940s was former President Ronald Reagan, who, while president of the Screen Actors Guild, was given the Bureau's confidential source code name "T-10." In 1947, Rea-gan testified before the House Committee on Un-American Activities about Communist infiltration of the film industry—the alleged result of which was known in Bureau newspeak as "Compic" for Communist pictures. He was followed to the witness table by the actor George Murphy, who was later elected United States Senator from California, and by Walt Disney, who had been an FBI informer and a confidant of J. Edgar Hoover since 1936 and remained so until his death, in 1966.

During his testimony, Disney settled an old score, charging that a strike for higher wages by animators at the Disney studio in 1941 had been instigated by Communist union leaders, although there was little if any evidence for this.

As with the CIA, there has been considerable talk of how the FBI intends to reorder its priorities now that the Cold War is over. Early in 1992, the Bureau announced that it had decided to shift 300 agents from internal security investigations to combatting gang violence and serious crime. Police chiefs across the nation applauded the reassignment, but government sources acknowledged that the 300 agents represented only about a fifth of the total number of agents assigned to conduct surveillance and investigative work in the Bureau's counterintelligence section. During this period, William Steele Sessions, the federal judge whom President Reagan had appointed to succeed William H. Webster as FBI director, was said to be working hard to root out internal problems in the Bureau, especially the problem of racism in the hiring, assignment, and promotion of agents. There was plenty of rooting to be done. Only 4.8 percent of the FBI's 10,000 agents were blacks, only 5.6 percent were Latinos, and only 10 percent were women. Of the Bureau's fifty-six field offices, only one—the office in San Juan, Puerto Rico—was headed by a black, and only three of 166 senior executive positions in the Bureau were held by blacks.

Sessions was forced to resign as director after a report issued by the Justice Department found that he had committed serious ethical violations, which included using FBI aircraft for private trips and charging the government $10,000 for a wooden fence he had erected at his home in Washington, D.C. He was replaced as director by Louis J. Freeh, who, in addition to the problems involving racial and sexual discrimination, soon had to deal with serious charges involving the conduct of the Bureau's Hostage Rescue Team. Its members had mounted an ill-advised tear-gas assault on the Branch Davidian compound near Waco, Texas, after a poorly organized sneak attack by agents of the Bureau of Alcohol, Tobacco, and Firearms had been beaten off. The tear gas, which had been supplied by the military, turned out to be highly inflammable and probably caused the tragic conflagration that incinerated most of the compound's inhabitants, including some twenty innocent children.

Attorney General Janet Reno defended the decision to attack the compound on the grounds that children there were being abused—an allegation subsequently proved to be false—and that the hostage-rescue team was exhausted after a fifty-one-day siege. Apparently, neither she nor anyone else thought to suggest that another hostage-rescue team be brought in to relieve it. Whitewash investigations conducted by the Justice Department concluded that although errors were made there was no way to avoid an armed confrontation with the Branch Davidians, and the whole affair was swept under the rug. Subsequently, it came to light that for days before the final assault, FBI agents had undertaken to unnerve the cultists and keep them awake at night by illuminating the compound in the glare of floodlights, by sending helicopters to hover overhead, and by playing music at full volume on loudspeakers. Ironically, few people in the nation's liberal establishment questioned the Bureau's conduct in the Waco holocaust—no doubt out of a desire to avoid embarrassing the already beleaguered young Clinton administration—so the outrage was left to fester in the paranoid fantasies of government-hating, gun-loving paramilitarists and psychopaths, until it emerged as a cause célèbre two years later in the wake of the bombing of the Alfred P. Murrah Federal Building in Oklahoma City.

# 31

## Sleeping Dogs

What didn't get swept under the rug so easily was the conduct of the Hostage Rescue Team during a confrontation that took place at Ruby Ridge, Idaho, in August of 1992. This incident had its beginnings a year or so earlier when agents from the Bureau of Alcohol, Tobacco, and Firearms enticed a white separatist named Randall C. Weaver into selling them a sawed-off shotgun. Weaver became a federal fugitive when he failed to appear at a court hearing after receiving a summons that listed a wrong date for the proceeding. On August 21, 1992, three armed federal marshals wearing camouflage suits encountered Weaver, his fourteen-year-old son Samuel, and a family friend named Kevin Harris on the mountainside near Weaver's isolated cabin. In an ensuing shootout, one of the marshals was killed by a bullet in the chest, and young Samuel Weaver died of a gunshot wound in the back. Carrying Samuel's body, Weaver and Harris retreated to Weaver's cabin.

Members of the FBI's Hostage Rescue Team, who were called to the scene, appear to have had little trouble convincing themselves that Weaver was a die-hard extremist who would not surrender peacefully. Accordingly, the commander of the team asked for and received permission from Larry A. Potts, head of the FBI's criminal investigative division, to shoot to kill any armed adult male its members might encounter on the mountain. (Eight months later, Potts and Attorney General Janet Reno would authorize the disastrous tear gas raid on the Branch Davidian compound in Waco.) Without making any attempt to negotiate with Weaver, eleven FBI sharpshooters armed with rifles equipped with telescopic sights took up positions in the woods around his cabin on the afternoon of August 22. Several hours later, one of them saw Weaver, Harris, and a young woman, who turned out to be Weaver's wife Vicki, leave the cabin. Acting upon the belief that one of the men might fire at an FBI helicopter hovering overhead, the sharpshooter fired a shot that hit Weaver in the back of the shoulder. As the Weavers and Harris dashed back into the cabin, the sharpshooter fired again. This time, he sent a bullet through the head of Vicki Weaver, who had picked up her ten-month-old daughter and was standing just inside the doorway. She was killed instantly and fragments of the bullet wounded Harris. Ten days later, Weaver and Harris surrendered.

During the trial of Weaver and Harris, which took place several months later in federal district court in Boise, the FBI released a report justifying the killing of Vicki Weaver on the grounds that she had willfully placed herself in harm's way. However, Judge Edward J. Lodge, who presided over the trial, issued an extraordinary sanction order in which he declared that the FBI's refusal to turn over documents relating to the true circumstances behind the shooting of Mrs. Weaver to federal prosecutors "served to obstruct the administration of justice" and showed "a callous disregard for the rights of the defendants and the interests of justice." (Four years later, it would come to light that FBI agents had indeed obstructed justice by destroying documents that authorized the agents at Ruby Ridge to shoot to kill on sight.) During the trial, Weaver's lawyers, who were led by the legendary Gary Spence, accused the FBI of using tactics in the siege of Weaver's cabin that amounted to murder. A jury quickly acquitted both defendants. The Justice Department later agreed to pay the Weaver family $3.1 million to settle its wrongful death claims.

In January of 1995, FBI Director Freeh announced that he intended to send letters of censure to twelve Bureau officials who had been involved in the standoff at Ruby Ridge. According to Freeh, the officials to be disciplined had "demonstrated inadequate performance, improper judgment, neglect of duty and failure to exert proper managerial oversight." Among them was Larry Potts, who had by then become the Bureau's acting deputy director. However, Freeh maintained that in spite of the letter he was proposing to send Potts for failing to properly oversee the rules of engagement at Ruby Ridge, he had "complete confidence" in Potts, and would call upon Attorney General Reno to name him deputy director. Reno did so early in May of 1995, but Potts was forced to resign shortly thereafter when the truth of what had happened at Ruby Ridge and his role in it was brought out in congressional hearings. During those hearings, Bureau officials had the appalling gall to suggest (without offering any forensic evidence) that Randy Weaver had shot his own son in the back.

No sooner had the FBI tried to put the tragic fiascos of Ruby Ridge and Waco behind it when a new scandal called the integrity of the Bureau into question. The latest imbroglio grew out of the discovery last year that aides of the Clinton administration had asked the FBI to furnish them with the confidential files of some nine hundred men and women who had worked in the Reagan and Bush administrations, and of the discovery that instead of inquiring about the purpose of such a sweeping request the Bureau officials had complied with it as if it were a routine matter. During the spring and summer of 1996, there was considerable speculation by members of the press and the Congress as to whether the White House was pursuing a political agenda in rummaging through the files, as well as harsh criticism of both the White House and the FBI for their obvious disregard of the privacy rights of individuals. All this was well and good, but an essential question went unasked. Why is the Bureau with its dismal record of civil rights violations allowed to amass confidential files on millions of Americans in the first place?

Instead of asking this question, various segments of the media embarked on a campaign of rehabilitating the FBI, not as a result of having observed any truly demonstrated reform within the Bureau, but simply because Director Freeh and officials of the Justice Department had the sufficient public relations sense to avoid a bloodbath when they undertook to resolve the conflict with the Freemen militants in eastern Montana in the summer of 1996. Just how grossly premature this campaign was can be seen in the fact that while FBI agents were showing unaccustomed restraint in Montana, Bureau officials in Atlanta were destroying the reputation of Olympic Park guard Richard A. Jewell by encouraging the media to consider him as their prime suspect in the bombing at the park, when, as it turned out, they had excellent reason to believe from the very beginning that Jewell could not have been involved in the crime.

What ought to be apparent to anyone capable of casting a backward glance over the past forty years is that no matter who the directors or what the circumstances, neither the FBI nor the CIA is capable of carrying out meaningful reforms in its methods of operation without strong and persistent oversight on the part of a higher authority. Since such authority can only reside in the presidency and the Congress—institutions easily influenced by the political expediency of the moment—it seems likely that Americans will continue to live in an era in which secret abuses of power on the part of the police and intelligence communities are tolerated, as they were throughout most of the Cold War, as a necessary evil. Nowadays, thanks to the terrorist bombings of New York's World Trade Center and Oklahoma City's Murrah Federal Building, as well as the gas attack mounted by cultists in the Tokyo subway system, Americans are being urged to approve the relaxation of the strict limitations on domestic surveillance and wiretapping that were imposed upon the FBI by the Justice Department twenty years ago, following the embarrassing disclosure that Bureau agents had penetrated anti–Vietnam War groups and spied on Martin Luther King. A proposed Omnibus Counter-Terrorism Act calls for sealing the nation's borders and making evidence gathered through secret surveillance and increased wiretapping available to government prosecutors in special courts. Proponents of such measures argue that if FBI agents had been able to operate as they had in earlier times, they might have tapped the telephones and infiltrated the ranks of the extremists who perpetrated the outrage in Oklahoma City. As a result of that bombing, President Clinton asked Congress for new legislation to create an FBI-led Domestic Counter-Terrorist Center and a special FBI counterintelligence fund that will increase the Bureau's ability to trace telephone calls and gain access to the records of consumer agencies, hotels, motels, airlines, and train and bus carriers. (The Bureau already has a Library Awareness Program, in which librarians around the nation are asked to report the names of people seeking access to scientific and technological information.) In addition, the president has lifted the twenty-year-old ban that prohibits the Bureau from spying on domestic groups without being required to show probable cause that the members of such groups are actually engaged in criminal activity. More recently, in the wake of the downing of TWA Flight 800, he has requested that police wiretap authority be expanded to enable FBI and other law enforcement agents to monitor all communications devices that might be employed by terrorists, such as cellular telephones and pagers, thus creating a situation in which the government will be in a position to intercept thousands upon thousands of private conversations with the push of a button.

Memory is the antidote to this kind of foolishness, but memory is elusive and sometimes goes on vacation, especially in an election year. Part of the present tendency to forgive and forget the abuses of freedom perpetrated by members of police and intelligence agencies in recent decades can be attributed to the historians, columnists, and others who, impelled by the end of the Cold War, are coming out of the woodwork to give rosy assessments of it. Some of them—the writers of espionage novels come to mind—seem to be filled with nostalgia for the Cold War's ritualistic joustings. Others take the sanguine view that the conflict was a system of political control that prevented local wars from getting out of hand. Still others—William Safire, for example—believe that we had every right to wage the Cold War as we did, not only against our Soviet adversaries but also against those whom we considered (rightly or wrongly) to be their surrogates. In a column that appeared not long ago in the *New York Times*, he acknowledged that many of the covert operations conducted by the CIA against leftists in El Salvador, Guatemala, Nicaragua, and elsewhere in Central America were flagrantly undemocratic, but took pains to assure his readers that "such dirty tricks that would save thousands of lives gain some moral coloration."

When you let yourself slide backward and forward over the last fifty years, you begin to realize how much the fear of Communism gave coloration to all our lives. You also begin to realize how easily that fear could be replaced by new fears that could begin the cycle of dirty tricks all over again. Fear breeds anger, of course, and when the anger could no longer be expiated by the sacrifice of young men and civilians in Vietnam, it turned inward and became the massacre at Kent State. Everyone has his own memories of the Cold War. Mine do not exclude the Counterintelligence Corps agents who knew what Klaus Barbie had done but helped him get away; the German scientists who stood by while slave laborers died of cold and starvation in the V-2 factories, but got to live in luxury when they worked at NASA's Space Flight Center; the American scientists who irradiated thousands of unsuspecting people for secret atomic research; the State Department physicians who lied to the women they tested for genetic damage; the admirals who tried to blame a dead gay sailor for the gun-turret explosion on the battleship *Iowa*; the high school teacher who kept Lonetree's civics notebooks all those years; and Attorney General Robert Kennedy giving J. Edgar Hoover permission to tap the telephones of Martin Luther King Jr. in order to determine whether King was being influenced by Communists.

Sometimes I find myself thinking that I should have interceded more forcefully in behalf of the medical captain from Orlando, and that I should have been more of a brother to Warshawsky. But that's all past. Water over the dam. Perhaps it's best to let sleeping dogs lie, as the saying goes, like the remnants of Lieutenant Ramsay's car moldering away beneath the abandoned sands of Fort Dix. Still, there's one thing I can't get out of my mind—the lengths to which our FBI guardians went to protect us from Jean Seberg—so before I close out my interest in the shallow deceptions practiced by warriors for whom the Cold War became a game, and in the foulness that floated in their wake, I recall again the gratuitous cruelty of what they did to her, and the cowardice that lay behind it, not to mention their contempt for women.

# 32

## Coda

Looking back, it is clear to me that my life took a profound turn at the end of the 1960s, when I began to devote most of my time and energy to writing about environmental and occupational health hazards. Whether that is a path I would undertake to follow again, I do not know. What I do know is that during the next twenty-five years, I was witness to a lot of human suffering that could have been prevented if it had not been for the ease with which industry and the military were permitted during the Cold War to contaminate the earth, the air, and the oceans, to circumvent environmental and occupational health regulations, and to endanger the lives of workers, consumers, and other unsuspecting people in the general population. During those years, I encountered shipyard insulation workers who were suffocating to death because their lungs had been irreversibly scarred by the asbestos they installed in navy ships; submarine workers who had developed leukemia as a result of being exposed to the emanations from nuclear reactors; uranium miners who were dying of lung cancer caused by their inhalation of radioactive dust; military and civilian radar technicians who had been blinded and made deaf by microwave radiation; and people from all walks of life, who, by virtue of living in the vicinity of army, navy, and air force bases across the nation, were being sickened by drinking water that has been poisoned by the millions of gallons of toxic chemicals and other waste that were dumped directly into the ground by military officials who apparently convinced themselves that the exigencies of the Cold War gave them the right to do so. Today, I am contacted with alarming frequency by people who have developed brain cancer, leukemia, and other malignancies after living in homes close to power lines giving off strong electromagnetic fields. Even more disturbing is the fact that the children of people living in such homes are developing and dying of cancer more often than other children. The death of children haunts me, as I'm sure it does most people.

During my career as a journalist, I have been called an alarmist by the captains of the asbestos industry, a scaremonger by the detergent manufacturers, a muckraker by the makers of chlorofluorocarbons, a sensationalist by officials of the electronics industry, and, more recently, an environmental terrorist by the paid consultants of the electric utility industry. People who are more kindly disposed toward my work tend to regard me as an investigative reporter. In frustration, I confess to having occasionally thought of myself as a kind of literary entomologist—one who overturns rocks in the dank garden of the private enterprise system as it presently exists and describes what he sees crawling out from underneath. The fact is, of course, I am none of the above. I am simply a writer who worked for a magazine during a time in which its editors believed that public health issues should be written about at length and in depth.

That time came to an end in the summer of 1992, when Newhouse dismissed Robert Gottlieb as the editor of *The New Yorker* and replaced him with Tina Brown, who has taken the magazine—sometimes referred to these days as *The* (new) *New Yorker*—out of the realm of issues and into the realm of personalities. As a result, I am no longer an investigative reporter, which is fortunate for the development of a sweeter and more forgiving nature, since one of the downsides of being an investigative reporter for any length of time is that it tends to make one skeptical and cranky. Nor, for that matter, am I an environmental journalist. I have retired from *The New Yorker* and the public health wars I waged in its pages and, thankful for the privilege of having worked at the magazine during its great years, have gone back to the fiction writing that was my first love.

But that's the least of my good fortune. The best of it is that my children are grown and thriving and that the wife of my later years—the luckiest find of my life—has a sunny disposition, an inquiring mind, and a love for travel. During the winter and springtime, we live happily together near the ocean in a small town in southern California, where she owns a bookstore. During the summer and autumn, she visits me on Cape Cod in "the house that Zap built." We have two cats. Their names are Gatsby and Daisy.